Not Tonig...

Not Tonight, Honey

Wait 'til I'm a size 6

Susan Reinhardt

KENSINGTON PUBLISHING CORP.
http://www.kensingtonbooks.com

KENSINGTON BOOKS are published by

Kensington Publishing Corp.
850 Third Avenue
New York, NY 10022

All Kensington titles, imprints and distributed lines are available at special quantity discounts for bulk purchases for sales promotion, premiums, fund-raising, educational or institutional use.

Special book excerpts or customized printings can also be created to fit specific needs. For details, write or phone the office of the Kensington Special Sales Manager: Kensington Publishing Corp., 850 Third Avenue, New York, NY 10022. Attn. Special Sales Department. Phone: 1-800-221-2647.

Kensington and the K logo Reg. U.S. Pat. & TM Off.

ISBN 0-7582-1124-4

First Kensington Trade Paperback Printing: May 2005
10 9 8 7 6 5 4 3 2

Printed in the United States of America

For Niles and Lindsey, who opened and occupied new pockets of my heart.

Contents

Acknowledgments

This book would not have been possible without the sacrifices of my husband, extraordinary father and jazz musician, Stuart "Tidy Stu" Reinhardt. His unselfishness with domestic duties allowed me the time and energy to create this book, assembling memories and stories often into the wee hours of the morning after the kids had gone to bed.

High on the list of people to whom I owe a huge debt of gratitude and maybe even a few internal organs are my parents, Sam and Peggy Gambrell, particularly my mother who "pre-edited" the book and made me take out all the cussing and really mean parts. Her heart beats a rhythm of goodness.

Other relatives to give a big fat thank-you or part of my Kate Spade purse collection, are my sister, Sandy, her husband, Internet Dave (for being a good sport), my wonderful in-laws, James and Jean Reinhardt, and the dear friends—especially Lisena Moss—who bravely allowed inclusion of their stories.

I can't say thanks enough to longtime and former beau William Holliday, who told me when I was just starting out that he spotted talent and encouraged the emerging gift.

Thanks to the members of the "Read It or Not, Here We Come" book club, formerly known as the "Not Quite Write" book club, a group of great women who didn't kick me out for not reading the selection a time or two. They give me a monthly Monday respite—each woman shining with her own unique gifts of the heart and tummy. Talk about fabulous cooks.

Others without whom this book would have never seen the gray of type include all those who told me, "Write a book," including and in no particular order, the great Cheryl McClary, who is an author, a lawyer, a professor, marriage expert, wife and mother.

Add to McClary's court author Ronda Rich who served as a wonderful and unselfish mentor, and those who gave me praise in the early days of the manuscript: Julie Cannon, Karin Gillespie, Laurie Notaro, Celia Rivenbark, Jill Conner Browne—all wonderful writers and women.

I'd like to thank the Dixie Divas for inviting me to travel with them and the fabulous women at www.implantinfo.com, including j.b.—a woman who proves that intelligent career women can—and sometimes do—get boob jobs.

Thanks to the incredible staff at the Asheville Plastic Surgery Center who packed my "Hope Chest" with two priceless treasures.

A big part of the project's coming to light can be attributed to the flexible scheduling allowed by the company that runs my columns, Gannett Newspapers. Thank you Gannett, and especially the *Asheville Citizen-Times'* editors and publishers, along with more than a few coworkers who had to hear about this thing night and day, particularly John Boyle who said, "Go for it. Make it a tell-all! Don't hold back a thing!"

I'll always be thankful to the many readers and supporters of my newspaper columns. You gave me unconditional support, confidence, inspiration, love, and many lasting friendships.

Perhaps the biggest thanks should go to my patient and hardworking agent, Ethan Ellenberg, who epitomizes excellence and professionalism and refused to give up—even after a pile of rejections landed on his desk for my first novel. And of course, mountains of thanks to Kensington Publishing and the thorough and expert edits of Audrey LaFehr, as well as the fine staff at this house who made this a better book.

One person I never want to forget is my grandmother, the late Jessie Mae Gambrell. I've got plenty of secrets keeping warm for when we meet again.

Another special woman who recently came into my life as if sent by angels to make me and others better people is Judy

McLean, someone who shows in her every move the joy of giving to others, even if you have little to give. Judy makes true the following phrase: "Friends are the gloves God wears when he touches us."

Oh, I almost forgot. What self-respecting girl can dare leave out sheer gratitude for the man who photographed her for the book? A man who spent three hours air-brushing away zits and wrinkles. Photographer John Whittington could turn back the clock on a centenarian and make her look forty. He's quite simply, the Magic Man.

Thank you most of all my dear and precious children, Niles Landon and Lindsey Hope Reinhardt. You are my reason for being and not only filled my heart when you came into the world, but filled my world as well.

Lessons from the Staircase

An Introduction to Life

Lying facedown on the top stairs, I could hear them. Smell their perfumes, a random mingling of different florals sprayed with the heavy-handed intentions of being noticed.

Their laughter was high, almost operatic, and with it the accompanying percussion of tinkling glasses filled with gin or vodka for tonics and Bloody Marys.

Cigarette smoke, like the funnels of tornados, rose up the stairs and into my nose, but I didn't care.

I wanted to see them, smell them, hear them. Be them.

The bridge ladies. Mama's bridge club.

I must have been twelve or thirteen, lying against the stairs, peeping. The blood filled my inclined head as I listened to their stories and heard the shuffling of cards, collapsing into hands softened with lotions and ending in long tapered nails polished in corals and reds.

They were glamorous. And old. To me they seem old, but they couldn't have been more than thirty-five or forty. They wore enough lipstick to leave prints on their glasses, and cake eyeliner rimmed their lids. Most styled their hair like Jackie Kennedy and Marlo Thomas from *That Girl*.

They talked about who was having nervous breakdowns

and whose husbands were cheating. They talked about exercises and clothes, their children and other people, but always said the required "Bless her heart" and "God love her" if their words weren't particularly kind.

One of their favorite phrases, which my mother uttered often and would affect me for a lifetime, was about people "going to pot."

"Pauline Bingham just up and let herself go to pot," my mother might say and all would nod knowingly and click their tongues, sip their Bloody Marys, and be happy it wasn't them. "Just flat-out let herself go."

"Pure T pot," another would add, the cards fluttering like wings as she dealt.

"Lot of married women do that," Mama often said, her hands usually fiddling in the bowl of chocolate-covered nuts. "I always try to put on lipstick and comb my hair before Sam comes home. I may get wrinkled and old, but I can at least make an effort."

"Peg, you look great," they'd say, because my mother really did. She was tall and thin, had wonderful high cheekbones and facial planes that only improved with age. She moisturized her soft olive skin and applied Vaseline under her eyes to prevent lines. Three days a week she took exercise classes in a spare room at the First Methodist Church, forgetting for that hour she was Baptist to the core.

Mama always told us whatever we did, "Don't let yourselves go." Getting married, she admonished, is not a free ride to the pig trough.

Her second biggest piece of advice was to "work on your minds."

"Beautiful women are a dime a dozen. You've got to be much more than that."

The rules were simple. Work on your minds. Think of others. Don't let yourself go. Don't go to pot. Don't smoke pot. And stay a virgin as long as possible.

Some of these we fulfilled. Others we did not.

Throughout the years Mama has always been a huge part of my life and my greatest influence. She is nutty and dignified, gracious and hilarious. Her mind works in ways that never cease to surprise, except in her unfailing and unconditional kindness.

Many of these stories contain her adventures and capers. And others contain mine or those of friends and family. It is my great hope that within these pages—this collection of stories taking readers on a carousel ride infused with lights and the music of laughter, the tears of love and even loss—you will find pieces of yourselves and those you cherish.

And that you will laugh like Mama's bridge ladies, a feeling all of us needs as we proceed through an up-and-down world without guarantees. We may be getting older, but it is possible to do so without going utterly mad and straight to pot.

It is possible, just as it was with Mama's bridge ladies, to grow older with grace and leave our own imprints on the lives we touch.

The Other Taco Bell Dog

My son has asthma directly related to cats, which means my family has always resorted to the crappy pets. Fish, hamsters, crabs, sea monkeys, Triops eggs that hatched into prehistoric and evil-looking tadpoles that grew huge and died belly up and bloated.

All of these starter pets croaked after just a short time. The hamster had a heart attack and we found it stretched out clutching its chest in rigor mortis, yellowed teeth long and jutting. I double-covered it in Reynolds Wrap, put it in a shoe box with a couple of toys, and buried it as deep as I could dig. The next day, the neighbor's dog ate it.

"Is that baked potato Hammy?" my son asked. He had watched the burial preparations, including placing the rodent in his Reebok coffin. "Why does the dog have Hammy in his mouth?"

"That's not Hammy, son. Lots of people have cookouts and throw the potatoes out into their yards for the squirrels."

"With tinfoil on them?"

What can a mother say?

It was time to get a dog. A real pet. Only problem was my

husband, Tidy Stu, hates dogs and kept telling us if we brought one into the house, he would up and bolt.

I obeyed for many years, but when my boy turned nine and my daughter was three and a half I decided the family needed a dog, an animal that would return affection, unlike hermit crabs and plenty of husbands.

Because of his job, Tidy is gone most weekends and we're home alone, the kids and I. A dog would be great. Part of the whole American family picture. Two kids, a minivan, an SUV, and a dog.

Giving it about three hours' worth of thought on a Saturday, I drove north toward Tennessee and bought a Jack Russell terrier. I didn't do a bit of research on the breed, like normal responsible pet owners would. I simply wrote the check and took the wild and wiggling thing home.

It peed and pooped everywhere. It jumped higher than acrobats and would bite holes in our clothing while we were wearing them. One day the tiny thing dug up four fully mature rhododendrons that Tidy Stu had spent years tending and coaxing into huge flowering bushes.

Needless to say, he was miffed. "Either find it a home, or I'm leaving."

"How 'bout I find you a home?" I said under my breath.

I mulled it over, and in the end, caved and found it a good home. The kids and I grieved. So we bought another hamster, which died two weeks later from a festering condition called wet tail, which gave my husband more fodder for his raunchy sex advances that get him nowhere.

"Here, Mama," my poor son said. "Here's the Reynolds Wrap."

Well, that did it. Giving a child's dog away just because it shredded bushes and clothing and made stinky pie on the carpet was pure mean. The nerve of some men. I'd show him who was Mother of the Century. Denying us a dog when we were allergic to cats was like denying a vegetarian greens when she can't eat steak.

One weekend, soon after Hammy II died of anus rot, Tidy Stu took off for a two-day gig—one of the perks of being married to a musician. During his absence, Putt-Putt entered our lives. I was reading the paper one Saturday morning and there it was, an ad straight from heaven.

Beautiful female miniature dachshund for sale. Unique markings! House-trained; great with children. Wonderful disposition! Yours to love and cherish for only $150.

I called the number and the woman was ready to jump through the phone and hand over her prized miniature dachshund. She went on about Putt-Putt's beautiful, one-of-a-kind markings and how she was the family's true treasure. I kept wondering and asking why they were getting rid of her, but the woman continued avoiding the question.

"You ain't gonna believe this dog," she said. "I got six people want her right now, but you sound nicer than them and plus you got young'uns and I want Putt to go to just the right person. She does best with young'uns. Only certain people Putt likes and I can tell it will be you."

After she told me that fate had intervened and Putt was "destined" to come into our home, I agreed to drive an hour down to Hickory, North Carolina, and meet this super dog, this divine canine that put all other dogs to shame.

"Bring cash," the woman said, voice turning rough and demanding. "I've had trouble with my other dogs and people writing me bad checks."

Other dogs? Lord have mercy.

"You know, I think I better give this some more thought," I said. "I don't believe my husband would approve and he can get really—"

"Honey, if you gone deprive them children 'cause you got some mean sumbitch in the house acting like King Hole, what kind of example as a mama you setting? The good Lord meant for children to have dogs. Pardon my language earlier. I just get so passionate about Putt-Putt, and I know this is meant to be. I got that feeling." She let her voice soften, realizing I'm the stupid sucker type who gives $5 to winos instead of the finger.

"Oh, well, all right," I said. "Could you give me directions to your house?"

She coughed a couple of times. "It's best we meet somewhere other than my home. How about the Taco Bell parking lot?"

Why didn't she want me coming to her house? Things weren't adding up. Cash, parking lots, beloved dog that was too adorable for words but not adorable enough to keep as a personal pet? Bad checks from other "customers" of her dogs.

The kids were overjoyed, hearing all the dog talk, and my heart soared. Just to see her babies happy, a mother will endure almost anything.

We sang all the way to the ATM, swiped the crisp bills, and then crossed over to Interstate 40 and drove forty-five miles to the Hickory Taco Bell. I pulled in and saw the woman's van. She was a fleshy-faced lady who glared at us, trying to assess the situation. She puffed her cigarette and then held up the little dog. All I could see was Putt-Putt's precious face staring out the window. I started to open the door and the woman about had a heart attack.

She rolled down her window and screamed from half a parking lot away.

"Don't dare come to our car. It will upset Putt. Let me bring her over to you. It'll be better that way."

My children were bouncing around in the backseat and overflowing with excitement.

"I love her already," my boy said.

"Me too," echoed his little sister.

The big jowly woman jiggled toward our car, preceded by one of those front asses split in half by her red polyester stirrup pants; what my daughter believes is a rare breed of humanity known as a "two-fannied" person. She insists people with front fannies don't have back fannies. I tell her some have both, but for the most part, she's a keen observer of the human form.

"Do not under any circumstance say a word about her two fannies," I warned.

The dog lady got closer to the car, her reddish-colored dachshund pressed against her chest and two children about seven and nine tagging along behind. She had her thighlike arms wrapped around the dog, covering up everything but Putt-Putt's heartbreakingly cute face.

I rolled down my window. The dog snarled. I saw two tarter-stained fangs.

"Here," the woman said, "I'll just toss her back there and let them get acquainted. Don't get out. That might upset Putt."

She flung the long red dog toward my children and they fawned over her just the way this conniving bat wanted them to. Oh, she had a plan all right. She knew how to trick a family.

"You bring the cash?" she asked. "I don't have much time to talk. You don't want her, eight more do." It had grown from six to eight overnight. "Three of them seem like great homes, too."

She had me. No mother likes that much competition.

"Well, I wanted to see first if the children would—"

"Look at that, would ya? The good Lord knows who to pair his pets with, don't He? I ain't never seen two happier young'uns." She held out her meaty hand for the money. I placed it in her palm and she licked her fingers and counted. She kept saying how she's gonna really miss Putt, the beloved family dog.

"Why was it you're having to get rid of her?"

"She's just like a member of our family, but Tuck, my live-in, he's right allergic to her, you might say. The two of them don't see eye to eye."

It was at that point I turned around and got my own eyeful. Oh my God. Oh, please, mother of the good and dear Lord above. I wanted the parking lot to open its mouth and swallow us up.

There, dripping and oozing, were what seemed like a dozen flopping teats, each nearly as big as my own. Poor Putt-Putt looked as if a fresh litter had been yanked off her swollen, achy chest.

"Has she just had puppies?" I asked and the woman's flab started trembling in the sun's glare. She squinted her raccoon-rimmed eyes.

"A while back," she said, the lies curling out with the Virginia Slims smoke.

Well, what about that milk pouring off her like sweat? I wanted to say, but the woman was extremely intimidating with her fake blond hair and front ass.

"How old is the dog?" I asked. "Your ad said she was a year old." The dog was covered in swirls of gray hair on closer inspection. She had more gray than my granny. Her whiskers were silver, her eyebrows, her paws flecked with gray. She had to be ten or eleven.

"I said all that in the ad. She's a year, give or take."

"How many litters has she had?"

"You a smart little thing, ain't you, with your fancy questions? This was her first."

Oh, you front-fannied liar, I wanted to shout, but she was digging in her purse for what I thought may have been a gun. Turns out it was a fresh pack of cigarettes.

"I was going to get her spayed, but I'm afraid I waited too late."

"Too late?"

"She's in heat, already. Them little wiener dogs get their pelvic itches right often. Weren't two days ago I saw a bit of the blood on her booger. I figured right then and there it was starting up again."

Blood on the booger? Her children snickered. I turned to check the dog's nose, wondering if it had a cold or something. But her nose was black and shiny. No blood. No booger.

"I'm not sure I know what you're talking about. What do you mean by 'blood on the booger'?"

She inhaled her nicotine and rolled her eyes up into the fat folds of her brow. Her daughter, who may have been about seven or eight, didn't flinch. She walked toward the window, poked her head in, and said, "Ma'am, a booger's a pussy."

The mother didn't do a thing but smile and her son cracked up, as did my own son. My daughter didn't understand what was happening, other than that she had sticky dog milk juices all over her.

"Mama calls the pussy a booger," the girl said again, because she liked saying it.

"When there's blood on the booger, the little old vaginer," the woman said, "you'll know not to let her get outside."

"She'll hump anything in sight," the little girl said. Then the boy stepped up to the window and explained what hump meant.

My son was on the floorboard laughing, grabbing at his sides, his new front teeth looking huge in his mouth. I thought he was going to wet his pants.

I tried to pry my daughter's hands from the old hanging-tit dog, but she screamed and cried.

"I love her. I want to take her home."

"See what I mean?" the booger lady said. "Putt's great with the kids. I reckon we best be going. I gotta get this money to the bank before Monday."

She walked off, this two-fannied human kennel who'd just ripped me off with an ancient, gray-haired, saggy-tittied dog that was beginning to howl and grieve, tremble and piss everywhere.

The ride home was the longest in my life. I was short $150 and my daughter had heard the words *hump* and *pussy* and she wasn't even four. I knew I'd made a second mistake. I knew before we got into the driveway that what was about to happen was not going to be a good thing.

"Oh, son, I just wish we'd gone ahead and looked at guinea pigs. They're a step up from hamsters. Oh, what have we done?"

Oh, why didn't I just let my husband rule his roost? Why did I have to go on yet another dog search and come home with this poor old trembling wreck?

Because, a voice in my head said, *it was meant to be.* That poor old wreck of a dog needed rescuing from any kind of fright who would rip puppies right off her chest and call her sacred parts a booger.

Yes, oh yes. It was meant to be. At least for six months, until my husband finally put his foot down. All because Putt hated people, especially men. Especially him.

He didn't like our four-year-old's new language either.

We were at our elderly neighbors' one day, precious Yankees of all things, chitchatting, when my daughter spotted their new dog. She picked it up and tried to look at its hiney.

"Does she get blood on the booger?" my girl asked, and my face flamed with what I knew would come next.

"I'm not sure I understood you, sweetheart," our neighbor said.

I squeezed my daughter's hand hard as a warning. "Ouch!" she screamed. "Let go of me." She turned to the neighbor and smiled, shaking her hand as if I'd broken it. "A booger is a pagina," she said, pointing to her crotch.

"Girls got paginas. Dogs got boogers."

Going to Pot

I figured I was pretty close to going to pot when my husband and I took a trip to Cozumel, Mexico, shortly before I turned forty.

Mexicans usually love me. I can always count on these sweet gentlemen to wink or smile or say something flattering, like *"La dama es muy bonita,"* which I think means "very pretty" or maybe it just means I'm wearing a fine bonnet.

I like to flatter myself and pretend they are seeking more than a green card when they follow me around town, getting all out of sorts even if I'm having a puffy-faced, fat-armed, retaining-fluid day.

My husband and I decided we needed a vacation from parenthood and signed up for one of those all-inclusive deals frequented by fatties and alkies, both of which I could qualify as being, depending on the day.

It was supposed to be four nights of romance and adventure away from our kids. It turned into four nights of my husband either sick with a cold or pretending to be, and me enrolling in every activity alone. Everywhere I went I was solo, and not one man, not even a toothless, wrinkled wreck or a staggering alcoholic, hit on me.

This was one of life's biggest wake-up calls, even bigger than when the postal clerk quit blushing when I licked stamps in front of him and he told me to move my business away from his counter.

I mean, here I was, a woman without a man, and not a single Mexican was wanting my affections and thus a chance to fly back to America—land of dreams—with me as his bride and ticket to better wages and a McDonald's in every town. Land of outlet malls and Tommy Hilfiger. Land of Gucci, Vuitton, Pamela, and Britney and other people and possessions those outside our borders find alluring.

This was as bad as walking through a construction site and hearing nary a catcall. This could mean one thing, and one thing only. Someone had gone downhill. Or straight to pot. All that motherly advice about working on my mind had left me with baggy eyes, loose skin, and a goiter stomach. Not to mention the boobs. Let's, for a moment, leave them out of this.

Each day in paradise as my husband flopped across his bed, hacking and snorting phlegm and bemoaning the bad food and concrete mattress, I'd lounge by the pool or beach in my two-piece suits and even the total drunks wouldn't so much as glance. If they did, they quickly glanced elsewhere because at these all-inclusives there are Sluts-a-Plenty!

One afternoon while my husband lay curled like a scorpion in the bed and snarling about how miserable he was, I decided to take this all-inclusive resort up on its free horseback rides.

The only ones signed up were me and a couple of geeks who looked as if they lived in a town where the sun hasn't come out for months. They were wearing matching "I Love Cozumel" T-shirts and were obviously on their honeymoon, thinking they were about to enjoy a romantic romp through paradise on a former Kentucky Derby winner.

A stout Mexican with a nice smile, tequila breath, and only one missing side tooth introduced himself. I was drinking a beer in a red tumbler that appeared to be the type Pizza Hut uses for its soft drinks. The beer, along with the watered-down liquor, was free, and though I'd later suffer a weeklong bout of E. coli, one doesn't think of such as she sips her diluted offerings and tries to envision the getaway of a lifetime.

The Mexican eyed my tumbler thirstily.

"You want me to get you one?" I asked.

"I'm not supposed to drink," he said, darting his eyes toward a counter where his boss was explaining the cost of rental cars. "Go now, yes. *Sí*. Get me one, *por favor*."

I brought him a draft from the bar and the honeymoon geeks gave me the evil eye. I believe they were Pentecostals, not that there's a thing wrong with them, but they don't like it when tourists and Mexicans fraternize over mind-altering substances poured from a keg and teeming with deadly parasites. They just wanted to get on their horses and pretend they were in a romance novel, the wind on their faces and in the armholes of their "I Love Cozumel" tees.

I, on the other hand, just wanted to drink a bit and escape my nose-blowing, mucusy husband who was probably sweeping the tile floors or making the beds. This is what he enjoys doing in fine hotels. Cleaning and pretending to be deathly ill from germs circulating on the plane rides. He is convinced airplanes are nothing more than petri dishes with wings.

The Mexican downed his beer in two gulps and led us across a dirt road to a patch of scrubby wilderness. He kept eyeing me because I had no mate, a slight buzz, and a snug swimsuit top paired with shorts. It was one of those padded push-up deals, part of a tankini, nothing slutty about it, but I was looking hot in that top. It might have all been an illusion, but it was working. Took me from a saggy B to a full firm D.

We rounded a corner and there they were, a group of swaybacked horses that looked as if they were ten minutes away from an Elmer's conversion. The honeymooners got the horses with both eyes and at least three decent legs. The Mexican winked at me and said, "*Los caballos son bonitos*," which I later learned meant the horses were pretty. I thought he meant my bonnet-style hat and thus I smiled.

He grabbed a set of tattered reins and handed over a snuffling horse that he called the "La Mula," and I knew what he meant. It was a damned mule. A mad-ass mule. I threw a leg over its dipping back and the thing snorted and turned its head and tried to bite me, nostrils flaring and shiny. The honeymooners had already taken off through the brambled path strewn with litter and discarded auto parts, while I tried to get my la mula to take one step forward.

The Mexican, who had swilled his one beer much too fast, stared at me with wobbly eyes. He tried his best to speak perfect English and get the words out just right.

"I like a mature woman," he said, his eyes going up and down my tankini.

Mature woman! What did he mean by mature woman? He must have been fifty himself, old geezer, and calling me a mature woman.

He trotted off with a wink, trying to catch up with the honeymooners, who were halfway down the path, viewing the scenic trash piles. Burning tires and stiff iguanas left the air redolent of reptilian death and toxic fumes.

I was trying to get my la mula to move. When I bit its neck and said, "La Mula is *muy malo* and I'm going to cook your haunch for dinner," the blessed animal stumbled like an old woman with two new hip replacements.

After ten minutes of me trying to get my mule to make some progress, the Mexican leader returned, smelling of belches and lust. He rode his horse next to my mule and grinned.

"I like a mature woman," he said.

"I know. You said that already."

"You have nice breasts."

"No, I don't."

Move, mula, move. I started to bite its neck again just to escape this man's conversation and boozy perversions.

"They are beautiful. I like a mature woman's beautiful breasts. Not like senorita Pamela Anderson's soccer ball breasts. *Muy malo. Comprende?*"

"You wouldn't like these," I said and my mule took off running on its three good legs because I had removed an earring and jabbed the post in its hide. I would apologize later with a nice green apple, but for now, I needed to beat it.

The mule would start and stop, pausing over something nasty and decomposing in its path. I could hear the hoof steps of the Mexican catching up to us. Where were those pale-assed honeymooners? Gosh, this was the ugliest countryside I'd ever seen. I thought when I signed up for this all-inclusive we'd get to ride horses on the beach like in the movies. This was the equivalent of riding through a trail of Dumpsters.

The mule wouldn't budge and I didn't feel right biting or poking it again. The Mexican was on my tail and sighed so heavily I could smell his sated, fetid breath.

"I just want to see one," he said.

I turned toward him. "One what?"

"I like a mature woman. One breast of a mature woman."

"Well, trot on up the path and find one. I'm not mature. You got that? I'm only twenty eight. I look older because I smoked when I was young and drank too much in college. I had that disease when I was born where you look eighty by the time you are three. Very sad, but I make the best of it."

"You are spirited and I like that in a woman. American women are like my horses. Spirited."

Your horses are two gallops away from glue, I wanted to say, but did not because he was staring a hole through my tankini top with the built-in mega bra.

"Let me see just one. Only one. A mature breast, please."

"I will not. They are ugly. I'm telling you."

"They are so beautiful. And mature."

I searched the ground for a big stick to hit him with, but all I could find were scrubby vines and old plastic cups. I was truly afraid by now. Not another person was in sight.

"Just show me one and I promise I will leave you alone. I promise."

"You will go away? You will run on up the path after the others?"

"*Sí*. Yes."

"Well, all right then."

He began to salivate and sweat. I knew he was in for a shock and the "spirited" American woman in me couldn't wait to see his face when he got a load of the goods this tankini was certainly boosting and plumping.

As he inched his old horse closer to my la mula, I began to have second thoughts.

"Just one," he begged. "The left one."

"Why the left one?" Oh, why was I even asking?

"It looks bigger. More mature."

Thinking I would be raped if he didn't get his peep show, I lifted the left side of my top and out flopped a long, eel-like tit that fell somewhere near the mule's saddle. His eyes squinted. His mouth curved downward. He nodded, kicked his horse, and fled the scene like the Lone Ranger after a bad guy.

"Hey," I yelled, offended to some degree. "What about the right side? Don't you want to see it? The right one looks a whole lot better!"

By then he was gone. The trip was over. My mula eventually made it back, drank some water, and crunched the promised apple I had in my beach bag. I cut my eyes at the Mexican before crossing the road toward the hotel.

He stood there staring, as if he'd been hoodwinked and robbed.

"Things aren't always what they seem," I yelled.

He nodded and turned away. I climbed the stairs to our villa, crawled into bed with my husband, and listened to him sniff and hack until time for my next solo excursion—snorkeling on three reefs in the middle of the ocean.

I dug around for a swimsuit that would hide nothing. I would show my breasts to be what they were, those of a woman who'd lived and loved and nursed two beautiful children. Those of a mature woman.

The Grumpy Vagina

As a reporter and columnist for years, I'm accustomed to interviewing people and asking all sorts of nosy and prodding questions. I'm not used to the tables turning, as was the case when a western North Carolina magazine named me Favorite Columnist.

A reporter from the publication called and I was in no shape for an interview. I was laid up in bed, eight months pregnant, trying to hold back a premature birth. With both my babies, I had to take medicines for a condition in which my big old fickle oven of a uterus wanted to pop out kids before the center's cooked.

"So, how does it feel to be named Favorite Columnist?" this sweet woman who sounded all of eighteen asked, as I rolled all two hundred pounds over in the bed and tried to think of something besides losing my mucus plug.

"Feels good," I said, sounding like some stupid hick. "Feels damn good." *Oh, why is it that pregnancy has turned me into Billy Bob Thornton? Just give me a PBR and a Confederate flag, a hundred-dollar coupon to Feed and Seed, and maybe a fetus tattoo.* "I'm honored," I said, trying to redeem a few brain cells and some class. They say when a woman is pregnant, the cranial brain dries up and the placental "brain" becomes the body's boss. I believe it. I had a feeling everything I owned or thought was stored in the placenta.

"Why do you think the readers keep giving you this honor every year?" she asked, and I was wondering the same thing.

"Hmmm. I would bet money it's my hair. It's my best feature and the only body part without a cartilage problem."

"Do you have bad knees?"

"Bad knees?"

"Cartilage. You know, in the knees?"

"Nah, I was talking about my ears. They flop like a piece of cloth, not a drop of cartilage in them. People say they favor Ross Perot's. And my nose, too. Way too much cartilage there. I have one pretty good feature and that's my hair, so I think readers appreciate that. Most of my mail is in regards to various and sundry hairdos. I try to change the style and color quarterly to shake things up a bit. A man threatened to kill me with that last change, the do with what he called the 'chunky skunk' highlights. He said he was of a mind to come in with a gun to shoot me and the stylist both. He said my nose had batwings coming off the sides, that the tip dragged too low, and that overall, my new picture would singe the eyes of every man's whose fell upon the page."

She cleared her throat and tried not to laugh. I was having a contraction and wanted to logroll out of the bed, but the doctor said if I got up for frivolous reasons, such as the need to pee, I might as well hold a bucket under my privates to collect the new family member.

I was hungry and my husband had left to play pinball at Frank's Pizza because he couldn't stand my pregnancy personality. He'd slid a cooler of food by the bed and refilled my water jug.

The interviewer wanted to talk about the secrets of my success, and I told her I never thought I was successful—except in getting men to fall madly albeit temporarily in love and propose—but I wasn't about to share those secrets with her.

"There aren't but three of us they could have voted for," I said to the young woman as I peeled a banana and stuffed half into my mouth. "There is Hooch McKinney, who writes about politics, but nobody wants to read about politics unless one of them's got his jibblybob where it shouldn't be, plus Hooch is bald-headed. Don't get me wrong. I love bald-headed men, but readers aren't going to generally vote for one. Then again, old Hooch should have won this thing 'cause he was the guy that broke the story on the Diapered Detective as you may recall."

"Diapered Detective? I'm new at the magazine. Tell me about this, please."

Ho-hum. "Well, the instigating detective had that cartoon piggy look to him and was one of those men with an unfortunate mad-baby face. You know, the kind of grown men who resemble angry infants all splotchy and puffed up? He was at least forty-five and got caught going to diaper parties at the local Best Western. A bunch of men just stand around in their nappies and give each other enemas. It's sick, sick, sick. Let me tell you, missy, I know firsthand about giving enemas."

"You do?"

"Well, I mean I don't trot over to Motel 6 with my hand in a glove and a Fleet by my side, but there was a time I got paid decent money as a young student nurse to do that kind of business. No way I'd stand around and do it for free or personal enjoyment. You have to be a real pervert to do that. Hooch wrote a few stories about it, even used the Huggies and Pampers logos next to his column sig, which was a riot, but I guess the readers didn't find him all that amusing, probably on account of being bald and having the Gorbachev thing going on up there."

"What do you mean the Gorbachev thing?" she asked. I guess she was too young to know who the man was. She sounded like a high school senior and I had to do most of the talking.

"He was the . . . Never mind. Hooch had that discoloration on his head like Gorbachev, only his is shaped like a . . . well, let's just call it a male member, and this got some people be-hind his back calling him a dickhead, only I don't 'cause I was brought up Baptist and you go to hell for saying those kinds of words, according to my mother. Besides Hooch, the only other competition was Regal Hildebrand, who lives near the Biltmore House and is married to a rich gynecologist and writes about things like decorating and the Junior League fund-raisers and when the daylilies are ready to bloom. That's boring as all . . . Hold on a minute, would ya? Something's trying to crawl out of me. Oh, help!" A contraction hit hard and I knocked the phone to the floor where it bounced across the hardwoods and finally hit a coffee table and flew back toward me.

"Sorry about that." The woman reporter said nothing. I couldn't even hear breathing, so I decided to finish my story before delivering a child.

"I was saying that no one can relate to those rich-woman tales of constipated living. If she was smart, she'd be writing witty prose about what it's like to be married to a gynecologist and how it sure helps they make a lot of money 'cause every-body knows what they face day in and day out. I dated one for six months who was partially fingerless, but don't put that in there because he's still mad on account of an incident with my old Subaru." Silence filled the phone and I was certain she had gone on a bathroom break. I continued talking as if my best friend were on the line.

"My family grew up near a gynecologist and before Mama got her renewed religion, she called him the Cul-de-sac Pussy Peeper, only don't quote me on that because Mama doesn't use the P word anymore. Anyway, what I'm trying to say is this Hildebrand woman really has it in her to be funny. She got drunk one time at a Christmas party, purely by accident, I as-sure you, and told about the time her husband had to open his secret drawer when an unwashed woman came in for her P and P—that's the lingo for pap and pelvic. He has this drawer, see, that has these things in them that look exactly like a Pest Strips but impart a lavender aroma, and Doc Hildebrand hangs them on one of the stirrups when the patient's not look-ing because he said a lot of these people don't bathe and have pubic vermin. That's exactly what Regal Hildebrand called them. Pubic vermin. I loved her that day. I loved her for an en-tire hour but haven't cared for her since.

"You know, both of them are really much better writers than me, but they just don't use their best material and I al-ways—"

"So you don't think you are a good writer?" Oh my gosh, she *was* still on the phone, meaning all that talk was on the record.

"I'm just saying I have better material. Better hair—most of the time—and better material, with the exception of the Diapered Detective series Hooch got hold of." Oh, why couldn't I shut up? The drugs to stop labor were kicking in and I was on the record saying all sorts of crude things and had no good food and was craving a Big Mac and large fries something awful.

"That's a good topic," the woman said. "Let's talk about your material. Tell me some of the more memorable stories you've done."

Oh, mercy. Here we go. The ceiling was spinning, my stom-ach squeezed itself into a tight ball, and the baby kicked my bladder so that I'm certain I partially wet my elephantine under-wear. I had panties so big that when it was all over I'd planned to use them as tablecloths.

"There's just so many stories," I said. "Let's see, there was the 105-year-old who tried to kick my ass and the—"

"Did you say a 105-year-old tried to kick your rear end?"

"No, I said she tried to kick my ass. She was having her birthday party at Miss Margaret's Place of Rest and Restoration and all her family was gathered, the both of them. She saw me and I tried to smile real nice and she said, 'Why don't you wipe that stupid grin off your face? You look like a little retard.' She sort of hissed her statements through a set of yellowed ham-ster teeth and I was taken aback. Old ladies usually just smile and nod in and out of sleep when they get past, say 101 or so. Not Miss Tolly, the one they kept calling Jolly Tolly for reasons unbeknownst to me."

"Did she physically attack you?" the reporter asked and I could hear her keys clacking away on the computer. Why couldn't I just shut up? Why wouldn't this medicine that's supposed to stop my uterus from throbbing keep my tongue from throbbing as well?

A vision of the woman appeared in my head. She wore her pink cardigan with the moth holes, her blue-and-yellow-print housedress and taupe granny shoes. Her face looked like a crinkled brown paper bag and she had a zigzagging line of orange lipstick going in all directions around her mouth. She kept raising her top lip like a dog will when it's mad and wanting to bite.

"She was a cantankerous thing," I said, "and tried, sure enough, to beat me about the head and chin, but I held her off. I said, 'Well, Miss Tolly, I'm here to do a nice write-up about your life and wanted to ask a few questions.' She raised up both her fists and her lips high enough to show off those dangerous teeth and started shaking like a little dog. She sorta kangaroo-pumped those fists straight out, jabbing them boxer-style. I was afraid, let me tell you. She wheeled her chair closer to me, got in my face, and said, 'What do you mean coming in here with your stupid nosy questions trying to pry into my bidness, you little idiot?' The staff had invited me, not knowing she'd behave like this. One of them started crying on account of Miss Tolly's horrible manners.

"After I asked her about growing up on a farm she got all upset, raised her fists again, and said, 'I'm ready to fight that little nosy thing sitting there next to me,' but the staff pulled her off. I tell you, I liked her. I was laughing away. I'll tell you another thing. She hated me the whole interview, but when it was time to go, I asked her if I could have a hug. And that's another reason I probably get voted this thing each year. Other than the good hair, I also give hugs."

Miss Tolly had shrugged her shoulders when I asked for a hug, but I leaned in and squeezed her gently. It was like hugging a withered tree. She was stiff and didn't respond, but she smiled. I saw it. A tiny little grin creeping from the side of her face. "I think the hug may have won her over."

The magazine writer typed so fast I thought her keyboard would explode. From experience I knew reporters liked it when they snagged a good quote, and I could tell I was a good one due to the medicines supposed to quiet down my uterus.

"Are there any more memorable stories; things you'd like to enlighten us with?"

I tried to think what I might be missing on TV by taking so long on this interview, and then I remembered we didn't have cable at this point in our lives. Might as well keep her on the line, this live human being. There was already a good chance with what I'd spilled so far I would lose my job, so I decided to pull out all the stops and gun it.

"There was the woman who kept calling about the ring of midget prostitutes living up under her single-wide," I said. "She claimed there was a band of them, about eight, and most were hookers. She kept saying, 'They's hiding under there and making the awfulest moaning sounds you ever heard. I can't get no sleep. That one little whore gets them all riled up and they bang on pots and pans all night and cook the smellingest foods up under my trailer. I can hear them moaning and hollering and doing the sex act all night long.'

"So I asked her, 'Why don't you call the police?' and she said, 'I do call them. Every time the sheriff's people come out and shine the light up under my trailer all eight of them midgets scurry like rats. They hide behind the hot water heater. Can't nobody find them. It's a mess, honey. Why don't you come on over and run 'em off for me?'"

"How did that story come out?" the reporter asked, exhaling what sounded like cigarette smoke.

"I called the sheriff and they told me not to worry. There

wasn't really a ring of midget prostitutes living in her under-pinning and that she was suffering from Alzheimer's."

"Wow. That is so interesting." The reporter's voice had that edge to it that all but says, "You're more nuts than the people you write about."

I could have stopped right then. The writer had plenty for her article about why my columns were favored over Hooch's and Hildebrand's, but I was bored and hungry and my hus-band would be playing pinball for several more hours so he wouldn't have to deal with my vicious placenta-ruled self. Might as well humor us both for a while longer.

"There was also a woman up in Yancey County who got kicked out of the VFW dance hall for dirty dancing. She was sixty years old, for goodness' sake. She said her husband had lost a leg and wanted her to enjoy going out dancing so he didn't mind when she put on her miniskirt and hit the dance halls. It was the other women who minded and got her kicked out. She sued the town and won. She got on *Inside Edition*, too. I talked to her one day and she said, 'Honey, I wasn't dirty dancing. I like to shake and throw my body around a bit, sort of an odd Elvis style, and then I just shimmy all over but I wear underwear. Ain't nobody seen my cat for nothing. I know women are jealous. Some old biddy got green as a frog and this is how all this got started. I don't do no grinding. We may bump a little bit but I don't make like I'm having no inter-course. Like I told you I's married to a one-legged guy they called Stumpy. He had the gangrene. He likes his TV and I like my dancing.'

"You may remember all this," I told the reporter, "because the *Star* had a big write-up and picture of her."

As I talked I wasn't sure anyone was still on the other line. I heard the occasional peck of a worn-out reporter's key-strokes and what sounded like someone blowing smoke rings, but figured as I rattled on, she was more than likely working on another story or e-mailing her boyfriend. I didn't care.

When you're confined to bed trying to hold back a birth, you'll talk to anybody, even a dead phone.

"There was an old lady, probably about ninety-eight, I met in a nursing home and we got to talking about marriage and she told me her husband had no interest in sex. She was so well spoken, and beautifully dressed, an accomplished woman, and I felt so honored to be in her company. All was going great as she spoke of her life and works, then she started back on her husband and how he never met her needs. If you're still on the phone, I'd like to add at this point in the interview that for some reason people tell me things I'd rather not hear. Or, well, I do like to hear them, but I'm not asking for such information. This woman tells me she was a real beauty, stunningly gorgeous, but her husband had no interest. She said, 'Some days I'd get so burning up hot I'd have to go off by myself and make things right.' I was shocked because she held up her third middle finger for me to see exactly what she was talking about and kept waving that finger at me. I wanted to run away. I was like, 'Way too much information, lady.'"

I heard the phone click. "Mrs. Reinhardt? Are you still there? Sorry, I was on another call, were you saying something?"

"No. Not really. Just eating my lunch, trying to keep my stomach calm."

"What's wrong with it? Do you have the stomach flu?"

"No, I'm eight months pregnant and doctors have me confined to bed."

"I'm sorry to hear that," she said, exhaustion in her voice. "Why can't you get up?"

"They call it an irritable uterus. Irritable uterus syndrome. It just won't behave."

We said our good-byes and one month later, on my way to the pediatrician's office for my brand-new daughter's first checkup, I picked up a copy of the magazine with our interview. There was the picture, an innocent motherly photo of me and my oldest, underneath which blazed a sentence I will never forget:

FAVORITE COLUMNIST SUSAN REINHARDT MANAGES TO SPIN YARNS DESPITE BEING CONFINED TO BED WITH A GRUMPY VAGINA.

Oh my Lord. I have never in my life laughed and cried so hard at the same time as I stared at that headline and wondered what my boss at the paper was going to think.

That afternoon the phone rang while I was tending my new baby. "How ya doing, honey?" my husband, who never calls me "honey," asked. "You want some loving tonight, or is it true you're suffering from a grumpy vagina?"

For years it's been hard to live that one down. But it does come in handy when looking for an excuse to avoid sex on the nights I'm too tired.

"Oh, not tonight, honey," I'll say. "I have a grumpy vagina."

Looking for Some Hot Stuff

Mama caught my sister and me dancing one Sunday afternoon on the carport and rushed out spewing Bible verses about the sins of our ways. This was the early '70s and thank God she's not like that anymore.

"Sabbath dancing will lead to nothing but a bad reputation," she said, cutting off the stereo and Partridge Family album, David Cassidy's voice extinguished and replaced with an echo of silent scorn. "First this. Then blue eye shadow. Next comes French kissing and ear blowing."

Sometimes children have to break their mothers in like saddles. After a couple of years of junior high and the screeching emotions of our puberty, my own Southern Baptist mama had whipped a 180 and was wearing half-tops, hitting the Moose Lodge and Country Club and dancing with my daddy after imbibing in a couple of bourbon and waters.

"It's OK as long as you don't slow-dance," she said, amending the rules of How Not to Sully Your Good Name and Ruin Chances for a Rich Husband. "But if you do slow-dance, make sure the boy does more than stand there and press into you. Make sure his feet are moving and his hands aren't sliding to your fanny. That looks hussified. Remember, slow-dancing leads to other things."

Yes, Lord, it does.

And I'm here to tell you about them.

In fact, the dance floor has led to the downfall of many a woman—and a man or two along the way.

Back when I was a bit of a boozer and young enough to have Farrah hair and Locklear thighs, the dance floor was where love sparked, lust ignited, and the hearts of many a young man or woman fell to the wood floors and bled to death under a disco ball.

Mama told us to be agreeable if a boy asked us to dance. It takes a lot for them to get up their courage and it's rude to say no or even no, thank you. My sister and I knew the pain of being uglyish in junior high and standing in a clump of girls, watching the popular sultresses being asked to dance as we leaned against walls and pretended not to care.

But my mama had no idea of the weirdo magnet implanted in our bodies, a microchip that drew hordes of duds, creeps, latent pedophiles, personality-maimed fellows, and future serial killers toward us—guys who would spot our Farrah hair from across the pulsating room and slide over to our table.

"Wanna dance?" a yuckster would ask, and a picture of my mother shaking her finger in warning flashed. "Better dance with him. If you don't, it will come back and haunt you. Remember, they're humans with hearts, too. Just God's Unclaimed Blessings."

So my sister Sandy and I danced with the eyesores of the world, the prisoners on work release and weekend furloughs, and the deranged or homeless who'd collected enough in their cups to dance in a bar and have a draft or two. Most of them were nice enough to share a single dance with. No harm done. But if one of them kept asking us over and over to repeat the mercy move, we had to take care of matters best we knew how.

And that is where the Howdy Doody dance comes into the picture.

"Watch this," I said to Sandy as I rose from my chair to cut the rug and pull the Howdy Doody on a guy who'd tucked his plaid button-down shirt into pants yanked up to his sternum, the crotch of which split his scrotum into something resembling a pig's hooves. I tried not to look at his cloven crotch because that always gives a guy the wrong idea and notions of future fornications.

Like a naughty twenty-two-year-old with skinny upper arms and no stomach goiter—a woman without the foresight to see that one day she would be forty-two and out of options unless one counts the advances and free swordfish from the seafood manager at Bi-Lo—I thought I was hot stuff. On the dance floor, I stuck out my teeth and all but brayed, extending one hand in a "Howdy" move, while doing a bit of the Hokey-Pokey combined with a John Travolta *Saturday Night Fever* pose thrown in here and there, that Statue of Liberty thing he does. I combined it all with a shock-eyed, crazed-woman grin and if I felt limber or tipsy enough, I'd arch and do a back bend and crab walk in a full circle around the guy.

At this point the men, even those with pig foot crotches and plenty of larceny convictions, would barely make it to the song's end before hightailing it back to Nerd or Penitentiary Land. Sandy and I invariably employed the Howdy Doody dance on many occasions when plagued by the outcasts of the dance club world who weren't satisfied with a single mercy dance.

The only bad part of that routine is that no cute men would ever ask us to dance once we'd pulled one of our best *One Flew Over the Cuckoo's Nest* performances. This was not nice, what we did. I knew it was mean. I knew one day I would be paid back for all this naughtiness. Mama told us countless times growing up we would reap what we'd sown. What comes around goes around. Make fun of someone and whatever they have, you'll get it. Call the lady with the huge fanny a "fat butt" and you'd wake up one day with an ass that could cart bags of charcoal and russet potatoes.

But I wasn't quite ready for the punitive end to this fun just yet. I had another round coming before I was willing to pay the price for my evil dance floor ways.

That time dawned when my dear friend Leslie was getting married and our whole gang threw her a bachelorette party, complete with a limo and stripper. Only she didn't know about the stripper. We'd booked him through Fantasies Alive and were told he had "the complete package."

"He'll do three or four dances and take off everything but his G-string," the woman on the phone told Lisa, maid of honor and in charge of arrangements. "He could be a Chippendale if he wanted," the woman bragged. "You oughta see his G-string. It's black with a red devil head rising out of his groin. And let me tell you, he's loaded. He fills out both the horns, if you know where I'm coming from."

Oh, how utterly lovely, I thought.

This stripper was to meet the party of wild women and bride-to-be at one of those cheesy hotel lounges where drunks and desperadoes hang out for the free hors d'oeuvres and house-brand hope.

Maybe they'd get lucky. They must. They keep coming back, these same types, clinging to the bars and the slim chance they'll see eight sizzlin' babes tumble from a black limo and enter this lizard's lair.

Here we were: Leslie, the bride-to-be, oblivious of the stripper on his way to this hotel, and the rest of us pretending as if nothing was going on but good old girl fun.

We all danced and waited eagerly for the Best Western lounge doors to swing open and Mr. Chippendale with the devil horns to sashay in. We danced and waited some more.

"He's an hour late," Lisa said, using the pay phone near the restrooms to call Fantasies Alive and getting only a recording. "What're we gonna do?"

"Give him another half hour," I said. "Maybe he's running over from another gig."

"But Leslie's already sloshed and is wanting to go home." That was the problem with Leslie. She would drink her white Russians too fast and then konk out early.

I surveyed the dance floor, seeing three bald men in golf shirts shaking their flat, concave butts with three ladies who appeared to be divorcées searching for husbands or overnight company. There was Leslie, tottering about with Teri, both bombed and laughing at nothing. There was Diane and some greaser bedecked in gold chains and then there was . . . Oh, Lord have mercy, there he was . . . our answer. Here was our substitute stripper.

He was tall, pasty, and so wasted he was out there hoofing it alone, trying to mimic a combination Michael Jackson and that Lord of the Dance man, but looking very much like he knew the moves to my Howdy Doody routine. I inched in closer as the lights flashed from overhead and Earth Wind and Fire pounded from the speakers.

The lone dancing man went wild. I especially loved it when he jumped up and fired off an air split before crashing to the floor, scrambling on all fours during the part of the song about boogying down. His red tattered T-shirt rolled up over his enormous gut like a window shade yanked too hard and his paunch poured over his faded black jeans. Hairs sprang in sporadic mangy clumps from around his navel, which by the way, protruded like a big toe. He wore the expression of one about to give birth and grabbed a set of abs that could have housed four to six fetuses.

He wailed and wallowed on the floor and I reached down and pulled his besottedness to his feet. His eyes, each seemingly independent of the other, wobbled like something on springs, one rolling in his head and getting lost and finally reappearing and focusing on my face. "I need you to do us a favor," I screamed over the music, taking him aside. This was when I noticed he perfumed the air with an odor that could kill locusts, a scent much like a cross between a urinal and un-washed skin folds.

"Whachu need?" he slurred, falling against an empty table and grabbing the railing. "I'm here to please."

I wondered just who he thought he could please. "You ever stripped?"

"Stripping's my middle name. I's a professional at one point."

I'm sure, I thought. "Listen here. The stripper we hired didn't show up, and see that girl over there?" I pointed to Leslie, who was almost asleep in her chair. "She's getting married next weekend and we need for her to have a stripper or it'll be bad luck. Her husband's getting one and we gotta balance the deal out. How much to strip? All we have is about twenty bucks left."

I could see his eyes counting the drinks that would buy. "I need thirty and to run home and get my good underwear. I ain't stripping in these." He tried to pull up the band of his briefs, but I stopped him. "I got me some good-lookin' Calvins at home."

"We need you now. I don't care what you're wearing. Just dance around to a couple of songs and then take off a layer. We'll give you a shirt to put over that one, and then you can throw off your pants. You know, sort of twirl them around. Do this in front of her face and when the second song's ending, turn around and show her your glutes."

His head toppled back as if his neck support had failed. I handed him my Michelob and he sprang to life. "I ain't about to strip in these drawers," he said.

"She won't care. When it gets to the grand finale or what-ever strippers call their last move, just shove your rump in her face and give yourself a wedgie so it will look sorta like a G-string real strippers wear. You gotta hurry. She's falling asleep."

"I ain't about to give myself a wedgie in these drawers. Look here, you crazy woman. I been on the road, my band and all's touring, and I ain't had time to change in six days. I gotta run home and get my black Calvins, you understand what I'm saying? I ain't gonna feel sexy unless I got on the right underwear to showcase my package."

I did not want to even think about his package. "We don't have time for you to run home and change clothes. I don't give a damn if you've got track marks up to Maine in those skivvies. Keep them on and I'll get you your thirty. Otherwise, I'll ask that man over there to do it." I pointed to a golfer type with fat red cheeks who looked one cigarette and erection away from a heart attack.

"Him?" The stinky potential stripper swilled the beer I'd given him.

"Oh yeah. Him. He used to do it full-time in Myrtle Beach."

"That's bullshit. He ain't done nothing in Myrtle but eat fried seafood platters. Look at his gut."

"He agreed to do it for twenty dollars, but we all thought you were much cuter," I lied.

Stinky Drawers grinned and let one eye have its own party somewhere in his thoughts. "OK," he said. "But I'm warning you about my underwear. Don't say I didn't warn you. They ain't my best or cleanest pair."

"We'll make do," I said, pinching my sides so I wouldn't start laughing. "Not much is going to show once you do the wedgie move."

"Get the extra money and you got yourself the real deal." He winked and gyrated back toward the dance floor.

"We gotta cough up some more money," I told the girls, pointing out our new stripper, who was spinning on his back on the dance floor, his legs rotating in the air like wild propellers.

"You're kidding, aren't you?" Lisa said and fell off her chair, unable to breathe she was laughing so hard.

Each of us went around the bar, borrowing a buck or two until we had $34 and change. We bought Leslie a Coke with the extra money and woke her up for her glorious moment—

the pinch-hitting stripper who was wobbling on his stork legs, hands clasping his region.

"It's time," I yelled in his ear.

"I ain't doing this unless that homo DJ plays 'Sweet Home Alabama.' That'll be my first number. The warm-up. After that he can play the Gap Band's 'You Dropped a Bomb on Me.' That'n always fires me up."

"I'm not giving you a dime unless you hike those drawers into a wedgie at the end. It's not a real strip unless butt cheeks are presented to the young virgin bride. You got that?"

He winked and did a chicken-wing flapping dance and I wondered what we'd gotten ourselves into. The DJ, thankfully, agreed to play both numbers because he was bored out of his skull and wanted to get in on the fun as well.

We scooted Leslie and her chair out into the middle of the dance floor. The disco balls glittered and the first strains of "Sweet Home Alabama" twanged through the speakers. Leslie tried to get up, but we pushed her back down.

Out of nowhere erupted a thunderous boom and the sound of breaking glass. Our stripper bounded from a table onto the dance floor, knocking down the furnishings and then falling to his knees. He popped right back on his feet, stomping the tiles with his black sneakers. It was as if he'd dropped from the sky.

He grinned at Leslie and bored his good eye into her while she tried to get up again, pushing at Lisa, who was taking off her belt to strap the poor woman in.

"This is your stripper," she said. "You aren't leaving 'til he strips."

"Oh my God," Leslie squealed. "I can't believe this. I'm going to kill all of you. None of y'all are going to be my bridesmaids. You're all fired."

As she ranted, the Stinky Stripper got going and the crowd clapped and cheered. Lisa was laughing so hard she choked. The stripper was down to his red window-shade T-shirt and his black jeans when the Gap Band number began.

He shook it and shimmied, mostly humping the air around

him. He grabbed Leslie and tipped his pelvis at her like a loaded weapon. She screamed and begged Lisa to undo the belt. The stripper undulated toward the center of the floor and tried to get out of his pants but they were tight and he was drunk. He fell in a heap of clumsiness and pretended it was part of the act and began doing the dead bug move, all while wriggling out of his jeans.

At last he tore off the pants, revealing a pair of the dingiest briefs ever with the elastic out of the legs and a huge chunk of unidentifiable man meat showing. He had three holes in those drawers and something resembling Kool-Aid splotches and cigarette burns on the defeated fabric. He stood up and headed toward Leslie, who was trying to escape from her confines. She turned her head but Stinky Pants turned right with her. At the end of the song, as instructed, he yanked up his drawers and flashed his buttocks, a white and partially hairy moon with several bruises and what appeared to be a skull tattoo.

He kept on dancing through two more songs until the manager of the club told him too much was exposed and he needed to put his clothes back on.

"I hate every one of you," Leslie said through her big smile. "I'm going to do something horrible to your bridesmaids dresses. Just you wait and see."

When my punishment finally came—the punishment Mama always promised—it hit hard.

A couple of years after Leslie's wedding, I had my own ceremony. And while slow-dancing to a lovely jazz band in the club of a swank hotel, my brand-new husband dropped a bomb on me.

"Musicians don't dance," he said, hand falling toward my fanny, feet suddenly frozen. "At least not the cool ones."

And that was the last dance I've had with the one I wed.

In the end, Mama was right. You reap what you sow. And I'd sewn an entire quilt.

Reeling in the Altar Chickens

How to Get a Stubborn Man to Propose

The news hit me like a hurled bag of Idahos. My ex-boyfriend, the one to whom I was semiengaged for eleven minutes back in 1985 and tap-danced on the hood of his ugly Mercury after catching him cheating, had gotten hitched.

I called Thurston Wallenborn Truitt, the former Altar Chicken, who lives in a certain part of coastal Georgia, and asked if the news was true.

"Did you do it? Did you really get married?"

"I really did," he said, his voice an odd combination of exhilaration and exhaustion.

"Why? I mean, I can't believe it."

"It was time," my ex said, and I pictured him as he was in the mid '80s, washing his face with ice water, lighting matches, and casting runes as he sat on the commode and pondered the day ahead. "I'm sixty-two years old, and I'd been with her ten . . . no, eleven . . . no, twelve years. It would have been morally wrong to do anything but marry her. All I need is one room I can call my own and I can bear anything."

Ah, what a trooper. I'll always love that neurotic old beau. He told me his life wasn't going to change a bit.

"Right," I said.

"No, really. I'm going to live here in my house in Georgia and she'll stay in Florida. It's not but a three-hour drive."

Back when I was dating him, I knew he was a lost cause as far as marriage material went. I knew the man feared the altar more than he feared growing old alone and in a nursing home, one of those men in nothing but damp underwear and drool who stick their big bony feet out and cruise the hallways, carrying on about nothing and fiddling with their geezer parts.

Thurston Wallenborn Truitt III was a nice man, a good boyfriend, even though he drank and caroused, was my mama's age, and the kinfolk were shocked speechless when I carted him home and announced my intentions.

"Those may be your intentions," one of the wise aunts said, "but are they his?"

It didn't take long to realize he would never marry me. A good clue is when you're "living" with a man part-time and he won't even give you a drawer in his dresser or a slot in his toothbrush holder.

Smart girls need to check out a guy's track record. If he's well into his forties and has never even been engaged, the red flags should wave vibrantly and the bells ding loudly.

I decided after the Mercury incident to cut my losses and leave town. I gave up a dead-end job at a coastal newspaper that required me to label all shark attacks as "incidents involving unidentified marine life." Even if the victim lay there with a missing leg and a huge bite out of his torso, I had to write, *A midwesterner is in a hospital recovering from lacerations from unidentified marine life,* instead of the truth: *A Nebraska man is in critical condition and on life support after he was attacked and eviscerated by a twelve-foot tiger shark later caught by the coast guard. He lost one leg and half of his small intestine, along with his spleen, six ribs, and two-thirds of his liver, a hospital spokesman reported.*

It wasn't as if I'd be leaving behind a world of journalistic integrity or a future with a man who would rather do ten in Sing Sing than march his chicken ass to the altar.

It was time to pack up and bolt from this town that had dried up on me like a pond without rain, leaving everything hard and cracked and without a base from which to flourish. Hard to make a living on $10,500 a year typing in obits and lying about fish bites and weather reports while watching one's boyfriend cheat every weekend.

Young girls need to know when to slice the line and swim fast. Those who linger on an empty hook could very well end up old and bitter and still waiting. If a man hasn't shown his cards after a year or two of willy-nilly, he's not in the game for keeps.

My precious and ultrarich Thurston may have owned every building and half the hotels on the Georgia coast, in addition to the five towns and six highways that bore his name, but I knew he'd never go down the aisle without a good fight and years of bribing along with countless sessions of psychotherapy. The second week I was dating him, he had us in a therapist's office for couple's counseling and I hadn't even slept with him. I should have run then and there.

Girls, let me tell you something. If you are dating or living with an Altar Chicken, listen up. There is hope and one or two surefire ways to get him to commit if he is even *remotely* heterosexual. The first, which I've tried on two occasions and both of which have produced fast proposals, involves moving or pretending to do so.

If you pack your bags and leave, a mechanism clicks within the stubborn psyches of these creatures and all of a sudden they are buying diamonds. There is something about telling these fellows you're moving away—even if it's just a town or two over—that triggers their instinctive competitiveness. This is why ugly girls with thick ankles and front fannies can snag cutie-pies. Men, no matter what the game or stakes, don't like losing. They hate the thought you may live somewhere else, and God forbid, find joy and another joystick. It drives them into buying precious stones and bands of gold.

I discovered this method purely by accident when I'd had

enough of Thurston's going home with vodka'd-up Realtors and nineteen-year-old strippers. I decided to not only leave town, but to also leave the country. I hopped a $79 one-way flight to Miami, caught another cheap flight to paradise, rented a tent in the U.S. Virgin Islands, and sailed right out of his life. Men can't abide the fact they've not only lost their girlfriend, but she's moved to a remote island and is running about in a bikini giving heart attacks to eighty-year-old leathered men motoring about in yachts. They don't like being back home and wondering why you're not answering any of their calls or messages. They want to know exactly where you've been.

"I'm on a yacht," I said one afternoon from the deck of an eighty-five-year-old *hottie's* fine boat.

"A yacht? Whose yacht? Who are you with?"

"Oh, you don't know him. You may recognize his last name. Does Rockefeller ring any bells?"

"Come on, seriously. Whose boat are you on? You know I love you. You can't just get on a plane and leave. Nobody does that, my Little Hurricane at Sea."

"I did."

"I'm about to have a heart attack. You come home right away, you hear me?"

"Come home? To your house where I don't even have a drawer in your dresser? I'm in the withered lap of luxury here. Several available men with the two Ts are after me. And you know how I feel about the two Ts."

"This isn't funny. My chest hurts. What are the two Ts? You aren't making sense at all, my Darling Tsunami. You've lost your mind. Finally gone crazy. What's this thing with the two Ts?"

"Well, since you've decided to fraternize with ho bags and floozies, I've decided to live on St. John and date only men who boat about and possess the qualities I love most—the two Ts, which I'll remind you, are, one, a trust fund, and, two, a terminal illness."

Within two days he was on St. John searching for me, a three-carat emerald-cut ring in his pocket.

The point is simple: You can read all the self-help books you want, but if a man is an Altar Chicken you have to scare the feathers off his carcass before he's ever going to drop down on one knee. You have to, first of all, act as if you have an entire fabulous and glorious life awaiting should they choose to remain on pause, like their remote controls during the parts in a movie where Nicole Kidman gets naked, which she loves to do more than any other actress who's not in porn, God love her.

There are various ways of frying an Altar Chicken, but as I've noted, the quickest way to pluck the fear from one is to move. If you really love the man, you'll pack it up, get a great job elsewhere, and show him what you're made of.

Before you do this let me bust a myth or two. My double-virgin mama always said a man wouldn't marry a girl he's slept with, but that's a load of bull when put to the test of a new century. Although most of the warnings she laid on my sister and me were correct, this virgin business was not, unless the man was Prince Charles in need of an unsullied maiden.

I've amended her rule to fit well into the modern world, and that is if you *do* sleep with them, you'd better be sheet-scorchingly good in bed. If you can't control your urges like our dog Putt-Putt and just have to hump something, then put on the Oscar-winning performance of a lifetime, making them think there's magic in their wands and that their precious weapons of male destruction aren't to be topped. Then walk out to lead the rest of your glorious and fabulous (even if fictitious) life and leave them hungering for more.

In other words, be the wild vixen one night and the next night tell him you just want a movie and a snuggle or better yet, that you've made other plans but will be thinking of him fondly. He won't know what hit him. Also, it's important to give him oral sex, which my mother pretends she'd never heard of until Clinton's great fall.

From sound research involving friends both male and female, the conclusion is that if you ignore his most beloved appendage and never explore this area as you do your favorite desserts, he won't be as eager to marry you. What man in his right mind wants to spend the rest of his life with a wife who won't bob for his apple?

Now, backing up a bit to that old expression, "Why buy the cow if the milk is free?" Well, here's why. If the milk's good, he'll buy the cow. If you've yelled his name in ccstasy and bragged on his manly parts, he'll crave you as one does water and need you like his very breath. You'll see. Just always walk away with him thirsting for more and remember my two rules for hooking a man for life.

First, act as if you have lots of options besides putting all your eggs underneath one Altar Chicken. Men can't abide a woman with options. Drives them crazy and directly into a blinding path paved with diamonds. Options can vary from moves to other locales, to hobbies and vacations that don't include him, as well as nights out with others.

And second, if you sleep with him, make sure it's after dating him so long he's about to die from his need for you. Then, once you do sleep with him, make it so unbelievably hot and memorable he'll never forget it.

I know, I know. Women have needs, too. One man's deprivation is another woman's starvation. One of my dearest friends is always telling me about men she dates who make her "mist" her panties.

"Jennifer," I say as nicely as possible, "if you've got the hots for him that bad, you've got to take action so you won't run him off."

"What can I do? I want him so much I can't stand it."

"Well, it's best to make him wait, but if you absolutely can't, go ahead and slam-dunk him once, give it your all, and then hold off for a good long while. He'll go crazy with desire."

"What about me? What about my needs? I mean, how am I going to control myself?"

"There are two ways for this besides taking matters into

your own hands. You must always be sure and wear your ugliest underwear when going out with him. Put on the C-grade panties with the permanent stains and the ugly bras that make your nack-nackers look saggy. Be sure the ugly panties and bra don't match. Since you'd rather die than have him see you in these clothes, your chances of slipping up are greatly reduced."

She started laughing.

"I'll have to drive extra careful when wearing this getup," she said. "I'd hate to be in an accident and have to go to the emergency room in my C-grade underthings. What's the other thing you said I could do?"

"It wouldn't hurt to ask your gynecologist for an SSRI."

"A what?"

"A bottle of Prozac, Paxil, Zoloft, or Effexor. Maybe some Lexapro. All of those will make you forget about sex. They're chemical castrators, believe me. The best side effect is you'll not only be completely frigid, you'll be the happiest frigid woman alive."

"How's that?"

"'Cause they're antidepressants. They'll keep you sane while he's at the jeweler's."

"You're crazy."

"Yes, I am. And between me and my sister, we've had more than a half dozen diamonds of the highest quality."

Men Who Have Maytags and the Women Who Love Them

Not long ago I ran into a man who took great exception with women who are trying to find decent men, even husbands, and the newspaper column I'd written on the subject. He fired off an e-mail that spread flames when I opened it.

Essentially, he said that all a woman really wants is a husband to buy her things, namely a washer and dryer. A washer and dryer? Come on. Where is he meeting his women? Fleece Night at the flea market?

I called him up, which I tend to do when people send blistering e-mails thinking that's going to be the extent of the contact. No way he was getting off so easy, believing he could sputter his evil and simply hit the Send key with no repercussions. No, sir. I like to hunt them down in the phone directory and call their sorry good-for-nothing arses.

He picked up on the fourth ring, sounding as if I'd awakened him from a Percocet doze. There is an entire subculture of people I've discovered through my work as a journalist, who stay home all day with "ailments" and exist in a state of narcotic somnolence. Occasionally, they call and babble all sorts of indecencies and indignities.

"What is it?" the sleepy man grumbled.

"I'm calling about your e-mail, Mr. Hicks. It smacked of misogyny."

"Say what? Did you say I was a pygmy?"

"No, I said miso—"

"Who is this a-callin' me at this ungodly hour?"

"This is Susan, with the paper. You sent an e-mail and—"

"Woman, it ain't even noon! All's I said was you women-folk is out to get men for all they got. In particular, a washer and dryer, if you know what I mean."

"It's true," I said, "that some men—and I have to say in all honesty you sound like one of them—would rather be neutered than commit their love and lives to a woman, but the point of my story was how to meet great men in this small city."

"You ain't in touch with reality," he barked. "All the women are out for one thing. To grab hold of a man and get married, then snatch all his money and everything else they can milk off him."

Excuse me, el Anusaurus, I wanted to say. "Women work, too. Some of us even get paid *better* than these men."

"Wake up and smell the wallet, woman," he screamed. "You need a reality check. You are like all the rest of them just looking for a house and a washer and dryer."

"What's with this washer and dryer business? I don't know a single woman who married a man for his Maytags."

"Well, they do. Pure and simple."

I decided to ask my husband, Tidy Stu, about this. He'd know. He once had to fight off a bevy of frumps chasing him for his authentic log cabin with the possum skeletons under the covered front and side porches. But come to think of it, he did own a stackable unit, and I imagine this intrigued a lot of his dates who were tired of changing dollar bills and sitting in the soapy humidity at Suds'n'Duds.

"Hon," I ventured, "do you think women are only after men for their appliances and such?"

"That's right," he said. "That and our hardware." He started laughing, thinking he was the wittiest person on the planet.

"You saw my '76 Buick wagon and then you had to sink your claws into me."

"I saw that car and nearly ran for my life. It was a motorized mess, a horror on bald Goodyears. I married you because you're neat and clean and can work a sponge better than Monet could work a paintbrush."

A few days later the evil Anusaurus sent another scorching e-mail, all about how women are only after what a man can give them materially, so I dialed his number, this time at nine o'clock in the morning.

"I'll have you know," I said in my calmest but firmest voice, "that I've loved many a poor man in my day and so have my friends. One of my best friends, in fact, once dated a man who took her to a fast food restaurant and used a coupon for the corn dogs. She didn't ditch him. They even got engaged and he didn't own a single credit card—couldn't qualify. As for a ring, he gave her an eighty-nine-dollar amethyst. She would have kept him, too, had he not gone to prison for robbing the Texaco. So there!"

He mumbled incoherently into the receiver, losing some momentum. "You women use your bodies as weapons."

Yes, I'll give him partial credit for that. Weapons of male destruction is what I like to call it. I've got a set of hips that could compact garbage and I'm considering buying a pair of enhancements that could double as flotation devices.

"Weapons, huh? Listen here. As for your comments about marriage being legalized prostitution, you are way wrong. We're not all a bunch of hookers wanting washers and dryers. You need the spin cycle, you . . . you . . . ogre."

He gurgled and tried to find his voice.

"Bye now. You have a lovely day and please refrain from e-mailing me again. I've put a hex on your address."

As for the whole notion of husband catching, why, it's something we've done since the dawn of man and womankind. Of course we want husbands—that is, if we've never had one. Those of us who've had one, if we are still half sane when the divorce ink is dry, would never have another. At least not for a while.

With men it's different. They are really hard to marry off until they do it the first time. After the maiden voyage down the aisle, they can't seem to want anything else. When the first wife leaves, they champ at the bit to get the second marriage rolling so the dinners don't stop and the sex is fairly regular. They need a woman like a bed needs a blanket. Women, on the other hand, can live half a century single and call those the best years of their lives. I've seen it happen over and over.

With men a succession of wives is like a lifeboat, offering in the form of domestic skills such pleasantries as missionary trips to the bedroom, a roach-proof house, toilets without the rings of Saturn crusting the bowl, fried chicken and limas, rice and gravy with flaky buttermilk biscuits every Sunday.

I knew something of that nature was going on when my phone rang about a week after my run-in with the washer/dryer psycho, and the past roared in like a storm surge. It was spring, which is the open hunting season on love in all its forms. There was definitely something in the air besides pollen when one fine afternoon in late April I had the great pleasure of hearing from an ex-boyfriend, the one with horse teeth and a high-pitched mosquito-whine voice. He was the boyfriend before Thurston Truitt III.

It had been eighteen or more years since I heard that soprano, but the spring heat, a wife who bolted, hormones, and the big yellow sun drove him directly to the phone where he dialed up his past as one would excavate a grave. He was in the mood for resurrecting and possibly getting laid and eventually having his shirts ironed and a hot meal on the table just like most of the other freshly divorced males, God love 'em. I imagined he'd called a fleet of us on his list, the girls from his personal recycling bin.

"What's up?" squeaked my old flame, who didn't like me quite enough in the '80s but somehow thought he might whistle a new tune now.

"Oh, not much," I said. "Just two kids, a mortgage, a marriage, and a mild case of going to pot."

"You got some pot?" he asked, and I remembered then how much he loved being stoned twenty-four hours a day.

"No. You know I don't mess with that. What's up with you? Why the call after nearly twenty years?"

"I'm divorced," he chimed as if I'd be deliriously overjoyed.

"I'm so sorry. Hmm. Wasn't she that sixteen-year-old you met a few years ago? That's the word on the street and in high school parking lots."

"She was almost eighteen," he said. "I see your sharp tongue hasn't mellowed."

"I guess you remember now why you dumped me."

"No, you dumped me."

"Wrong," I said. "You traded me in for the California Hemp Queen. Remember?"

"We were just friends. She had good weed."

"That's right. Dumb me. I forgot friends sleep together for a year and a half."

"I don't want to talk about her. When can I see you?" he had the nerve to ask. "I think about you all the time."

"It's been almost twenty years," I said. "*Twenty years!*"

He cleared his throat and sniffed a few times. Obviously spring had rendered the guy 100 percent insane or divorce had shoved a Roman candle up his sphincter, certain to send him rocketing for the altar. That's one more thing I must mention. Divorced men, as I've said, are fairly easy targets for one who is really hungry to marry. You don't even have to pretend to be moving to another area or leading a glorious life to snag a commitment from them. I'm told divorced men make good husbands because they've learned a few hard lessons and are beat down enough to know it won't kill them to say, "Yes, dear," and keep their mouths shut on other topics first husbands can't leave alone. The other bonus is the captivating children he'll bring to the mix, stepchildren sure to love you so much they plot daily the various ways to make your life a living hell.

For a good long while, I sat in shock and silence on the phone, not ready to answer this old flame with the sudden urges to go through his little black book. I wondered how many he'd called before he got to my name.

"I miss you," he said unconvincingly.

"How did you find me?" My daddy had run this particular fellow off in 1984, a year before I met Mercury Man Truitt. And then I remembered the wonderful new world of Finder's Keepers—the Internet. Google.com.

"I'll bet you look exactly the same as ever, don't you?" he said.

I put a hand across the flesh mountain that used to be my flat stomach. "Oh yes. Unless you figure in the twenty pounds and teats that hang like two old-lady stockings. Not to mention the fact I could very well be a candidate for a future front ass."

He laughed and it was so high-pitched I heard two dogs barking in the background. It was the same pterodactyl cry that used to cause my eye muscles to twitch and left arm to seize. "I saw your pretty picture online."

I didn't have the heart to tell him the photo was taken seven years ago.

"I'm not getting any younger," he said.

"Neither are your wives," I countered, feeling mean saying such.

"Seriously. I'm going to be an old man with liver spots by the time I finally get to see you again. I won't have any hair and my back will be covered in moles. I guess I'll be calling you from the old folks home. Maybe then you'll see me."

"Maybe in the summer of '42—2042. You might want to brush up on your shuffleboard and bingo. Keep flossing your teeth. The men with original molars seem to get all the rest home babes."

"That's pretty mean, Susan. You used to be the nicest girl I ever dated. That's what I tell everybody."

"Oh, right. Your sisters laughed at my shoe selections and your bipolar poodle bit a hole out of my ass while your mother sat there and did nothing but pet the killer dog."

"Come on. Let's just get together for old times' sake."

"I'm sorry, really. Memory lane isn't my destination of choice. It's just that I'm completely married and up to my scalp in debt. My husband has an eBay addiction and we're paying off the fourteen trumpets he ordered in addition to the Lexus with no bumpers or hubcaps; plus there're the PTA meetings for the next ten to twelve years. I'm on the covered dish committee, along with my volunteer work with Hospice and the Leukemia Society. There's no time for fraternizing with old flames, hon."

He cleared his throat and I swear I could hear the swoosh of pages flipping in his little black book. I felt his defeat in the silence.

"You got any single friends?" he asked, and all I could do was take pity on him. I knew how he felt. This is how women feel when the men we have given our lives and years to won't budge on the issue of marriage. It's frustrating and heartbreaking.

"Maybe if you act like you're moving away," I kindly tell my ex, "the girls will come rushing back begging for your attentions. Or better yet, go to Sears and get the best front-loader and matching dryer money can buy. I'm told that works like a charm. A girl just can't resist a man with Maytags."

Mama's Bridge Biddies

As a child I learned many of life's lessons eavesdropping on Mama's bridge club parties. I loved those late nights when the ladies I'd known only as someone's mother became real people, characters who did more than drive us to school and yell when we didn't clean our rooms.

They became almost like celebrities on bridge nights and worthy of study from a hidden perch at the top of the stairs. This was where my sister and I camped and learned the secret worlds of grown-up women.

I can close my eyes and still see their animated faces, their lacquered hair and nails, the spirals of smoke that built as evening wore on.

My sister and I gazed as if at a fashion show at their clothes and accessories: bell-bottom pants and midriff tops, pastel shifts, and short dresses, wide patent leather belts, and big wooden beads. We inhaled the strong scent of Maxwell House percolating in a silver pot, the coffee burbling in dark waves against the glass knob and making a sound we could hear three rooms away.

I was twelve or thirteen, and to me, their trilling laughter was like nothing I'd ever heard, this layered and multioctave mirth that seemed rich enough to tell its own story. I wondered why my young friends had never laughed in that way, what could be so funny to these "old" women who had to be way into their thirties. I'd strain to hear their whispers and to smell their Kents and Salems as the tobacco smoke mixed with the perfume de jour—Estee Lauder's Youth Dew.

On bridge nights after the biddies had finished a couple of Bloody Marys, I heard stories I knew I wasn't supposed to ever know. Stories of divorce and cheating, stories of gambling, debts, other women, children gone astray, and the message that stuck with me most—that if you get fat and let yourself go to pot, your husband will likely run around on you.

I learned there were times in these other mothers' lives when they didn't feel like getting out of bed in the morning and doing the day, putting on makeup and superficial fronts. I learned about nervous breakdowns and people falling apart—how that for a woman of a certain age and circumstance, it was as expected as a man's midlife crisis. He gets the red convertible and home-wrecking mistress; she gets the feeling of fleeting beauty, lost time, and finds herself in a corner unable to do much more than mutter and wonder how to coax her spirit into seeing reasons to rise each day and put another pound of ground round on the right front burner.

Bridge nights rekindled lots of spirits. And most of Mama's bridge ladies found comfort and escape through each other, through chocolate, caffeine, nicotine, and moderate intakes of alcohol.

"Proud Mary and Jesus are my drugs," Mama used to say, speaking of the song by Ike and Tina she liked to dance to on Saturday nights followed by the Sunday mornings she'd plant her long narrow bones on a church pew if her stockings didn't have a run.

My daddy was in charge on Mama's bridge nights. He'd let us eat junk food, skip baths, and go to bed with candy in our molars. He made up stories instead of reading them from books and didn't mind when we climbed onto his back as he galloped through the house on all fours. With him, it was like having a sleepover because he pretended the rules didn't apply. We ate Swanson's chicken potpies and drank Cokes instead of milk.

I loved it best though when it was Mama's turn to host bridge, those nights I never knew what I was going to hear as the blood rushed to my head, upside down in spy position on the staircase, and their voices and stories filled my mind.

These were nights my mother became more than a two-dimensional figure, when she transformed from her alternations of loving and nagging, into an exciting woman living life beyond the borders of her daughters' whims and husband's desires.

I'll never forget the evening I overheard her talking about her first day on the "job" as a volunteer at the local nursing home. She was trying to become a housewife who did charitable works so as to help define her when the working mothers were always asking, "What exactly do you do all day long?" a question that really irked her.

If she'd been a mean-spirited woman, she could have answered honestly, "I cart your children to and from school, to ballet and Girl Scouts, and keep them while you're working." But Mama's not mean-spirited so she kept her mouth shut.

On this night she was on fire with the adrenaline of a hostess who'd mixed the Bloodys with a heavy hand and whose cards were quite possibly the best of the deal. She held her friends spellbound with her words and pacing, and my sister and I were afraid to breathe, scared we'd miss a part of this story.

"I quit volunteering after only two hours on the job," Mama announced with precise timing and pitch. "I'm telling you, it was something else." She paused for effect, her nail tapping an ace of diamonds. "The men patients were on one wing and the women on another. The head nurse told me to go fetch the men and wheel them back to their rooms for a nap."

As Mama told her story, the cards ceased motion. None of the ladies could move, except to drag nicotine or sip drinks.

"After I carted a few of them to their rooms, I went up to this man in a wheelchair with his back facing the wall. I turned that little withery fellow around and Lord have mercy all of a sudden his hand jumped away from his exposed . . . his shining . . . penis."

The laughter reaching the top of the stairs was as explosive as fireworks on the Fourth. "I was mortified," Mama said. "I ran to tell the head nurse what had just happened, and she said, 'Oh, well now, he does that all the time.'" Pause. Sip. Tap. "You know what else the nurse said?" The women shook their heads and waited, their eyes huge and expectant. "That nurse had the nerve to laugh at me and ask, 'Well, do you have one that looks that good at home?'"

By now the bridge ladies were all but rolling on the green carpet, and my sister and I were about to tinkle in our pants. We had never heard our mama saying such things. We didn't think she knew what a penis was, actually.

"I swannee," Mama said. "I looked at that nurse with my eyebrows shot up real high and my eyes as wide as they could be and she said, 'I sure don't have one at home that looks as good as his.'

"I have to tell y'all, it *was* a fine-looking thing for his age. It was about the only thing healthy on him."

I knew the lady telling this story had my mother's face and voice, but someone else had occupied her body for the night. She was no longer the Baptist Sunday-school-teaching prim and proper etiquette maven. She was a woman set free, the ropes of properness slashed with friendship and chocolate, Chex Mix, and two Bloody Marys. She was a real person with feelings and emotions, not just the lady who made spaghetti and taught me how to set a table, the woman who delegated chores and discipline.

When the cards flapped and fluttered to the table, the coffee mugs clinked in their saucers and ice tinged in glasses, when no husband was around to put a damper on her spirit or children nearby to disappoint her, Mama grew as bold and lively as a fabulous character in a book.

When life got hard she played bridge and sat with seven other women in living rooms all over the small towns in which we lived in Georgia and South Carolina, talking of things I would finally understand after the birth of my own children.

It was soon after my first child arrived, I discovered the world of Mama's bridge biddies, the feeling of being a nervous wreck and riding the waves of hormone havoc. The more children, pressure, and commitments, the more a nervous breakdown threatened to consume me. It seemed a gracious woman's due, her rite of midlife passage.

These breakdowns—also known as hissy fits, conniptions, and meltdowns—were as expected as replacing spark plugs and transmission fluid in cars with sixty thousand miles. Every month at bridge, I heard Mama and the ladies mentioning the latest to succumb. And now I was one of them, only I had no bridge club to commiserate with and lighten my load by spreading it around and coating it with Maxwell House, vodka, and chocolate-covered nuts.

I *wanted* a bridge club, a circle of close friends to share the pain and joys of life with, but there never seemed enough hours in the day for deep and connecting friendships, particularly in the early years of working and motherhood. It was hard enough to find fifteen minutes to cook a real dinner once a week. When I did get together with women, it was with other "mom" friends and we'd end up at play parks and school events, chatting mostly about kids and parenting travails and how one day we would finally fall victim to a good old-fashioned fit or breakdown.

I fantasized about that day often—dreaming of the day I could succumb to my feelings of being dog-tired and overwhelmed. I pictured the uniformed sanity enforcement officers knocking at my door, stethoscopes slung around their necks, clipboards by their sides. I had worked for years to earn a pathetic HMO card and copay, and was ready to put them to use in a serene setting whereby I'd learn guided imagery and hear a voice in a monotone chanting, "Rest, relax, release. Be mindful of every muscle in your body going to sleep."

It would occur on a day from hell at the office, following a morning from hell at home when no one would get to school on time or have combed hair or brushed teeth. Lunch money would have been forgotten and one of the kids would have said the F word and the other worn a tragically unwashed and mismatched outfit that would have me worried about an imminent visit from the Child Welfare Department. On this particular day from the depths of misery, when the morning sun had forgotten to rise on my side of the bed and everything went downhill from there, I would decide now or never for my nervous breakdown.

"It's time," I'd mumble semicoherently at work as I slid under a colleague's desk. "Call Peace Release at St. Merciful Medical Center. We're on their plan. I checked an hour ago." As the sweet coworker dialed the hospital, I would point out the urgent need to run home and get supper on the stove. "My in-laws are coming for dinner and if I wind up in the hopper, they'll think I just didn't want to cook. I'll have the chuck roast and green beans ready and warm for them. The only thing missing will be me and they won't mind that a bit.

"Tell the sanity patrol to meet me there. I'm already packed. Been packed for three years," I'd say, crawling to my feet, grabbing my purse and stumbling out the door.

A few hours later they'd turn their white passenger van into the driveway and two men and a woman would hop out, wearing those pinched smiles of concern and carrying papers as if bouquets.

"Mrs. Reinhardt?"

"Yes."

"We're here to take you away."

"Bless your hearts. The pot roast is on, the beans are tender, and I've been waiting for this moment for three years."

"We know how you feel. It's been crazy the last few days, no pun intended. It's just that all the moms are suddenly checking in. We got a backlog of working mothers and they can't do anything at this stage but stutter and drool so you may have to share a room for a while."

"I'm sure these stutters all mean the same thing, poor dears," I'd say in all earnestness. "No one at work appreciates them, then they go home and their children hate them and dinner never satisfies anyone. Their husbands are always wanting sex at midnight and yet none of them has said, 'You're beautiful' in five years. You know how it is."

The woman sanity enforcement officer would nod and I could honestly tell she'd been through several of life's more cruel wringers. Somebody had long ago forgotten to dry her on the delicate cycle.

"OK. I'm ready," I'd say, breathing the last gulps of air from my home in the burbs. I'd caught up on enough laundry to find time to work this breakdown into the schedule. I finally clipped everyone's fingernails and toenails, trimmed and washed their hair, got prescriptions renewed, their dental cleanings in order, and made enough frozen meals to last a month. My husband wouldn't have to do a thing but sit upright and blink.

Once he discovered eBay he forgot I even lived in the house. And the kids? That's all taken care of, too. They don't start back to school for thirty-four more days, so I'd have time for my breakdown with a few days to spare for back-to-school shopping.

This little fantasy was beginning to sound perfect. Just think, three squares a day, no dishes to scrub, scrape, or load. No job to report to. No husband wondering what's for supper, when is he ever going to get laid again, where's the remote, and why does his wife wear ratty pajamas when she used to shop at Victoria's Secret?

I'll tell everyone good-bye from the unit phone at Peace Release and promise to see them in a few weeks when I come home a brand-new rested, relaxed, and released version of the old self, a woman who promises not to wake up every morning shouting, "Brush your socks! Put on your teeth! Eat your shoes!"

"Ma'am?" the sanity patrol officers will say as they watch me slipping into a stand-up coma, that condition of mothers who zonk but still manage to open jars of Prego.

"Ma'am, where are your children?"

"They're at Nana's. I can't break out of my domestic chains with them staring at me with those big sad eyes and crocodile tears." Oh, the thought of it would tear me up, a knot clogging my throat as I clutched my chest and felt pain rip my gut like a fist. Oh, my babies. Oh, my wonderful, precious, mean, fighting, mother-hating, messy, loud, obnoxious, brilliant, charming, troublemaking, loudmouthed, adorable, and delightful babies. They were calling to me from Nana's; I could hear the phone ringing in my heart.

"Uh. Wait," I'd said to the sanity patrol. "I . . . um . . . Let me check the calendar once more."

Vacation Bible school. Basketball camp. Piano lessons. Beach trip. Allergy shots. Eight special projects due at work plus a mandatory defensive driving school and ethics and diversity training.

I'd bite my thumbnail, knowing that having a nervous breakdown was something I'd have to postpone, at least until I could get my children old enough to babysit themselves. As of now, they require me like teaspoon-size kangaroolets need a mother's pouch. I'm their cook, shrink, social director, entertainer, doctor, nurse, teacher, preacher—you name it.

"I'm so sorry," I'd have to say to the men and the lone woman in white. "Could we schedule this thing in ten to twelve years?"

Until then, I've come up with a short solution to midlife meltdowns, something my mother taught me years ago every time she cruised the aisles of Kroger and tossed stalks of celery, tomato juice, Tabasco, and Worcestershire into the cart: the mixings for Bloody Mary bridge night.

I learned from those nights about the medicine found in a circle of women, a soothing release of emotion that bandages hurts and rinses the soul. And while I never learned to play bridge, I do read and I joined a book club a couple of years ago. A dear friend who'd lost her precious daughter and her way in life started the group, and the therapy these nights bring is immeasurable.

There are eight to ten of us who meet the first Monday of each month to eat, drink, and discuss everything *but* the book we were supposed to have read, a book some of us never even open. We call ourselves the "Not Quite Write" book club or the "Read It or Not, Here We Come" crew, and we pass the time as Mama did on bridge nights, talking our way out of stresses and into laughter. We bring delicious hors d'oeuvres and the hostess turns on the charm and her blender.

Humor and friendships heal the strain of our busy lives. The husbands are in charge of the kids, just like the daddies of my mama's day. They give them too much sugar, too much TV, forget the baths, the teeth, and the thirty minutes of reading before bed.

Sometimes, as the night wears on and we get carried away longer than we anticipated, I'll see tiny heads peeping around corners. I'll hear fits of giggles and spot spying little ears listening to things they'll play back in their minds for a lifetime, lessons learned from a mother's book club. They'll see us as real people and not the PTA presidents and room moms. Not the women who yell for them to pick up their clothes and finish their homework.

They will, on those nights, see the other sides of their mothers and realize we're real people with lives that sometimes jump the boundaries of the expected and venture far away from the carpool pickup lines.

They will remember these lessons forever. Just as I learned them from my own mama's bridge club.

Bebo

It was a Sunday afternoon, October 12, and the sky shone so blue it looked as if someone had thrown a bucket of paint across heaven's floor and told it not to dry.

Everyone said it was a beautiful day. But I saw no beauty.

Several days earlier doctors had told me I'd lost my baby, just two months into the pregnancy, and that any day now I would miscarry the one whom I'd wanted so much.

On that cloudless Sunday, I heard a knock at the door. It was noon and I was wearing mismatched pajamas, had dirty hair and eyes swollen with unmet dreams and heartbreak.

No one understood. To them, it wasn't a baby. Just a chance, one of many we later would have, like something as expendable and plentiful as disposable diapers.

My mama stood at the door wearing her typical big smile and slim-fit Levi's. She smelled of wind and White Linen laced with ribbons of wood smoke from neighboring chimneys. Her arms were loaded with three grocery bags packed with comfort foods like Pringles and Little Debbies and the canned salmon and Carnation Evaporated Milk she was never without.

Not being the kind of woman who calls and asks, "What can

I do?" she stood there on the porch until I opened the door wide enough to let her inside where she would take charge only in the way of a mother who never thinks of herself.

"What are you doing here?" I asked, wondering how I would have made it without her.

"This is what mothers do," she said, entering the house, her heavy bags rustling.

She was, at the time, fifty-eight years old and wore her hair strawberry blond and in a blunt cut that accentuated her high cheekbones and ageless face. My mother comes from a small mill town in South Carolina, a place where the people are friendly and have learned to be happy with little. She looks to me like Princess Diana. They are the same height and have similar faces and builds.

I had told her not to come, that plenty of women have miscarriages and somehow manage to cook supper and vacuum, put in a load of laundry, mix a pot of macaroni and cheese for their clueless toddlers or preschoolers.

But she lives to bring others joy, doing so by creating a sense of order where none before existed. She leaned over my sink and stove, peeling potatoes, boiling water, and simmering a fat yellow onion until it turned mild and sweet, free of the pungency that brings tears.

She filled the house with the sounds and smells of love. Of life going on.

She opened cans of Carnation milk and poured them into a huge pot with a stick of butter and creamed corn, stirring in the potatoes and onions. She added the canned salmon, pulling away the spines the way she knows I like it though she laments about the loss of calcium.

Next to her stood my four-year-old son, happy now that his "mama Peg" was there, no longer faced with wondering why his own mother was sleeping so much and smelling like the sick.

Mama gave him what he needed: unwavering attention, a roll of frozen cookie dough to cut into animal and monster shapes before baking, and unlimited time in her lap.

I watched her. This woman from the poor South Carolina mill town who never had a role model. Her own mother had died from a faulty gas heater when she was only eight, and from then on, it was just her and her two sisters shuffled among relatives, learning bits and pieces of motherhood from the aunts who took them in and loved them so thoroughly that they, too, would acquire the selfless dance of putting others first.

I had hoped I'd be half as good at the dance as she was.

The first mistake I made may have been telling my son about the baby too soon. He seemed excited. He called him Bebo. He'd look at my growing belly, carefully placing his little hands on his mouth as if to form a megaphone, and say in that way of a boy his age, "Helloooooooo down there. Is anyone listening? Hellooooooo. Bebo, can you hear me?"

We told him about the baby early, too early, ignoring the old-timers who say wait three months just to be safe and certain. Life in its earliest stages was as fragile as that in its latest, they would say, but I always thought, *Sure. Maybe so for other women. Not me. I'm healthy.*

Seeing the pink plus sign appearing on the pregnancy test like a winning Lotto ticket had been the most exciting moment since my son's birth, and I found myself consumed with the eagerness of a child before Christmas, one who sneaks under the tree and peeks through the wrapping, making sure wishes contain realities.

I had waited four years to have another child, begging my husband for one more. It was asking a lot. He had given up his career as a jazz musician to stay home with the first, and had loved every moment, but only wanted one child.

And yet soon after my son was born, I felt not only a sense of completion, but a tug of longing as well. The smell and feel of this little boy, the way he gave me a different love than I'd ever known . . . was powerful. And I wanted the feeling repeated. He needed a brother or sister. That was my argument, and finally, my sweet husband relented.

The positive sign that appeared on the test was faint but visible as I dashed from one light to the next, sunlight to fluorescent, hoping for clearer confirmation. Not fully satisfied, I rushed out and bought another test and still another. Positive. Positive.

I phoned for an appointment with the ob-gyn, then drove to Eckerd's to pick up some prenatal vitamins. I cut my only addiction, caffeine, to one cup of coffee a day, and took long rests, midday naps, and tried hard to eat leafy green and yellow foods.

Soon, I began to feel good, too good. The morning sickness had vanished as well as the bloating and heaviness, the overwhelming fatigue.

The morning of my son's fourth birthday party was also the day of my first doctor's appointment. I was happy, so happy. Finally, my family would number four, the way it was when I was growing up—traces of the traditional bringing comfort in a world that at times seemed to unravel.

The doctor was kind and wore her hair long and curly, her face round and dusted with tiny freckles. "Everything seems to be OK," she said, pulling off her gloves and tossing them into the wastebasket. "We'll do an ultrasound next time and you should be able to see the baby's heartbeat."

I left the doctor's office feeling a smile that wouldn't go away. In two hours my little boy's skating party would begin and fifteen preschoolers would squeal and roll around the rink and eat Batman cake and vanilla ice cream.

Two days later, on the actual day of my child's birthday, I called a friend.

"You know, I really just don't feel right. I don't *feel* pregnant."

"Count your blessings," she said. "I threw up for six months."

Later that night as I lay in bed reading *What to Expect When You're Expecting,* I noticed a few mild cramps and light spotting, which caused alarm and continued throughout the night. I slept restlessly and called the doctor's office early the next morning, the nurse scheduling an ultrasound "as soon as you can get here."

After taking my son to preschool, I drove to her office, plagued with those intuitive "something doesn't feel right" thoughts, even though friends and even medical books said light spotting was typically no cause for alarm.

I watched, legs shaking, as the doctor squirted cold gel onto my abdomen and pressed her equipment into my skin. Her eyes, however, were on the screen above, the fuzzy images of my womb, which she scanned with her wand, trying to get a clear picture, and sometimes stopping and pausing, her face giving away nothing.

I waited. She grew quiet. She ran her hands through her curly hair and clicked off the machine, walked to the beige phone on the wall, and called for another physician.

"I don't know how to work this machine well," she said, trying to spare me. "It's new and the other doc is more familiar with it." She patted my shoulder and tried to talk about Atlanta, a city we both had ties to. She might as well have been speaking a foreign language, because my mind was miles away, in a place where hope and facts face off and only one comes out the winner.

The other doctor entered with a brisk and busy manner and squirted more gel onto my belly. He searched with his eyes pinched and forehead frowning, trying to read the screen that predicts or steals futures.

I expected to see something, some sign of life, but there was nothing but a shadowy cross section of organs. Empty. Seedless. No heartbeat blipping like treasure discovered deep against the ocean floor.

My doctor and this man exchanged glances, and he walked out the door, leaving her alone with the worst and me. I closed my eyes and again heard the machine shutting down, as if it were life support.

She sat next to me and I felt her hand, cool and dry, against my bare shoulder. "It just stopped growing," she said. "It's really common, nature's way . . . one of those unfortunate things . . . one in five pregnancies end this way . . . a positive sign of fertility . . . you can try again in three to six months."

Then she saw my tears, falling as silently as dawn's dew, and she hugged me, my mascara leaving a black trail on her blouse.

After taking a few moments to compose myself, I left the office through a side door and drove to preschool to pick up my son on this day, this very day, I had given birth to him four years ago. This healthy boy who appeared with robust energy on every ultrasound ever scanned.

The house was dead quiet when we returned. My husband was off somewhere playing his saxophone and wasn't due home before midnight. I reached for leftover cake from my son's skating party and lit four new candles.

I sang "Happy Birthday" to him and let him open the rest of his presents, watching his oblivious delight as he unwrapped a Batmobile, Power Rangers, and a toolbox kit as complete as any home builder's.

I continued staring at him with the deep joy of one who's felt love without having seen it. I hugged him more than usual that night, knowing he was an even greater miracle than I'd ever imagined. A child who'd made it past those first critical weeks when life is so fragile, as uncertain as it is for the man with a new heart, the woman awaiting a donor kidney, the child with chemo running through her blood.

Later that night I tucked my son into bed—with me, this time. His warmth was life and he smelled like Dove and bubblegum toothpaste.

We read new books, party gifts. *Pippo Goes Shopping. Where the Sidewalk Ends. The Very Quiet Cricket.*

I looked at him and saw his face flushed from the excitement of a boy whose birthday had come and gone. I kissed his pink cheeks and said, "Sweet dreams, my precious child."

He lifted the covers, as he had done so many nights before, and looked down at my stomach.

"Good night, Bebo," he said.

"Good night, Bebo," I repeated. One last time.

It was three days later that my mother had appeared with her love, food, and mission of getting a family back on its feet. She floated through that blue-sky afternoon pouring watermelon Gatorade for my son, scooping up oddly shaped cookies from the hot oven, and stirring the salmon stew bubbling on the stove.

Throughout the house, I could hear her laughter everywhere, my son's following like an echo, and never had I loved either of them more.

Soon—too soon—Mama had to leave, the smell of raw onions strong on her hands as she pressed them against my cheek to wipe away another tear. I kissed her good-bye and wrapped my arms around her shoulders. They were still warm from her grandson's lingering hugs.

The Uterine Comptroller

Everybody deals with weirdos in the workplace. It's what shakes the martini of life and keeps us marching into our offices like ants straight to corporate battle, flashing our name badges and fattening our 401-Ks.

When all else fails to hold our interest and we're considering hanging up our worker bee wings to slog forth into new worlds, it's the weirdos who save us.

We want to see what they're going to do next.

When I was pregnant with my second child, an advertising sales rep and natural birthing zealot began eyeballing all the women with occupied uteruses in the building, monitoring growth and activity. He figured since he had a Bradley class under his belt among other things, he had every right to see to it we were treating our wombs with care. We nicknamed him the Uterine Comptroller and if he hadn't been such a cutie-pie, plenty of us would have marched his ass up to H.R. That is a bad word in corporate America. When you get dragged to H.R. you leave with cardboard boxes to tote your coffee-stained junk home in.

Four of us were pregnant on the second floor, and the Uterine Comptroller's wife had recently delivered their first, making him an expert on a woman's matters south of the border. I hated passing him in the hallways because he'd stare at my belly and I could see his fingers trembling, wanting to touch it so badly. He ached to tend to another ripe womb, now that his wife had pushed their baby out with no meds, no tubes, wires, monitors, or such. She simply glowed in the light of motherhood and her body's primal abilities. Guided imagery tapes played on the boom box they brought to the hospital and the smell of sandalwood filled the air. When the pains became too intense, she would sit in a tub full of warm water and chew chips of ice, hand-fed to her by the U.C.

He told us if we dare order an epidural, our children's IQs would plummet and we'd be lucky if they got accepted into Happydale Bead Stringing and Humming College.

I had already given birth to one child and wasn't about to do this again without the second best thing to Jesus and Whitman's Samplers—the almighty epidural.

The way it was with my first was simple: he was breech and wouldn't flip. At that time no one would attempt trying to manipulate the abdomen manually because of the risks doing so carried. I had a birthing instructor who offered a few creative suggestions.

"Shine a light down low where you'd like the head to be, because some babies will swim to the light. Or you may want to try playing music at your pelvic floor. Lots of babies love the sound and go toward the music. Try the Rolling Stones."

That very night upon receiving her advice I laid out my flashlight and Walkman and proceeded to give it a shot. When my husband came home smelling like pepperoni from playing pinball at Frank's Pizza, he dropped his groceries as he spotted me sideways on the bed.

"Why do you have headphones on top of your panties?" he asked. "Did you sprout a pair of pussy ears I'm unaware of?"

"Shhhh! Don't talk ugly. I don't want that to be the baby's first word."

He moved closer to the bed. "Why is a flashlight shining between your legs?"

"Shhh! I'm playing Aerosmith's 'Dream On,' which has a good beat, so the baby may try to seek the source."

"Seek the what?" He frowned and bent toward the headphones. "Please explain why you have headphones and a flashlight all but up your ass."

"Don't say ass. The baby can hear you. I'm just trying to get him to turn the right way." I tossed the equipment, trying to sit upright myself. The doctors had ordered complete bed rest due to a condition called irritable uterus syndrome. Or what that magazine writer called my "grumpy vagina."

"I don't want a C-section. I'm trying to do like Rosalee suggested. Could you go clean something, please? The grout is molding in the shower and I heard bats again in the attic."

While he rustled around and made those noises men make when irritated, I opted for plan C and stood on my head because Rosalee said sometimes babies would somersault if you did that. It's not an easy thing at eight months pregnant.

In the end, nothing worked and my son sat like a stubborn king on his throne, thus when the time came for delivery, I knew I wasn't about to lie down and deliver a child feet or buttocks first. I also knew that whatever drugs they had on tap, I'd beg for each and every one. To the devil with Bradley, Lamaze, and anything natural. I'd wear less lipstick—that would be my contribution to a natural birth. Maybe no blush either.

Two weeks after trying to lure my son down the canal with music, lights, and standing on the head, the doctor called with good news. "You're thirty-seven weeks today. The baby's lungs are mature enough at this stage, so don't be surprised if you go into labor within a week. You can stop the medications and the bed rest."

I heaved my walrusy self from bed, footsteps thundering like a T. rex as I dressed in our best sofa slipcover for the first meal out in months.

"I want a fried seafood platter at the House O' Fin and Claw," I announced, my husband astonished upon seeing his two-hundred-pound bride on two pulpy feet. "I also want some steamed crab legs and lobster-stuffed mushroom caps. Maybe a side of she-crab soup and some coconut-battered shrimp. Some key lime pie would be good, too, or a hot-fudge brownie with ice cream."

It took two hours to eat everything and as soon as I got to sleep that night the contractions began, accompanied by a loud pop and rush of warm water. I woke up my husband, who called the doctor, who said get thee to the hospital right away. Yelping in the car, I was convinced I was going to die. The pain was enough to make my head swivel.

"Faster, you . . . you . . . Beelzebub," I yelled. "If you don't step on it, I'll knock every tooth out of your blisteringly large head."

He didn't bat an eye at the evil words I heaved. "I'm not going over the speed limit or we'll get a ticket. How would you like that?"

"How would you like a squiggling fetus on the floor mats?" He frowned and clicked on the emergency flashers, increasing the speed by five miles an hour all while wearing the mask of male horror—that long and ashen face of a man on the threshold of unfamiliar territory. This wasn't ESPN. This wasn't aisle 10 at the Bi-Lo where the cleaning supplies whispered sweet nothings in his ears and gave him erections.

This was *childbirth*. And I'm sure what was going through his mind was, *Why can't I be like my daddy and his daddy before him and not have to go into the room and see all sorts of overstretched vaginas and blood? No decent man thirty-five years ago had any idea what a placenta was, and if you ask me, that's a good thing.*

At the hospital, as doctors plunged a needle into my spine and wheeled me to surgery for the C-section, I gazed at my husband dressed in scrubs, mask, hair net, and horror, and started laughing. He looked exactly like the servers at the cafeteria who wore expressions of dread and weariness, as if they wanted to shout, "Eat something, you fat pig, 'cause I'm not going to stand here with this metal spoon and carving knife in my hands much longer." I imagined Stu waving a huge spatula, his eyes darting left and right toward the chicken and roast beef and then at the baked salmon and spaghetti pie.

I couldn't stop laughing. The operating team peered from their masks and protective eye goggles to see what fool woman would be cackling during a cesarean. My husband stood there in complete shock.

"Serve you a meat?" I said and the entire O.R. crew winced. I imagined them thinking, *Who is this idiot? We'd better call Child Protective Services and the fifth-floor psyche unit. Can't send a new baby home with this fruitcake. Going to need parenting classes for sure.*

"Serve you a bread, sir?" I said, feeling the pressure of someone tugging on my belly. "Serve you a fresh piece of strawberry shortcake or pecan pie? Serve you a cold glass of iced—"

A head appeared over my face, hovering. The nurse. "Congratulations. You're no longer at the K and W Cafeteria but are the mother of a beautiful baby boy."

Needless to say he ended up a semigenius despite the flow of drugs throughout my bloodstream.

With the second pregnancy five years later, it was good to have the Uterine Comptroller around with all the Bradley classes to his credit. The U.C., with his fetish for all gestating women in the office, designated himself an amateur ob-gyn and birthing coach. He was the rah-rah man, the childbirth cheerleader, who was rather amusing—at least in the beginning.

At first he was just another guy with a freshly delivered kid and a few birthing classes tucked beneath his fertile belt. But within weeks he'd zoomed to the extreme, brandishing his teachings like verbal swords and wildly uttering orders and epiphanies: "Make sure you're exercising." "Don't forget your three to five servings of fruits and vegetables each and every day." And the real clincher: "A drug-free birth means a smarter baby!"

I paused at this absurdity. "Where in the world did you find this gem of information?"

He stood in front of me and spouted birthing tips the way other men talk cars and pro football. "Just say no to the brain-damaging effects of the epidural. It's the only way to go," he exulted. "Your baby will thank you for it. Her I.Q. will soar. Scholastic achievements will fly off the charts."

I assured him that when the time came, I'd wear less mascara and foundation, but that was as natural as I could promise being an epidural aficionado and believing after my first that God's greatest gift to women was that series of meds known as spinal blocks. Not that I don't admire women who are able to withstand the deliveries the U.C. claims will bring forth geniuses.

"I'll make a deal with you, Mr. Womb Warden. I'll forgo the epidural if you promise when it's time for your vasectomy, you'll employ the Bradley techniques and focus your way calmly through a few choice slices in your scrotal sack. Deal?"

"Funny. Ha, ha, ha. I was wondering . . . are you doing your twenty minutes of cardio a day in addition to staying within the recommended seventy percent or less of your target zone?"

"Listen here. I'm going out on bed rest for the remainder of this pregnancy same as I did with the first. My uterus can't handle the upright position. If you'd like to come over and do a few jumping jacks at the foot of my Serta, so be it."

The U.C. slammed his briefcase on a table and caused a scene in the office snack shop. "You can't go out on bed rest! You haven't completed your birthing classes. It's important you talk your husband into reading some Bradley or, in the very least, Lamaze literature. It's the only way to go."

I unwrapped a candy bar. "We did go. With the first. He was breech so I was forced to have an epidural. No need to focus, pant, and breathe when you're so numb you could swear you had no legs."

"No, no no! Women are made for this," the Uterine Comptroller shouted, his cheeks splotching. "They can do it. You can do it!" By now his voice was sheer euphoria and he'd drawn a crowd. "The female body was designed the same as animals of the wild. You don't see them asking for epidurals, do you?"

"They would if they could," I said and stuffed a Snickers in my mouth just to give him palpitations.

It had been hard enough watching my rear end grow at such a rate it could double as a dinette set. I certainly did not need the U.C. monitoring my every prenatal move. "The additives in that candy bar can kill fetal brain cells!" he yawped.

"I guess by now I've got a kid destined for special ed. And throw in the high-powered epidural and Demerol I'm planning to soak in, we may not get that far up the academic ladder, but I'll love her all the same. She can loop beads or bag groceries and I'll adore her tooth and nail." I grinned wickedly and waddled off.

Hours prior to leaving for this doctor-ordered three-month vacation in my Serta Firm Sleeper, the U.C. grew bolder than usual. Desperation can do this to a man.

"You don't have to take these bed rest orders lying down," he said, standing at my desk. "Those doctors are just trying to prevent lawsuits. Your body was designed to work in fields and carry a child. You lie in that bed and all you'll get is a sluggish infant who may score lower on future achievement tests."

"Give it up. Please."

"You don't have to become a complete vegetable in that bed."

"I don't plan to. My plan is to become a slug, which is a meat, and watch *Oprah* while my husband plays pinball at Frank's."

"Oh, please have him reconsider the 'Father knows all' birthing classes. Your child will thank you when he graduates from Harvard."

"My child will thank me that he doesn't have a mother

telling birthing war stories about how he nearly ripped her apart coming out. I'll be in pharmaceutical bliss and the entire experience will arrive tender and sweet. No screaming and sweating and hair tearing. That's so primitive. Why have it?"

The U.C. was clearly frustrated beyond words. He kind of choked and sputtered and emitted a few grunts.

"Please . . . just . . . just . . . do your kegels."

"Excuse me?"

"Kegels. That's the least you can do for your body. Tighten those vaginal walls while in bed to help season the passageway."

There is no comeback for a woman when a man suggests she season her passageway. The only thing I could do was try to close my mouth.

Of course once I found myself marooned in bed, about the only thing I could do was kegels. A couple of months later I went into labor and my husband drove like an old geezer to the hospital. I tried to focus and breathe and count the minutes until I could have my special-ed-inducing meds.

The Uterine Comptroller came to mind as my husband puttered along at twenty-five miles an hour on a deserted street at 5:00 a.m. I hollered and tore at the glove box and seat fabric. At least the U.C. would drive fast. He had bragged about doing ninety because his wife was so brave she'd stayed home until she was eight centimeters dilated like the rest of the super earth mamas who eschew anything but extreme pain in order to feel 110 percent womanly. I'd just as soon be a big fat whiny woman and beg for drugs.

When we finally arrived at the hospital, the nurse checked and said I was only dilated one single centimeter and couldn't get an epidural for a good long while. I thought I would die and that cutting my leg off with a cleaver would hurt less.

"Please, I need something."

She came back with a mild form of Demerol she shot through the IV, which immediately caused double vision. For the oddest and completely inexplicable reason, it seemed a good idea to seduce my two husbands. Oh, they were looking so handsome. I'd never seen two of Stu at once and was enjoying the effect of his Siamese twin. I could pretend the other head was sweet and romantic and didn't spout profanity.

"Come here, sweethearts," I slurred. "Y'all are looking good today. Either of you want to fool around while the nurse is gone?"

He was startled as if I'd lost my mind. "I'm not sure who you're talking to, but if I'm included in this conversation, sure! How come you never want to do this at home when you aren't in labor and having hallucinations?"

"Listen. I'm wanting it now. I'm hot for y'all, so surely one of you wants it."

He inched slowly over to the bed. "You're hooked up to an IV that's made you insane, and top that off with that beeping strap across your stomach . . . Oh my God. I saw it wiggle. I swear I saw it *move* a second ago, I'm serious."

"It's been moving for the past five months, but you're the one who chose not to look. You chose to play pinball for six hours a day like you did with our first baby. Why don't you focus lower? I shaved my legs and put on dark native woman tanning cream. I'm wearing a thong, too."

His cheeks puffed up because he's the kind of man who when mad suffers from inflatable features. "A thong! What kind of woman wears a thong to deliver a child?"

"It's all I had. It was the red thong or your boxers. I didn't want them to get the wrong idea."

"Oh, they'll get it all right," he said and his nose swelled from a long thin structure to a new potato. I saw two potato noses, actually.

"Come here, pooh loves," I said, digging in my purse for my pink frosted lipstick so I'd look pretty when Mama arrived with her new camcorder to film this miraculous occasion.

"What could this medicine be doing to our baby?"

I threw my plastic vomit bowlette at one of him. He was sounding like the U.C. "It's preparing her for remedial math,"

I said, and though it was mean, I couldn't stop laughing until a contraction hit and knocked me flat again.

The pain finally subsided and I begged my husband for some affection. He must have remembered how long the dry spell had lasted after the birth of our first, because he leaned in and planted a big passionate kiss on my pink lips right as the nurse came in.

"Well," she said, "I do believe I've come at the wrong time."

"You got that epidural?" I asked. "If you do, then it's never the wrong time. I'm sure I've had enough contractions to have dilated five centimeters in the last fifteen minutes."

She snapped on a glove and checked. "No, you're still at one. Go walk the halls and see if that eases your pain," she suggested. "Or keep doing what you were doing. I'll knock next time I enter or I could put up a do-not-disturb sign."

When an hour later I was still only at one centimeter, she finally got tired of hearing the screams and ordered the epidural along with a drug to speed up contractions. She turned to my husband. "You'd better go get something to eat. Could be a long day." He'd been gone no more than fifteen minutes when I had a sudden urge to push. I rang for the nurse.

"I think something's happening. I feel pressure, lots of pressure."

She checked around in there. "Oh, goodness. That's the baby's head. I've never had a woman go from one to ten centimeters in less than half an hour. Oh my God. I'm going to have to run and get the doctor, so hold off on the pushing whatever you do."

"My husband's in the cafeteria. He'll miss this entire moment. Could you please page him?"

"We don't do that. It's against hospital—"

"Well, I'm not pushing until his face darkens this doorway. Please?" About three minutes later he stood at my side, panicky, and held my numb legs for the pushing session I later referred to as "dramatic theater." They tried to hoist a big mirror in front of my parts and I yelled in shock, "Get that thing away immediately!" By that time a small crowd had gathered, including my mother with her video camera, saying she was ashamed to death her daughter wore a thong to deliver her grandbaby. She kept talking about my sister's dignified birth and how she had worn Little Bo Peep ruffled panties and had her hair in the cutest little braids and white eyelet bows.

Mama continued telling me to cover myself up after the doctor ordered me to remove my thong. I wouldn't have been surprised in the least if she'd said, "Cross your legs," as she had for the last thirty years.

"It wouldn't hurt you to bring an ounce of dignity to your birth," she said. "No need to spread yourself that wide unless you plan to deliver an eighteen-wheeler."

My husband decided this was a fine moment to take advantage of the situation: the drugs, my loony mama, and the bonus money I'd received for an award-winning story on the 105-year-old woman who wanted to kick my ass.

He held a leg as if it were a massive drumstick. "I sure would like a new TV," he said, winking seductively.

"Do what?" I'm sure I hadn't heard correctly. I was out of breath, straining to push out a child.

"A wide-screened TV. Circuit City's having a sale."

"Have you lost your mind? I'm trying to give birth here and you're wanting a damned Magnavox?"

"Not a Magnavox. A flat-screened Sony. Circuit City has them for twenty-two hundred with a hundred-and-fifty-dollar rebate if you act now."

I spun my head around a few times like an owl, while Mama rushed to the bed to throw a blanket over my privates. The doctors reprimanded her, saying they needed that view she found so unpleasant.

"I don't want any X-rated footage. My daughter wasn't raised that way."

"We have to see to deliver this baby," the doctor said.

"Please go and do something of a grandmotherly nature. We have a vending machine down the hall."

"I don't want a candy bar. I brought my own. Y'all never have Kit-Kats. I want to get pictures of my grandbaby and that's my daughter, by the way, whose . . . whose . . . pussy you can't seem to take your eyes off of."

Oh my God! My mother has used the P word. I would have fainted but was already lying down. Oh, I wanted the floor to open up and swallow me whole.

"I'd really like that Sony," my husband said. "There'll never be a time like this to—"

"Cover up, Susan." Mama snatched a handful of sheet and tossed it across my bottom half. "This isn't a classy look."

"There wasn't but one Sony left other than the floor model and it has scratches across the screen, so really now is a good time to—"

"We can't show this video to any kinfolk if you keep spreading your legs like a tramp." She turned to the doctor. "Can't she sort of sit up and squat instead? My other daughter didn't have to lay her wares out like a centerfold."

A nurse pulled my mother to the back of the room and shoved her into a vinyl chair. She then told my husband this wasn't the time to discuss TV sets.

"What's the baby's name going to be?" she asked, trying to get everyone's mind on a more pleasant topic, having no idea this was the sorest of all possible subjects.

"I want to name the baby Lindsey," I told my husband between pushes.

"I like Jenny."

"You dated that slut named Jenny. I'll never name my daughter Jenny."

"I never dated a slut or even—"

"Susan, there's no need to say vulgar words or to open your legs that wide unless you're planning to give birth to Big Foot."

"That's enough out of you," the nurse said to Mama,

who'd popped out of the vinyl chair. She patted my arm. "Jenny and Lindsey are both lovely names."

While pushing and listening to all the banter, I had an idea, the perfect solution. "Tell you what," I said to my husband. "If you let me name her Lindsey, I'll let you buy that wide-screen TV and we can even order cable."

He smiled with pure love and kissed me with a hunger the birth staff didn't like. "Focus," someone yelled. "The head's almost out."

Mama rammed her camcorder through the crew of medical experts to get a good shot. "Don't worry, Susan, I've got a feature on this thing that will block every hair from the tape except the hair on my precious new grandbaby's sweet head." She grabbed my numb leg, the one Stuart wasn't holding, and pushed it aside for a better view. "Hey, baby doll. Come on out and see your Mama Peg. One day I'll tell you the story of your mama wearing a thong to your birth."

The Perfect Mom

Once in a while, just when you think you may be a pretty decent mother after all, you meet her.

You know who I'm talking about. The perfect mom. The one who does her Pilates and kickboxing classes up until she delivers her fourth child and never once gobbled down anything with Little Debbie written on the wrapper.

The one who managed fresh highlights and Demi Moore's body throughout the duration of her four pregnancies.

The one who flew in a well-renowned midwife from California to help her deliver the babies at home, with Mozart on the CD player and candles flickering in every room so that she could experience true and natural womanhood. All while the rest of us begged and screamed for our epidurals and Demerol at one centimeter.

She's that same woman who jumped up from the delivery ready to hit the Baby Gap—only hours after wallowing around nude with her also nude baby for some perfect skin-to-skin bonding and breast-feeding, which of course, came effortlessly.

She's the one who two days after the glow of the World's Most Splendid Birth, slips into size 2 jeans, which amazingly fit more loosely than before, and drives in her spotless white BMW SUV to Dinner for the Rich, the gourmet and organic food store where a stalk of broccoli costs $6. She'll buy a free-range chicken and virgin vegetables for the stir-fry she'll serve tonight, after Pilates and three thousand sit-ups as she and her husband and four children stare at one another in sheer bliss and grateful bounty.

I see her at least once a week, this lovely reminder of everything I'm not. As soon as I spot her I feel myself swell and bloat, knowing full well my facial pores have decided to open at full force, holes big enough for small rodents.

The stains on my shirt magnify in her presence. The dirt beneath my children's fingernails makes them look as if they've been playing in a landfill.

The perfect mom isn't only in my neighborhood making all of us appear slobbish and slovenly. She looms in every town and city. She's that much-maligned, pulled-together woman who looks as if she's never had to shout, "Time out!" or, "Go to your room!" or consult the kiddie psychiatrist about the pros and cons of Zoloft and the Benadryl IV drip for toddlers.

She's the woman who would never yell in her yard, "Y'all come home. Supper's ready!" No way she'd raise her voice to corral the herd for dinner.

I'm always dumbfounded when I step into the manicured lawns of the Perfect Moms. Their children are playing as quietly as if in a library. The Perfect Mom steps out with a tray of fresh-baked cookies, a pitcher of lemonade, slices of lemon and strawberries atop each glass.

Every time I run into her, everything is in place and orderly. Her children, impeccably dressed, intelligent, and well mannered, are all under six and reading three- and four-syllable words. No one hollering for Little Debbie snack cakes, no one getting testy or hurling Smuckers from the shelves.

Standing next to her, I immediately feel myself shrinking, feel my teeth yellowing beneath the hideous fluorescent lighting. Then I see all the fresh fruits and whole wheats and grains in her grocery cart, noticing no boxes of opened Pop-Tarts, Trix, or Coco Puffs tumbling out of her children's hands.

Her children would never need the Keebler elves to elicit decency.

Maybe she won't see that my dingy "capris" sweatpants are ripped near the crotch or that my legs could use a few strokes with a sharp Venus triple blade.

Maybe she won't spot the blackberry and coffee stains on my shirt or chipped polish on my reptilian toenails.

Maybe she wasn't real, and this perfection must be a fraud, a big cover-up. Maybe this impeccable public facade was simply a shell of her real life, a thin coating that would crack open and her true self would come oozing out once the doors of her own home shut behind her.

It was my one comforting thought as I threw into my cart, along with a gallon of sugar-packed Sunny Delight, some Green Giant baby carrots for good measure. It was all I could hang on to as I looked down at my own children, my son's knees muddy and grass stained, and then at my baby, the globs of prechewed and partially digested graham cracker gunking up her sweet cheeks, Beech-Nut squash smeared all over her pitiful Onesie. Oh, why hadn't we worn our Gymboree smock and matching leggings? We were in a dingy white Onesie, the equivalent of a redneck's ribbed undershirt.

I had to picture this woman's house a mess just to make it from bread to produce without falling into the aisle and giving up, arms and legs straight up in the air like a dead bug's, muttering unintelligible phrases like "Fish fry on Fridays," and "Fettuccini on Saturdays."

I had to imagine her pearly whites as false, and hold fast to the sound of her dunking those clacking choppers into a jar of water by her bed every night. I thought of her rolling over in a plaid housedress the size of a piano and gazing at her husband with her sunken toothless mouth and saying, "Wanna hab sex?"

I had to imagine her husband with an enormous belly, covered in random red moles and wiry black hairs, her shower a carnival of mildew and bad grout, just to keep from crying.

And then when the most horrible thought of all swept over me—that everything perfect in her world was real and natural and effortless—I had to imagine her as a neurotic female Felix Unger, a girl who found it more thrilling to spray Tilex than eat an entire tray of Whitman's Samplers.

Finally, I had to picture her in a cheerleading uniform, pom-poms shaking as she shouted, "Give me an O! Give me an X! Give me an I! Then add *clean!* What have you got? I said, 'What have you got?' Oxiclean! Yes, Oxiclean! Say it again! Say it louder!"

It was enough to nudge me toward the checkout line, especially after I noticed the stubble peeping from my high-water leggings like thousands of tiny quills poised for attack.

Even on the days I have my children scrubbed and cleaned, threatened them with no TV or video games for a week if they acted ugly, my gene pool always comes home to roost.

There are times in one's life when a mama wishes to sweet Jesus the chair in which she sits would open up wide and swallow her whole—just as my own mama wished on countless occasions during the parenting of my sister and me, two hellions who nearly did her in.

Not long ago I attended a PTA function at my kids' school. I was in charge of salads and had made a huge Greek platter with all the fixings: black olives, feta cheese, purple onion, cucumber, and tomato with a delicious Greek dressing. I was so proud of my salad but didn't have a chance to stand by it and let everyone know it was mine, as any cook will do, especially at Baptist covered-dish dinners.

For it was this very evening, when all the awards and honors were being doled out to teachers, that my then preschool daughter went on a public bender. She decided, on this night of all nights, to showcase each and every recessive and hideous gene we'd been working so hard to mask—heredity's bounty such as the:

1. Laughing out loud inappropriately gene.
2. Wallowing and rolling on the gross floor while making Linda Blair noises gene.
3. Another two holes in my tights gene.
4. Watch as I jump up and run away gene.
5. And finally, the I have to potty every two minutes gene. Just because flushing is so much fun.

I plain froze with shock and humiliation as my sugared-up sweetheart pawed the air like a drunk squirrel and seemed to be break-dancing on the nasty floor where a pool of grease had spilled, making it easier for her to spin.

"Wouldn't have happened in my day," I heard one of the teachers whisper. "Her brother's pretty loud, but this child's a piece of work."

I felt myself burning with anger, but ate a brownie instead of biting off a head. When their chatter about my child's behavior continued, I'd finally had enough.

"Listen here. See that Greek salad on y'all's plates? I stayed up till 2:00 a.m. making it. And see that child y'all are yakking about? That's the baby the doctors told me might be born dead or profoundly handicapped. You can't imagine how happy I am that she is able to wallow around and cut up. You just can't imagine how I count my blessings every night for her."

They stared at me in shock.

"I want you to know she's not usually this rowdy." Then I pulled out the excuses we all use. "She's had too much sugar. She's tired. I think she's cutting a tooth."

They raised their eyebrows and curled their lips in a teacher-ish smirk.

"One more thing. She's the class teething ring of her preschool and she never bites back. She's mine through and through. I love every bit of her, even the rare bits that don't make me proud enough to pop buttons on my blouses."

I picked up my daughter, wedged her onto my hip, and held

on tight as she tried her best to wriggle free. It was one more event we had to leave early. But my baby would only be this young once.

I cherish all her quirks and behavioral challenges. How many mothers can say their three-year-olds are smart enough to loathe and despise back-to-school shopping?

Well, my child must be one of those geniuses. She knew instinctively that if a store had the word *Mart* or *Discount* anywhere on its sign, she was in for a miserable time.

She learned this during that summer horror known as the "back-to-school" shopping nightmare. Our state decided to have no sales tax on school supplies one weekend, making these marts almost impossible to enter and thus navigate.

There were fistfights over the last jug of Elmer's glue and jumbo box of Kleenex. Women pushed and shoved and snapped their beaks like feisty macaws.

"Move!" one old witch shouted as she bumped her cart into mine, my little girl rattled and possibly suffered whiplash. "Can't you see I'm trying to find a three-ring notebook binder?"

A woman released a bloodcurdler from the floor where a buggy track had rolled over her white blouse. "Somebody shoot me, but first put the sixty-four-count Crayolas in my cart."

Just when I thought I would keel over, my then three-year-old decided this was the perfect moment to showcase her budding hormones and the colorful language she'd learned from her older brother (and parents, to be honest).

She stood up in the buggy, stepping on the antibacterial soap and pencil box holders. She put her little hands on the railing and shouted, "*Asshole!*" at the cart-ramming woman as loud as her lungs allowed. The frenzied shoppers came to a complete halt. I tried to hide, but my cart sat trapped among twenty others.

I knew I had to save face or someone would call Child Protective Services. "OK, honey," I said sweetly and then hollered: "We'll get you a *bass pole* as soon as I find the loose-leaf paper."

No sooner had we reached the checkout line than I saw the Perfect Mom, suntanned and glistening with creams and scents, carting her four spotless children, none uttering a peep. It seemed to me that the Perfect Mom's waistline had shrunk another two inches since I saw her last year and that her thighs were perhaps even thinner.

"Hey there," I said, because Mama advised us to always act friendly.

"Hello, how are you?" she asked, followed by a chorus of children saying, "Hello, ma'am. I hope you're having a lovely day."

Heaven, help. "Are you here for school supplies?" I asked.

"Oh no. We never come here for that. We always go to Office Serenity because no one else in town knows about it."

No one can afford to pay four dollars for a glue stick when Big Mart has them for twenty-five cents each, I wanted to say. But all that came out of my mouth was, "Good to see you. You look wonderful. I don't know how you get thinner each time I see you."

"Oh, now," she purred. "I'm not thinner. I'm four months pregnant with our fifth angel. But I guess I have lost fat since I've started teaching power yoga in addition to kickboxing and two spin classes daily."

This was way too much for me on this maddening day in a Mega Mart. I once again pictured her without teeth and saying to her children, "I'm tho habby you chirrin' behabe tho bell." And then sneaking a Little Debbie Swiss Roll from under her bed and eating all six double-packs. It was the only way I could manage the drive home.

In Sickness and Health, and Trips to the Goodwill

I can't tell you the number of days I look over at my husband and wonder how in the world we ended up together. No two people could be more different, and sometimes I truly believe we have no common interests but the kids.

It is true that opposites attract, fall in love, get married, and subsequently spend a hefty portion of those married years wondering what they're going to do with themselves and each other.

OK, so he's not perfect, I tell myself. But who is? I'm certainly not with my quick temper and propensity to stack and pile items, the genetic disorder of turning clothes dryers, sofas, tabletops into storage areas for papers and other where-to-store-it whatnots.

On that opposite extreme is my husband, a man so neat and orderly he gave off blazing clues during our courtship, which *love* insisted on shrouding, even blinding. Otherwise, we'd surely have seen what was coming.

There he was on our second date on aisle 10 at the Bi-Lo supermarket scanning cleaning products as if he were judging the bikini contest in the Miss Universe pageant. His eyes were wide and expressive, his breathing rapid. His hands reached slowly for the Comet, the Lysol, the Windex, and the Dow Scrubbing Bubbles as he stuffed his cart with what looked like a hotel housekeeper's weapons against scum and grunge.

"What about the Cornish hens?" I asked, thinking we'd come in for dinner items.

"Huh? Hens?"

"Do you still want to cook dinner together?" I noticed he was flushed and for a moment he said nothing.

"Hens. Sure."

That right there should have been the big clue this man meant business as far as a spic-and-span environment went. If that hadn't registered, I should have listened as his mother told stories of how when she'd ask him to clean out a drawer as a teenager, he'd empty the entire contents, the good and the bad, everything not anchored to wood, including perfectly good calculators and expensive fountain pens.

But no, it was blind ignorant love that sent me marching down that aisle wearing a size 8 wedding dress (impossible today) and dreams of bliss and hearts pitter-patting with love until neither of us had teeth, until he'd lost all his hair and I'd grown a crop on my chin.

I moved my belongings into his life and should have woken up when I saw that he was completely infatuated with my Dust Buster, held on to it same as he did his "unit" while watching TV.

But I didn't. I kept dreaming of our synchronized love, my eyes shunning clues as if wearing mule blinders.

He was neat and I was a "piler." He liked lots of sex. I liked lots of romance. And on and on.

One day shortly after our honeymoon, I noticed one of the uglier wedding gifts was gone.

"Sweetie, where's that piggy footstool Aunt Barbara gave us?"

"Huh? What footstool?"

"You know. The one you hated. The one I kept putting in bed with you at night as a joke."

"That big fuzzy hog thing? I have no idea. Haven't seen it and hope I never do again."

"Haven't seen it? It's three feet wide and weighs sixty pounds."

He turned red and quickly left the room. I later learned that sweet pig packed our woodstove one frigid night when we ran out of split logs.

Maybe it's such differences that fuel a marriage, each opposite characteristic just another log on the fire. Who knows? Plenty of times I've looked at couples from the surface and thought, *Lord, what in the world are they doing married?*

No one is able to guide a blind heart; it holds its own reins. Only sometimes I'd like to take those reins and tie my husband's ever-scrubbing hands until he learns his lesson: that cleaning doesn't mean throwing out a person's special belongings.

On the day he carted a load to Goodwill that included my old high school cheerleading shoes and tap dancing costumes, I called my mother in tears.

"I can't take it anymore. I went to Goodwill the very next day and someone had actually bought those ugly blue and white saddle oxfords. Why would someone want blue shoes? Why would they need my orange sequined jumpsuit? I'm leaving him. First, he throws out things he deems unworthy. Then he up and burns Aunt Barbara's pig stool and decides my memorabilia from the past, including my *cheerleader* shoes and tap dance outfit, needed to go to Goodwill. It's over. He can just go expose himself on aisle ten at the Bi-Lo. He can unzip his blue jeans and flash the Clorox bottles."

My mother assured me the first year of marriage was far worse than all the others combined, and that if I could survive one year, I could live through them all.

"Does he drink, smoke, hang out in bars, or beat you?" my practical mother asked.

"No."

"Well, that's a start."

"Mom. Haven't you heard a word I've said?"

There was a long pause. Finally she sucked a deep breath and said, "Look, you know that lamp of his you think's so ugly? Pack it up and take it down to Goodwill. Nothing like a taste of their own medicine."

I did just that. Within five minutes of discovering it missing he hit the roof and sent me down the road with a fistful of money. I had to buy the monstrosity back and wouldn't you just know it was still sitting there?

I'm telling you, that first year nearly killed me, and the fifteen that followed were no day at the park either, God love him. I figure it's my load to put up with all his business such as the fact he won't allow bath mats, dust ruffles, or curtains in our home and that he plans to take down all the existing window-wear the former owners left behind.

The first several years of our lives together were spent in a log cabin built in the 1800s and replete with hairy wolf spiders, baby rattlesnakes, and other biting creatures. His mother had decorated it for him, as he was young and single and she knew a girl's heart would soar when spotting a man who had drapes that matched his sofa. When I moved in, the curtains hung beautifully and even sported ruffles and white lace.

Don't ask what happened when we built our first house. Every time I brought home a bath mat, it ended up in the basement. Each time I tried to cover the box springs with a dust ruffle, he screamed as if someone were branding him.

"We really need a dust ruffle to complete the bedding ensemble," I said. "Please quit throwing them down the stairs or in the trash. The garbage collector kept thanking me for the home décor items and it finally dawned on me what you've been up to. I'm going this afternoon to replace all that you've disposed of."

"Oh, how redneck. Only hicks have dust ruffles. I hate that word. Dust ruffle." He made a yuckster face. "You need to get you a double-wide if dust ruffles are what you want."

"I've seen plenty of trailers I'd rather live in than here. This makes the Amish look opulent. Why do you like the box springs to show? I don't get it."

"Our beds aren't the kind you put a ruffle around. Our box springs are nice and match the walls. You're trying to Hootin' Gootin' up the place."

"The beds look naked."

"You oughta take a lesson from them."

Ha, ha, ha. "Why not just toss a few bare mattresses stained with old-lady tinkle onto the floor? Scatter them about. Forget sheets and comforters."

I was mad and tired of seeing my friends' well-appointed houses with all the sofas and window treatments, their bedding and decorative pillows piled high and matching the gorgeous Roman shades and lavish window-dressings. Everyone knows texture and fabric bring layers of warmth to a home. Everyone but Tidy Stu.

I got depressed and went shopping. To the devil with his undecorating and the fact he burned my fleecy pig and tossed my cheerleader shoes into the Goodwill barrel. Every decorative wrong he'd committed I was planning to right on this day.

I gripped the charge card as if it were a loaded gun and bought bed skirts, careful they weren't ruffled, bed pillows, and—God forbid—bath mats. I purchased hand towels for the kitchen and place mats for the table, all the small details one loves when warming a home.

As soon as I scattered the wares about the house and on the beds, all hell broke apart, like a frozen lake cracking.

"We aren't the kind of people who use these," my husband thundered, ripping off the bed skirts and whipping the bath mats up in his arms. "We have beautiful mattresses and I want them to show. We've got nothing to hide. Only people whose grannies have peed in the bed need dust ruffles." He reached over and picked up a green and yellow polka-dotted pillow and held it out as if it were covered in the Ebola virus.

"What the hell is this?"

"A pillow."

"No. What is on this?"

"That's called a pillow sham, hon."

"It's called white trash décor. And this?" He held up a bath mat.

"That's what people use when they get out of the tubs and showers."

"We have tile, beautiful tile."

"Yes, and when it gets wet, the kids or I could fall it's so slick."

"That's why we have an HMO. No one puts a bath mat down to cover tile. That's for linoleum people. We are *tile* people."

I was ready to shoot him. I had once chopped up one of my SSRIs (Selective Serotonin Reuptake Inhibitors) and microwaved it so it would turn to powder before pouring it in his tea. The plan was for him to sip his apricot tea and over time the world wouldn't become such a hostile place for him. He would, after two weeks of Zoloft tea, be able to tolerate a pillow sham or maybe even a hand towel in the kitchen instead of using seven rolls of Bounty per week. He might just drink the special tea I was brewing and decide having a couple of curtains in the house wasn't a bad idea, either; that window treatments weren't just for trailers as he had previously insisted.

"I hate the term *window treatments,*" he snarled in the days prior to my tampering with his teapot. "Sounds like the windows are sick and in need of medical care. That's more of your country bumpkin décor. We have gorgeous windows just like our box springs and bathroom floors. Why are you trying to cover up everything with your redneck shopping trips?"

My doctor doubled my prescription for antidepressants, knowing I was planning to medicate my husband. It was hush-hush, but I knew the shrink thought it best.

Every day I chopped the Zoloft the way he chopped my fleece pig and mixed it in his tea, telling the children never to drink Daddy's tea and making them their own fresh pitcher of lemonade each day.

For weeks he sipped his happy poison, and slowly I began noticing a change. He quit asking for sex. Yippee. He quit fussing and grumping about the piles of papers and stacks of things around the house, and lo and behold, he quit cleaning. Just up and ended his obsession with dirt and scrubbing.

I shopped every day and spread fabrics everywhere. He said nothing and cleaned nothing and cooked nothing and quit rubbing on me from behind like some old dog in heat. He was a Zoloft Zombie, sitting at the computer all day long playing solitaire and pinball. He was pleasant enough, but no one was inside. After a while, I missed his ferocious demeanor and his grumpy ways. I missed the fact nothing would irritate him because aggravating him used to bring about great pleasure. And . . . and . . . well . . . truth be known . . . I missed his hideous and vulgar sex advances. This was like having a Stepford Husband. I'm sure the SSRIs work great for some men, but they zapped mine and he turned into a bore, sitting on furniture and staring into space. He stepped on bath mats when he got out of the shower and didn't scream in decorative horror. He laid his zombied head directly on sham-dressed pillows and never once convulsed or levitated.

He couldn't play his grand piano, nor could he blow those fabulous notes from his tenor or soprano sax. He even quit fondling the fourteen eBay trumpets. He quit cleaning and dirt and piles climbed higher and higher. Dust blew and coated everything. Stains took root in tubs and toilets. I tried, I really did, but didn't have the magic he possessed to keep things neat and organized.

I cut back on the poisons and little by little allowed the old beast to return. When he did, the bed skirts vanished, as did the bath mats, curtains, pictures I'd hung on the walls, hand towels, pillow shams, and other items he once again found offensive. He grabbed his balls and asked for sex. He was back. Mercy, he was back.

The saving grace was that the house became clean again. Two weeks after his tea therapy ended, and thus his mind clicked back into obsessive-compulsive overdrive, he high-tailed it like old times to Home Depot and bought an array of mops and brooms. He came home prouder than a hunter with big game in the trunk.

"Look at this," he said, and I noticed his ears reddening with sexual excitement. He was holding three mops that looked exactly alike. "This is for the wood floors and I've marked it *wood*. See the typed labels? The other mop," he said, holding it up, "is for tile. See the label typed *tile*? That third mop is a backup. See that label marked—"

"Spare me!"

My son entered the room. I had high hopes for him being neither a neat freak nor a slob. Something in the middle would be nice. And then he had to open his mouth full of oversized preteen teeth. "Those mops are killer, Dad."

I reached for the phone. Surely there was a self-help group for this type of disorder. I was interrupted by the sideshow and smells of cleaning fluid. "Watch this, son," my husband said euphorically, never getting quite this happy on Zoloft tea.

He lifted the mop high in the air and pressed the lever as the head of the contraption folded itself into a self-ringing motion. "Awww, sweeeeet!" my son exclaimed. "Let me try it."

"So this is genetic?" I asked, hearing no reply, only the sounds of battery-operated Swiffer Wet Jets and the spray of Murphy's Oil. Tidy Stu had hauled out every cleaning product in our cabinets and lined them on the shelves, as if soldiers preparing for battle.

After this father-son mop-fest had run its course, Tidy moved along to the row of cleaning products. "This," he said, gently clutching a bottle by the neck, "is Kaboom." His voice held reverence. "Gets the stains out of everything." I thought he was about to genuflect or at least light a candle as if spiritually moved.

"Kaboom is, and let me emphasize this point, only for bathroom use, you understand? Sinks and stuff. Comet is for toilet use. Cinch for the countertops and mirrors. Murphy's

Oil is for the wood floors and Lysol for toilets and trash cans after, say, a stomach bug."

This was the last straw. I knew he'd crossed the line of sanity. That night Mama called after the weekly conclusion of her only obsession besides death and Jesus—the show *Big Brother*. I heard my husband yelling from the shower where he was Kabooming his sanitized heart out.

"Tell your mother that she would love Kaboom," he shouted. "Tell her Kaboom can perform miracles just like Jesus."

"I'm not telling her that. It's sacrilegious."

"What did he say?" Mama asked.

"He said Kaboom and Jesus were close kin."

"You need to seriously consider getting him into church. I'm afraid when the sky opens up, no one's going to reach down and pluck him up."

I know not to argue when Mama starts in about the skies opening up and certain individuals rising while others become ash.

Later that night as Stu was alphabetizing the fridge and pantry, he announced he was headed to Bi-Lo. He quit letting me go because I coupon shop and he said I buy white trash items like Little Debbie Swiss Rolls, which are the most delicious PMS food a woman could possibly eat.

While he was in the store, I slipped into CVS pharmacy next door to see if they had any good lipsticks on sale. When he finished his shopping, his bags stuffed with cleaning supplies, milk, and Special K with berries, he must have spied in the windows of CVS and viewed a potential domestic disaster under way.

He sent our son in on a mission. "Dad sees that sixty-four-pack of Charmin in your cart," he said. "He told me to tell you if you don't put it back, he's driving off without you."

I stared at this mini version of my husband. "Is that so?"

"He said to tell you he's not in favor of toilet tissue the size of doghouses."

"Tell him I plan to toss a roll in the doghouse with him if he's lucky. Otherwise, he'll get my old *Redbook* magazines."

The clerk stared, her fingers poised above the register, unsure whether to ring up that bad boy or listen to my son.

"*Ring it up!*" I said as she raised her painted-on eyebrows. "Go ahead. I'm not worried about him. He hates any kind of multipack. It's a phobia, a multipack disorder. When I joined Sam's Club he ran off for three days all upset because I brought home a bottle of Advil the size of a milk jug. He didn't like the cereal because the boxes were bigger than what our dishwasher came in."

I asked my son to help me lift the QE2 multipack from the store, him holding one end, me the other, as we stepped outside to see my husband and daughter already in the car by the curb.

His anger flashed and he motioned for my son to get in the car. "Sorry, Mom," he said, dropping his end of the multipack. I heard doom in the form of doors automatically locking, like the cells of jails. Tidy Stu grinned like a stinker and flipped the car into Drive. He had the nerve to slowly inch away, leaving me standing in the darkness, holding on to something that could easily double as a spare bed. Eventually, as all men who want to get laid will do, he returned and unlocked the trunk, loading the mammoth pack of Charmin into the car and grumbling because he couldn't see out the window.

"If I wreck it's because of you," he said. "Because your irritable bowels needed two hundred rolls of toilet paper instead of the four most humans buy."

When we got home, he opened the closet door and chose the perfect weapons to wipe away his frustration—the mop marked *tile* in one hand, the bottle of Kaboom in the other.

Marrying Ma Ferguson

My best friend in the world is Ma Ferguson. Her real name is foreign and lovely, but I call her "Ma Ferguson," because some days we wake up and feel like old grump pots and grannies and thus the name suits.

She was once a gorgeous model and fashionista who dated the rich and famous, including a Saudi prince and an heir to a perfume dynasty.

Ma, at thirty-two, is still a raving beauty and her groom, though pushing seventy-five, is every bit the hard-bodied grandpa who could kick butt if need be. He's a fine person and Ma decided she would up and marry him and have the yard man who moonlighted as a preacher perform the nuptials.

In these parts, that's what people do. They don't just get married. They "up" and marry. She'd found her a fellow some forty-odd years older, but much better looking than that thing Anna Nicole lured into her trailer by wiggling naked on a pole, grinding it like a dog on someone's sofa cushions.

Ma Ferguson has bigger headlights than Anna and hers are real. She never danced naked, either, or had a bunch of hicks without teeth for kin. All Ma's kin are refined and cultured and from swanky parts of the globe, including Finland and Italy.

She had dated this elderly man for about five years and when the two decided to up and marry, they asked me to be the matron of honor.

"We're getting married in the yard," Ma said. See, she's not pretentious. She really lives with her fiancé on the most beautiful property in town, more like the grounds of an estate than a yard. "It's just going to be me, you, Dwight, and Dane." Dwight being the groom and Dane, Ma's son by a previous husband closer to her age.

"Who's marrying you?" I asked, figuring she'd drag the priest from the Catholic church to her manor and set him up with a nice plate of homemade cookies and a few pounds of fish.

She started laughing. She couldn't stop. She fell over on her fine leather sofa and hee-hawed like a drugged chimp. She held her bottom and said she was going to wet her pants so she jumped up and flew to the bathroom, still carrying on. When she came back her face was streaked with mascara and she was holding her stomach and stifling more laughs.

That's when the guilt took over, as it will with Ma since she's Catholic. She excused herself and went into her laundry room where she's set up the Jesus vigil, wall-to-wall photos of Jesus and Mary illuminated in the flickering glow of about fifty burning candles. This is where she washes her precious geezer's Fruit of the Looms and all their dirties, machines rumbling and tumbling while the scent of Tide and vanilla candles spreads throughout the room. She'd dragged in an old cardboard table that's about to collapse from the two hundred spare candles on hand and the different saints and Bibles, religious knickknacks I'd never seen in a Baptist church.

Food and water bowls for her six dogs share space with Niagara Spray starch, OxiClean, Mary, Jesus, and all my dear friend's guilt. Poor Ma is eat up with guilt and goes to the Jesus washeteria to release it and set the record straight with the Lord.

When she'd returned from praying for forgiveness, she

flopped back down on the couch as if drained. "Oh, I'm so sorry," she said. "I love Shorty and I think he's the best man in the whole entire world, but was wondering if—"

"Who?" I interrupted. "Shorty?" Slowly a face formed with the name. Shorty. The sweet pumpkin-colored stump of a fellow who helped mow the fifteen rolling acres of her soon-to-be manor.

"You mean the yard man is going to marry you?"

Ma Ferguson nodded and sat up. "He's the most precious person on earth. Oh, I love him so much and he goes into my laundry room after mowing and stays for fifteen minutes, so you know he's of the holy nature."

"Maybe he's washing himself."

"Did you not know he's an ordained minister? He does marriages and funerals along with yard work. I'm lucky. I can get married and my grass mowed all in the same day if I so choose."

She likes to really build someone up if she's overcome with guilt. "He's a saint, that sweet, dear godly man."

"I thought he had stomach problems and couldn't mow anymore."

"He does, but he's getting better since the surgery. He seems to do fine with the colostomy bag."

Mercy. I knew all about colostomy bags from my days as a young fool student nurse.

Hearing about Shorty's colostomy reminded me of that former career prior to going into journalism. I had decided nursing was the field for me and worked a couple summers in various hospitals and rest homes. My jobs mostly entailed the tail ends of folks. I was an ass-wiper, an enema giver, and once, armed to the elbow in a latex glove, the de-impact woman. I had orders from the head nurse to dig out the fossilized pellets of this poor old lady not responding to less invasive treatments. Seemed to me a person would need a medical degree to go prowling in a rectum that wasn't her own. I greased up my glove and turned my head, hoping to find the right opening.

"Ohhhhhhhh," the constipated woman moaned as the excavation began. This is not the kind of work for twenty-year-old women in their prime. "That's so much better. You's a gift from God, sugar pie."

"Glad to help." I covered her up and ran out of the room as fast as possible to gag, only to discover on my assignment chart orders for a "hot soapy enema for Mr. Bonner in room 314 and a bulb enema for Mrs. Marshall. Don't forget she doesn't have legs, so you'll need the bedpan."

That was some summer. The summer of asses. And of falling in love with those sweet people. I lost twenty pounds on what I like to call the Doo-Doo Diet. It's hard to swallow hospital chicken-fried steak after being assaulted by a dozen sets of bowels on a daily basis.

That was also the summer I saw my first penis. Step back. Make that my first penis over age ninety. Old Mr. Hinson was due a sponge bath and a condom catheter and Nurse Susan was sent in to provide him his first erection in God knew how long.

I bathed him, carefully avoiding all erogenous zones. He must have had the cleanest hands and forearms in town because I kept going over the same areas of safe skin as much as possible.

He got tired of it. "Go lower," he said, and I was shocked because I'd worked there two months and had never heard him say a word. "Loooooooower."

I scrubbed his chest and abs and then his thighs and everywhere but *there*.

When it was over I had to dry him off and figure out how to apply the condom catheter around his penis, which I was trying not to look at because several times during the bath I could tell from my periphery it moved like a snake, coiling and trembling and trying to take flight.

"I'll be right back, Mr. Hinson," I said and left the room to find Linda, the other student nurse who was extremely gorgeous and who dieted by chewing tobacco and spitting into patients' trash cans. I caught up with her in Miss Bessie's room, assuring the woman for the tenth time her nightgown wasn't ablaze and that the windows had no flames licking the panes, nor did any of the nurses have a secret agenda to burn the place down.

"Please, Linda," I begged, inhaling the sharp smells of ammonia and bodily breakdowns. "You've got to help me."

Linda bragged about how she knew her way around a penis and marched straight into Mr. Hinson's with a wicked glimmer in her eye. She spat her tobacco juice, adjusted her cultured pearls, and snapped on a pair of gloves. I handed her the equipment and she went to work, not making eye contact with Mr. Hinson, who fortunately, had gone back to sleep.

Linda took a medium-size condom catheter and set it aside. "We have to wash the penis first. Did you do that?"

"Um. No."

She shook her head as if I were an errant child. She set about her duties, refilling the bowl of warm water, opening a fresh soap, and grabbing a clean washcloth and hand towel. Little Miss Red Man Efficiency. As if all my former bathing of the man didn't count. She started washing Mr. Hinson and he awakened with a start, his eyes wet and wobbling around, unable to still themselves. She treated his manliness as if it were just another body part and not *the* body part.

As she dried the thing, it shot from limp to flagpole rigid and then quickly toppled before twice rising and falling again. Linda said nothing. She held the penis at an angle as it wriggled in her hands and firmly wrapped the sheath holder around the condom.

"You don't want to wrap this too tight," she said, cheek bulging with Red Man. "If you do it too tight, it'll stop the blood from going to the penis."

That might be a good thing, I wanted to say.

"Next, I'm taping the catheter to his right thigh next to the base of his organ." Linda attached the equipment, peeled off a glove, and hawked her plug in the man's trash can.

"Don't go," Mr. Hinson cried. "I loooooooooovvvvve youuuuuuu."

Linda didn't bat an eye. "Make sure you place the bag below the level of the bladder so he won't back up. Understand?"

"Yep." I sure did.

And I understood when Ma Ferguson was telling me about Shorty's colostomy bag exactly what she was up against, wondering how in the world her lawn-mowing preacher could possibly perform an outdoor service in the blazing heat with a barely stitched and healed new doody route.

"My uncle had a colostomy," I said. "He wasn't able to get around for a while."

"Shorty's doing great. He'll be fine when the day comes."

"When is the day, again?" I asked.

"Next Saturday."

"You mean a week from tomorrow? I thought we had 'til the end of August."

"Dwight's ready to get on with things. And we wanted to go ahead with it before Dane starts school."

The way she talked, it sounded like a farm chore: like milking the herd or bringing in the harvest.

"What do I wear?"

"Anything you want."

Well, when the big day came I don't recall what I was wearing, but Ma and Pa Ferguson looked great. Ma was radiant in a lovely lavender number and her groom appeared not a day over fifty and smelled like Halston and yellow Dial.

Truth was, he looked better than most men half his age. He didn't even have a paunch and sported the tight little body of the sort of fellow who runs around with lots of energy and forgets to eat unless a wife plops a meal on the table.

My best friend was to be his fifth or sixth wife. And Shorty was to marry them.

Only when I glanced over at Shorty, my breath caught. His shirt had risen from his unzipped pants and several buttons had either given up, exploded, or were in a state of firing like bullets from the cloth. His brow poured sweat and his skin took on a shade similar to the inside of an acorn squash. He wiped his face and breathed with great difficulty, like a creature in a monster movie.

We were to walk the wooded and hilly property to the creek for the nuptials Shorty would perform, but I didn't think he was going to survive the stroll.

The man needed to be in a hospital, hooked to an IV and prepped for surgery. His organs, it appeared, were swelling and malfunctioning.

"Is he OK?" I whispered as a beatific Ma Ferguson floated through the woods, ripping away branches and yanking bothersome vines with her strong, German woman arms. She either ignored or didn't hear me. "Here, Shorty. I've cleared the path for you. Come this way." He grunted and stopped to emit a sound that was unmistakable. Oh my God. Stop the wedding. The minister has bagged a fart.

"Ohhhhh," he mumbled and ripped the remaining button from his shirt, letting his poor belly puff like a tire being pumped up. "Ohhhhhh."

Ma Ferguson patted him on his dripping wet back and scooted ahead to remove a tree that had fallen during a recent storm. She is strong, that Ma. She has a shot put thrower's arms and with one hand hurled the tree across the creek. Her husband-to-be and son stood at the bottom of the valley, wearing suits, trickles of sweat, and nervous smiles.

"Ma, your reverend isn't well," I said.

"Shhh! He'll be OK, honey. He's much better now." She led him by the elbow over a series of roots that had pushed through the earth and threatened to tank Shorty and his musical bag.

I kept walking. We were almost there. Almost there.

"Oiyeee, Oiyee. Argghhh. Mrrrmp." Shorty collapsed on one knee and Ma Ferguson, who'd waited five long years to marry her senior citizen with the hot body, yanked up this fallen reverend and replanted him on her soil. There was no way she was going to have her day ruined by a dying reverend. No telling when she'd get her fiancé down the aisle again, if ever.

"You're fine, Shorty," she said in a sweet, angelic, and saintly voice. All the while she lifted this man as a mother would a toddler and carted him on her waist down the rest of the path.

He writhed in her grip and turned wetter and more orange. His clothes were nearly gone and his pants only partially zipped.

"Ma," I said as she set him down and watched him stagger before her fiancé and son. She promptly fetched him and propped him up by a dogwood. "Ma, he's not doing well."

My best friend, now perspiring but glowing in her beauty and determination, cast her eyes on me. "He'll be fine. He just has gas."

At that point, Shorty burst forth with a chorus of bag and upper gastrointestinal tunes. His poor belly contorted and changed shapes as if his innards were playing musical chairs. Ma Ferguson, true to her giving and kind and oh-so-devout nature, petted the man. "Everybody toots, Shorty," she said and I burst out laughing and couldn't stop. "Well, they do," Ma said. "All God's creatures have gas."

Ma made the sign of the cross or whatever that move is Catholics are always doing to appear gloriously pious. She reached for her son and beloved senior citizen husband-to-be.

I stood next to them with my flowers. Shorty managed to face us, his black Bible shaking in his hands. As he began, the bag accompanied us with a series of unusual sounds, the melody of Ma's marriage, her personalized wedding march. I noticed a video camera perched on a tripod and figured we'd at least have proof if Shorty died, that we didn't kill him.

I didn't know whether to laugh or call 911. It was a strange moment, Shorty blowing up with gas, his clothes peeling and erupting from his body, and my best friend in her lavender and high hopes willing him on with the desperation in her eyes.

Shorty turned to me. "I think I may need you to read this

for me because I didn't bring my glasses," he said, trying to save face, poor man.

He handed me his spare Bible and I nearly passed out upon seeing the traditional wedding vows. He was asking me to perform the ceremony and my best friend gave me a look that said I'd better freakin' do it or I wouldn't get any of the lavish Italian wedding cake or finger foods later.

Shorty leaned against a tree and was trying to put his clothes back together. He roused himself enough to hobble forth and say, "Dearly beloved, we are gathered together here in the name of God to join together this man and this woman in holy matrimony, which is—" He continued sputtering out the service for a while, but I couldn't stop staring at his bag, which was detaching and making quite the rumble.

"Which is . . . which is commended to be honorable among all men; and therefore—"

His knees buckled and I caught him in time. "You mind finishing this up?" he groaned. "Here, right here." He pointed to the passages in the book. I had no choice, Ma Ferguson giving me the evil eye and the reverend hovering near death.

"Well," I began, coughing and trying to sound religious and official. "On behalf of the Reverend Shorty, I'll read for him as he is the one really and truly doing all the marrying here. I'm simply the reader, the one who will—"

"Get on with it," Ma said, casting an eye toward the panting reverend, who had given up standing and rolled in the grass as if aflame. "Go on, hurry."

I found my place in the book. "Marriage is the union of husband and wife in heart, body and mind," I said, suddenly finding my voice, my preacher woman, fire-and-brimstone evangelical voice. Ma Ferguson appeared alarmed. "It is intended for their mutual joy and for the help and comfort—"

"You can skip all that," Shorty said, heaving and gripping his stomach. "All that's frills."

He needed an ambulance and wasn't about to wade through unnecessary vows. He had directed me straight to the crux of the matter and I continued. "On behalf of the Reverend Shorty," I'd say before every passage read, including the words the bride and groom must repeat and the exchange of rings. By now, Shorty was growing sicker and more orange.

"Inasmuch as Ma and Pa Ferguson have consented together in marriage before this company of friends and family—"

"Skip!" Shorty hollered.

My goodness, I thought. *No way this deal will seal.* "What therefore God has joined together—let no man put asunder. And so by the power of the Reverend Shorty and the power vested in me by Shorty and the state of North Carolina, and Almighty God, I now pronounce you man and wife, on behalf of Shorty."

"Shut up," Dane yelled and Ma swatted him.

"You may now kiss the bride," I said, and shut up as ordered.

The happy couple kissed, and Shorty began rolling around again as if covered in bees. Ma had barely gotten hitched, and I'm not even sure it was legal since I have no degree in reverending, before they had to call an ambulance for their dear yard man.

Ma carried him sideways on her hip like a kicking baby and waited on the EMS crew.

"It'll be all right, Shorty," she said. "Everybody toots."

Later, during the reception held at her new manor and attended by a dozen friends and family members who weren't privy to the private ceremony, she couldn't stop laughing once we heard Shorty would be all right. Ma's elegance and held together stress unraveled and she felt so guilty she hit the prayer room and put in a load of wash before rejoining the guests.

A few weeks later, I was at my in-laws' house and saw a familiar white truck. I peered around the backyard, and there he was—Shorty, mowing my father-in-law's grass. He looked less orange, less bloated, and like a man who could knock death out of the ballpark every time he stepped up to bat.

I turned around and got back in my car, ashamed I couldn't

face him, afraid we'd committed a terrible crime by having the matron of honor marry the bride and groom.

"I don't think my marriage is legal," Ma Ferguson often says to me. "I can't even bear to watch the video."

"It's as legal as any," I say, as she rises and retreats to her laundry room, mumbling prayers and pouring out the Tide and Kibbles and Bits.

Little Miss Ungrateful

I have to say that my mother is the most innocent person alive. She married at nineteen and was on her wedding night a double virgin.

For those who don't know what a double virgin is, she is a woman who not only hasn't had sex or anything remotely close to it, but one who also knows none of the terminology. A triple virgin, which Mama also partially qualifies for, is all of the above plus complete ignorance when it comes to all words related to body parts below the belt and their functions.

Here's what I mean.

Once when Mama was working at Sears to help put Daddy through college, she had a coworker whose name drove her crazy. For, you see, along with complete innocence, my precious mother can't pronounce multisyllabic words. Of course, she has no trouble inserting three syllables into one-syllable words—such as when "hey" becomes "haaayyyyeeeaaa"— but throw a two-syllable word at her and whew! All sorts of odd things unfold.

This is what happened at the candy counter at Sears where for eight hours every day she and this coworker with the name

Mama couldn't pronounce would scoop up ten cents' worth of chocolates for hungry shoppers and their whiny children.

This went on for several months, my mother always avoiding calling the woman by name. She'd say, "Here, hon, you take a break while I clean the chocolate-covered peanut trays." Or she might try, "Morning, hon. You have a good night?" Hon it was, and nothing more.

All was going well until Hon needed a ride home from Sears one night after closing. My dad, fresh from higher learning, was picking Mama up. She started to panic. She knew he'd want an introduction. So Mama stared at Hon's name tag as hard as she could, trying to go over the pronunciation in her mind. It was just a little word. Almost like Anne . . . but not . . . was it . . . was it . . . Annis? . . . or would you say it like "A Niece"? How do you pronounce Annis? None of the customers had ever tried to say it either. Or had they? Oh, my mother was in a snit. Variations rolled over her tongue in silent word warfare.

She and Hon got in the car. My father grinned and turned his head to the backseat where the woman sat smelling like burned popcorn. "Hello there," he said, then looked over at my mother with the face that said, *OK. Time for introductions.*

Mama swallowed and her heart pounded and she felt her head go half numb. She stared at the name tag and formed the consonants and vowels around in her mouth, working them like a piece of Sears's best fudge.

She had it. She finally had it on the tip of her tongue. It was . . . It was . . .

"Sam," she said with great confidence, "this here is Anus." Silence filled the car. "Anus," she said, as loud as one giving a speech, "this is my husband, Sam."

My daddy laughed so hard he had to pull the car over. Annis laughed too. Later that night Mama, embarrassed, asked my daddy what was so funny. "What was wrong with how I said her name?"

He grabbed my mother close, hugged her, and kissed her cheek. This innocence is what he has always loved most about his nearly triple-virgin bride.

"Sweetheart," he said, gently, "an anus is a rectum."

"A rectum? I'm not sure I understand what you—"

"For heaven's sake, Peg, it's a butt hole. Do you know what a butt hole is?"

The next morning Mama had to be pried from bed and physically deposited at the Sears candy counter. She continued to call the woman "Hon." It was just a whole lot easier that way.

Even many years later, post children and enough bridge parties to have learned a few things, Mama's innocence continued to be a big part of her charm. My sister and I were almost grown when at forty, Mama decided to go back to school—beauty school at a technical college in a small west Georgia town. And this is where she met the wonderful Tee for Terrific as well as the foulmouthed Little Miss Ungrateful.

This is where she got more sex education than she ever received on the Sealy Posturepedic with her own husband. All she had wanted was a diversion, a distraction since one daughter was in college doing God knows what, and the other was a senior in high school.

She needed something to occupy her days and decided on beauty school where she'd sharpen her scissors and work on her mind. She'd been pretty good with hair while putting my father through college, a job she took after the Sears candy stint, standing all day long in a salon that smelled of ammonia and bleach and wishful thinking. She'd take home her tips and a feeling of satisfaction and decided these feelings would be nice to repeat now that she was forty, the scariest age she'd entered thus far.

All was going well that first semester, and she was the matron of the class, the pro they all looked up to, thinking if she knew this much about how to give a perm, then my mama must know and enjoy all kinds of things, including sex and trash talk. Beauty shops and schools are famous for salacious chitchat.

The very first week Mama heard about her classmate Tee's mother who ran her own shop and relayed plenty of wild stories from the customers. Since these stories didn't involve penises and vaginas, Mother could handle them. Throw the words *penis* and *vagina* at her and she purely convulses and will exit a room.

"There was this one time," Tee said as they practiced cutting a dummy's hair, "that my mother was called to go to an elderly client's house to do a haircut. The lady had been such a good customer for thirty years, Mama couldn't tell her no. So she goes, and upon her arrival, the daughter says to Mama, 'My mama's on the bedside commode and you'll have to cut her hair while she has her morning B.M.'" Tee was cracking up as she told the story, her scissors snip-snapping the dummy's head. "My mama said, 'No, that's all right, I don't mind waiting.' But the old woman's daughter jumped up and would hear nothing of it.

"'Oh no,' the daughter says, 'sometimes Mama has to sit on the bedside commode for over an hour to empty up, so go ahead and start cutting; she won't mind.'"

Tee's mother reluctantly proceeded with the cut but said it was an awful experience standing behind someone on a commode, hearing them grunting and straining all the while trying to give them a haircut.

Lord, have mercy, my mama thought. *This place is going to give me more than just an education in hair follicles and color correction.* This would end up becoming a year of not only making new friends and straight As, but also one in which she would learn dozens of lessons, preferences, and perversions.

After she got to know Tee, whom she adored, along came "Little Miss Ungrateful," who showed her true colors soon enough.

Little Miss Ungrateful was the skinny young woman Mama at first really wanted to help. Because that's how Mama is. Tee was funny and didn't need Mama's help, but Little Miss Ungrateful did.

"I could tell the girl had a hard life," Mama said. "Her hair was blond and greasy. She had to be in her twenties. Her eyes were hollow with dark circles. I felt like I needed to get to know her. She was too young to be letting herself go to pot like that."

After a few days of practicing perms and cuts on each other's heads, Mama learned her name was Faye Lynn something or other and that her boyfriend was in prison.

"I visit him on the weekends," Faye Lynn told Mama, a long cigarette hanging out of the side of her thin lips. Faye Lynn didn't smoke like the bridge ladies who would always use their hands and manicured fingers and never speak with a cigarette bobbing in their mouths. A lady must be sitting down while smoking. Everybody ought to know that. In fact, my mother had decided years ago smoking in any form was trashy and had quit altogether, but she didn't mind if others smoked as long as they didn't do it without hands.

Mama said her cheeks about caught fire when Faye Lynn told her about her boyfriend and the conjugal visits. Mama didn't know what conjugal meant but guessed it had something to do with food or dinner on the grounds. She was in for a shocker.

"I'd go visit him," Faye Lynn explained, "and I'd get up on his lap and he'd be so happy. One day he said, 'Faye Lynn, honey bunny, please cut a hole in your pants so I can enjoy your visits all the better.'"

Mama's skin scorched with heat.

"Your cheeks sure are red," Faye Lynn teased.

She wondered what she'd gotten herself into. All she had wanted was to pass the time and not think about her daughters and the possibility of their pairings with young men, wondering if they were drinking or remaining virgins or acting like this little tramp. She simply wanted to learn a trade and find herself once again useful in this world. But she couldn't stop wondering if all of Faye Lynn's pants had a hole cut in the crotches or if this was a joke. She'd never heard such a thing in all her life.

"I thought, *Oh, my goodness, I'm in for a rude awakening at this beauty school*," Mama said. "But I decided that I liked the hussified Little Miss Ungrateful in spite of her crudeness. She was just young and needed a little guidance. I thought maybe I could help."

Every morning Faye Lynn always brought a single piece of fruit for lunch and nothing else. She was skinny as asparagus and had a hungry look to her face.

"Most of us would buy our food in the cafeteria," Mama said. "Faye Lynn always sat with us, and sometimes when we had food left on our plates, she'd eat it. I started getting more than I wanted because I knew she was hungry. It never bothered her to reach over and snatch it up."

One day at the lunch table, the ladies smelling of Clairol and Aqua Net and cigarettes, Faye Lynn started in on a raunchy story. It seemed that since her boyfriend had been locked up, a whole pack of strays had come sniffing around her trailer door, growling like wild cats in heat.

"The guy in the trailer next to mine wants to have sex with me," she announced, her voice registering nothing more than a ho-hum while my mother tried to swallow her sandwich and found it stuck against her dry throat. "He says since my fellow's in the slammer, he can keep me satisfied with his nine-incher."

Faye Lynn sat straight up in the chair, a change of pace from her usual slumping. "I told him I didn't need his services, that I have a dildo."

Every other beauty school student roared with laughter. Mama did not.

"A what?" she asked. The others hee-hawed even harder.

"A dildo," Faye Lynn said. "It's the same thing as a fake dick."

Mama was mortified and jumped up to run hide her shame in the bathroom. A drunk coming off two weeks of Mad Dog couldn't have been any redder. After lunch, they all returned to the rubber heads they were working on, and for a long time, not much was said.

Then Faye Lynn walked over to Mama and apologized.

"I didn't mean to say that in front of a . . . um . . . lady. I wish I was more like you, is all." Mama, who would forgive about any sin on earth, hugged the young woman.

Two months later she came to school wearing a maternity uniform. Everyone had noticed she'd been putting on weight, but hadn't said anything until now.

"We thought it was the lunch food we were giving her," Mama said, "but it must have been the hole in her pants. She told us the boyfriend in prison was the daddy."

Sometimes Mama wondered if Faye Lynn really had circles of fabric removed from the crotches of all her jeans and slacks. *No. Probably not.* She'd more than likely been yakking and running her mouth the way some of them liked to do in beauty school. No subject was off-limits for these ladies.

One day Mama got to school early and began cleaning her combs and brushes, getting everything ready for class to start. At the station next to hers was a genuine human heifer queen, a thunderously large rectangular woman who was stout as a sequoia and looked a great deal like a male wrestler.

"She was sitting there that morning kind of quiet," Mama said. "I was getting my station ready and all of a sudden she looked over at me and said, 'Did you know husbands play with themselves?' Well, what could I say, Susan? She made that little motion with her hand and I nearly got sick. Then she up and says, 'I caught mine cupping his genny-tales last night.'"

My mother had no answer for that one. She wasn't sure what genny-tales were, but she sprang from her seat as if a curling rod had burned her and ran toward the bathroom where she had to squeeze her head with both hands to try and stop the ugly thoughts.

"I was thinking—and this sounds awful—but if I was married to her, and I know this isn't the Christian thing to say, but really, if I was married to that big old cinder block of a woman, I'd be doing the same thing he was doing. Who can blame the guy?"

Mama and the rectangular woman didn't talk much after that, and upon graduation, instead of becoming a hairdresser in a salon, the woman went on to barber college.

In the meantime, Faye Lynn had left school, big and pregnant with the son of an inmate who was conceived, according to Faye Lynn, via the hole in her jeans. Beauty school had ended before the baby was born, and Mama earned all As the entire year, possibly highest in the class. She made Faye Lynn promise to stay in touch and let her know when the baby came.

One day she called and told Mama the baby had arrived and gave her directions to the trailer. Mama immediately drove to the nicest department store in town and carefully selected the gifts, choosing the most expensive wrapping. She found the trailer park, unloaded her presents, and stepped onto Faye Lynn's front porch.

"I knocked on the door and she yelled to come on in. She was sitting on this pitiful old sofa smoking and feeding the baby. The baby was adorable."

Faye Lynn opened her baby's gift first. His was a sailor suit and hers a beautiful nightgown, the kind a princess or virgin might wear. She looked at the gown, held it up, and said, "Good Lord. It has long sleeves and this place has no air-conditioning."

Enough, my mother said to herself. *Enough*.

"I told her good-bye, and as she got off the sofa to see me out, I noticed something odd. You aren't going to believe this, but there it was. A hole. Right in the crotch of her pants. You couldn't help but see it. She'd uncrossed her legs pretty wide to get up and there was that hole big enough for anything to get in and move around. I decided then and there, I'd had enough of her."

And while my mother chose to remain a housewife and not enter the field of beauty, she has kept in touch with Tee all these years later. Every now and then Tee will share a story of life in the beauty shop and all Mama's been missing.

"The other morning," Tee said, "one of my older ladies was telling me about going to Panama City with her daughter and was saying they had the best time staying in a condom."

Tee started chuckling. "I said, facetiously, 'I'll bet that was a tight squeeze,' and the old lady said, 'Oh no. We had two bedrooms.'"

It made my mama feel good that other people, sane and normal human beings, had as much trouble pronouncing words as she did. The condom comment, she figured, was certainly on the same level with calling a woman an Anus.

Die Rear

Tidy Stu, my precious soon-to-be ex-husband, took cleanliness to new heights one Saturday morning.

He strode into the house shortly before noon and muttered his giant announcement. He was red-faced, which is unusual because he's typically pale from breathing so much Clorox and Comet, his drugs of choice.

He approached with caution.

"I ruined the cars," he said, with the same enthusiasm as if he were telling me he'd turned in the tax forms.

"You did what?"

"They're ruined. I wrecked them both."

"But how? You've been outside scrubbing oil stains from the asphalt, right?"

Stu, God love him, had been loading his van with tons of music equipment when he decided he'd better shoo the dog out of the way. With Putt-Putt long gone and adopted into another family, he'd bought a black Pomeranian, which for a moment made me question his testosterone levels. He had parked at the top of our driveway, and my car was at the bottom, directly in front of the glass doors to the basement.

"What happened?" I asked.

"It was dumb, really. God, I can't believe it." He explained that Flamer, the name I call his new Pomeranian, was having die rear in the passenger seat. "He was in the squat position and it was pouring out of him. I had to do something."

Mrrrrrrrpppphhhh! It would have been much simpler had the dog just chewed up a chair leg or peed on the carpet like Putt-Putt did. If Tidy had only gotten to know Putt-Putt, had put the incident behind him when Putt tore into him as he lay on the couch clutching the remote, his "software" partially displayed, he could have avoided this entire scene. But you see, he had to be the man of the house. He had to be the one to choose the dog. My choice, the white trash dog Putt-Putt, wasn't good enough.

So he gets Flamer and wrecks the cars.

It seems my beloved husband yanked the pooch up mid-poop and jumped from what he thought was a parked vehicle. He had no idea he had failed to put the van in Park as he ever-so-gently *hurled* Flamer onto the grass. Meanwhile, his gray Ford Aerostar took off like a stampeding elephant.

Down the driveway it gathered speed, weighted with all those speakers and amps, until it slammed into my car, leaving a multithousand-dollar trail of damage. My first thought was, *Thank God the kids are inside playing with knives and matches and aren't in the driveway.* My second thought was, *We are going to be bus people. The bus stop is three uphill miles away.*

I surveyed the damage to my Rodeo. The door wouldn't close and the mirror hung by two wires and lapped against the dented side like a giant buffalo tongue.

What's a girl to do when her husband wrecks her car with his own? In the family's driveway, for heaven's sake?

His dysentery-soaked Ford minivan had that look and odor that said, "You're totaled, hon." With nearly fifteen years and more than a hundred and fifty thousand miles on it, the insurance adjusters were most certain to be about as forgiving as a fundamentalist is of divorce and public nudity.

The thing a decent girl does when her husband crumples

both cars due to a gay Pom with die rear, is to hop in what's left of her own vehicle and spend the day test-driving adorable new cars.

I drove twenty-five miles an hour down the interstate toward the dealership, window open, the scent of Bradford pear and dogwood blossoms on my face, the mirror cupped in my hand so it wouldn't lop off and tumble into the path of cars. This proved a good position for putting on a coat of frosted pink lipstick, sure to knock $1,000 off the price of whatever sat unmoving on their lots. I also tightened the straps on my steel-belted radial push-up bra and hoped the ground-sweepers would rise enough for some pretend perk and major discounts.

First stop was the Subaru dealership. I decided to try cars I'd been admiring, and assumed affordable, including a Forester and an Outback. The Forester, it turns out, may be cute as pie, but is the Chihuahua of SUVs. Great on gas and precious to boot; however, not the best choice if one has children who talk loud and throw objects from the backseat. Perfect, though, for the childless and elderly who want to look sporty. Then I tried the Outback, a wonderful wagon, but I couldn't stop picturing Crocodile Dundee or that oddball who wrestles reptiles and seems to get erections doing so.

The salesman, who was nice enough not to get angry when he saw my Burger King bag upon exiting his vehicles, whipped out scrap paper, a pen, and a calculator. He punched and scribbled, scratched the numbers, and nodded to himself, as if he were coming up with the deal of a lifetime. He didn't once look at my chest, but called me "ma'am" so many times I realized I was going to get the price quote only idiots and big-underwear girls who have let themselves go to pot have to pay.

What he offered, payment-wise, shocked me so much I couldn't swallow. I sat there and hacked like Flamer after he swallowed a neighbor's Kotex. "You want some water, ma'am?" a bald-headed one asked.

"How old are you?" I snapped. "I am just curious since you've sat here and ma'am'd me to death."

"Forty-three."

"Well, how old do you suppose me to be?"

He tapped his pen and then thumped his front teeth with it. "I never try to guess a woman's age."

"Well, do me a favor, Mr. Clean. Don't call me ma'am until you've sprouted at least four hairs on that crown, got it?"

Poor man. He kept punching his calculator real hard, probably pretending it was my PMS-bloated face. I held out some leftover fries as a peace offering. He was not happy. "You wanna car or are you just here to drive around and eat garbage in our new vehicles, *Ma'am?*"

"I was hungry. I didn't see a sign that said, 'no fast food in car please.' Listen, I'm sorry. We have gotten off on the wrong foot. I love car salesmen and once thought about a career in this field or a husband along those lines, and I especially love Subarus. I had one when I was twenty-five and it was great until I hit the power pole and knocked out an entire subdivision's electricity. So please, tell me, how much? What's your best price? 'Cause if you don't have one my daddy can get one on the Motor Mile."

"Oh, the Motor Mile, huh? Daddy gonna work the starving salesmen on the old Motor Mile?" He looked at his partner. "I say she oughta just go on down there with Daddy to the Motor Mile. What about you, Term?"

"Term?"

"Term for short. We call him the Terminator. He creams people who prance in here and try to take us. Pick us like crabs. We gotta eat too, you know. People don't treat car salesmen as good as they should. We ain't criminals. We're here to provide a service." He took out a cigarette and lit it, even though it was supposed to be a nonsmoking environment.

I pulled my trump card. "I got a car I could trade. Nice, beautiful Rodeo. Drives great. Has a few minor cosmetic issues." I thought of the Putt-Putt ad from the two-fannied lady at the Taco Bell. "Beautiful markings. One of a kind. Needs a good home." The two men exchanged that look. Crazy woman on the lot. They knew it. I knew it. Only hours earlier my husband's gay dog had sprayed his seat with die rear and thus sent two cars to their graves. My period was due in three days and I was between antidepressants, thinking I might possibly live as a normal person with no serotonin reuptake inhibitors mellowing my world and giving a false sense of joy and zero sex drive. Who was I fooling? One more week without my prescription and jail time was likely.

I clawed at my swollen belly, wishing to God I could sell my uterus on eBay for $20,000 so I could afford a nice Forester. Uterus or Forester? Hmmm. "Y'all want to see my adorable car?"

"Let's take a look," the salesman said and winked at the Term.

Rule number one: unless you're rolling in dough, skip the whole trade-in scene. The two salesmen checked out my car as if it were a Mee-Maw at the bottom of the waiting list for a bed in Croaker's Rest Home. The main salesman picked up the mirror, rubbed the frosted pink lipstick off, knuckled the dents, and said things like, "Test, test, testing the biggest piece of shit on our fine lot," as he kicked the tread off my $300 tires.

"She's got some wear and tear on her," he said, stubbing out his cig near my fine wheel. "She ain't what she once was, for sure."

"She ain't a she," I said. "It's a boy car."

He put his hands on his hips and stared at me dead-on. "It's a what?"

"It's a boy."

"How's that?"

"Anybody can tell a girl car from a boy car, besides the fact trucks are always boys and anything over thirty thousand dollars is always female." I was messing with him now. Ohhh, it felt good. Mama would be so ashamed. Mama, sweet Mama, my mean old swelling uterus made me do it. It's all my uterus's fault. I'm sending it away, that bitch in a bag. Scarred and stretched, useless organ.

I heard her voice, which was destined to chime in my head and ring the bells of guilt until I died. "If you lose your female organs you'll grow a beard and talk real deep. You just remember what happened to your great-aunt Goodie Gert. Never forget when she lost her organs, when she up and decided having a uterus was a curse . . . Don't you forget that less than two years after they hauled it out, she grew a full beard and an Adam's apple."

Mama tells us how Aunt Goodie Gert shaved for the rest of her life until she went into the nursing home when she gave up and let the hairs have at it. "We went twice a week to trim her beard, and I'm telling you, she had a prettier beard than any man's I'd ever seen. Only problem was she had to have a single room because no one would let their kin share a space with her. If that's what you want, then have them cart your uterus off to the incinerator."

"I don't think that would be—"

"Let it be a lesson to you. If it's not broken, don't ask to have it removed. The week before she died a doctor told me she was growing quite a bumper crop of teeny testicles."

I decided to keep my uterus and see if I could afford to have both the organ and a new car. "Listen, guys, um, gentlemen. I just want a car. I'm tired and my husband has done the unthinkable." They thought I was talking about an affair. "Please, let's see if we can come to an agreement that works for all of us."

"Before we do that, I wanna know what you mean there's boy cars and girl cars. Term wants to know more about that theory if you don't mind."

Oh, what would it hurt to humor them? I'd been mean on account of my uterus so I owed it to them to impart laughter. "Boy cars are always dropping their mufflers all over the road like dirty underpants. Girl cars never shed their parts on the highways. Then again, the El Camino is the only car that's neither male nor female. A hermaphrodite on wheels, so to speak, and uglier than a Pinto."

They stood smoking, eyebrows twitching. "Tell me again why this here Rodeo is a boy car?"

I walked closer to them and whispered, as if it were a secret, "It's lost two mufflers and its tailpipe sticks out six inches. Could have been worse. Could have only had a three-inch tailpipe like some of the less endowed male cars you see here and there."

That got 'em.

My salesman and the Terminator began doodling and refiguring, coming up with a payment close to my price range but one I still wasn't ready to take on.

"I love the cars, fellows," I said. "But I'm also in the market for something I'll just for now call an 'upgrade.' I can't at this moment decide which takes precedence. I'll get back to you. It's been a pleasure."

I thanked them for their time and drove home holding my side mirror so it wouldn't bounce across the highway. Some women, I figured, were meant to drive Gremlins.

Not Tonight, Hon: Wait 'Til I Get My New Boobs

Married monkey business can be about as exciting as watching the same movie five thousand times. Most couples lose that tingly feeling after the birth of kids and ever-increasing demands for our attention. We still love our mates but we've run out of steam.

I've been married for what many a night has seemed like a hundred years and so have most of my friends. We occasionally talk when we shouldn't, giving our state-of-the-union address in terms of how infrequently we've gone to the mat, or in this case, the mat-tress.

Psychologists and sex therapists worldwide are making a fortune off the waning libidos of one or the other partner in a relationship. Even the ads popping up on our computers shout for us to enlarge or recharge. For men it's a pill to pump them up to the point of combustion and for women it's Texas Pete of the panties. I'm sorry, but no way I'm putting some sort of Ben Gay cream in my drawers.

Most of my friends who haven't gone to complete pot have the same problem, and that's fighting off our husbands so we can get at least one decent night's sleep or see an episode of *Sex and the City*.

I've heard excuses ranging from "Sweetie, I'd rather postpone the bliss tonight since I have a zit in my ear and my balance isn't good," To this, "You are the cutest thing in the subdivision, hon, but I've been watching you bite your long yellow toenails for so long I'm ready to cut them off."

My all-time favorite excuse was cooked up by a clever member of our "Read It or Not, Here We Come Book Club— eight to ten of us who love to read, eat, drink, and laugh until we fall off couches.

When she's not in the mood, she looks over at her deprived husband and purrs coquettishly, "I'm like an oyster, sweetheart. You can only harvest me during the months that end in R." He's a happy man in fall and early winter, but the rest of the year . . . poor baby.

Another member of the book club says sex is based on a point system. She believes a woman can earn points *and* get out of sex by being smart and knowing when to make her move.

"When he's sick as a dog is when you pursue him," this vivacious blonde said. "That way he'll say no and you'll have made the effort for extra points. You get the credit without having to put out."

Then there's this other woman in the club who says we're mean and that she gives it to her husband whenever his eyebrows so much as twitch or raise a notch.

"Well, no wonder the man served as PTA president for four years and Scout leader for three and has run for five public offices," I said. "He's one happy husband."

Most of us wives love our mates, but frankly are in the Humpty-Dumpty mood far less than they. It's human and animal nature. Sorry. It just is. Ever see a lioness run? See the does dash? Hear the girl birds screech? See a female human pretend to be asleep or having her second period in as many weeks?

But just how often are we ladies saying those dreaded words "Not tonight, hon, I'm feeling a little tired," and thinking that which we dare not vocalize? *And probably not tomorrow night either, sugarplum.*

We married women who work and are raising children and trying to keep careers afloat have more energy to peel a sack of potatoes than hop in the sack every time our beloveds get the itch.

It's just that we are too tired and sleep-deprived to do the mattress mambo twice a night like some of them prefer. We know all about their poor old achy prostates and that lie some tell about how if not serviced regularly they might end up dragging a scrotum big as a grain sack.

"Did you know," my husband said one night, "they discovered a 154-pound pair of balls that are two feet in diameter? I take it his wife wasn't paying him too much attention, huh?"

"Are you talking about elephantiasis?"

"No, I'm talking about deprivation."

My husband relishes telling me about the 154-pound testicles on a regular basis. As soon as his chicken or pasta has digested and he's all laid up on the couch like some sort of middle-aged male centerfold, he starts in about his prostate and his aching neglected private region. It's hard to heat up when you see your mate of fifteen years sprawled out in dingy Hanes briefs, leg hairs illuminated in the lamplight. It's tough to feel that warm tingle while watching him grin wide, his hand reaching forth to grab what we have not.

My husband—to his credit—is the king of quality once the act begins, but he's clueless about why he doesn't get it more often. I guess he doesn't understand it's all in the presentation, which has changed from the good old days of "You sure look beautiful tonight" to the tales of super-sized balls and what I consider mildly vulgar come-on lines from watching Howard Stern when I'm not around. The art of asking for love has gone down the drain and into the septic tank.

I should have known what was coming. It's not like I wasn't forewarned. During our hot-and-heavy premarital days he turned to me one evening and said, "My friend wants to know if you'd like to meet his two little buddies." He pointed to his male area and smiled.

"Excuse me?" We love the captain of the boat, fellows, but most of us would rather not hear about his oarsmen. Leave the testicle festival for male bonding. We're delighted you've got all your parts, but we don't want to hear about them, OK?

It is hard enough going to the petting zoos and seeing them swinging off the asses of lions and llamas. It's even tougher when your four-year-old daughter asks, "What are those bubbly things, Mama?" and you have to lie and say, "I reckon he has the mumps, sugar." Or in the case of my son, "Sweetie, those are his storage tanks."

But to have your husband showcasing them like three-thousand-carat solitaires? I don't get the bonding going on with men and their balls and never have and never will.

Plenty of nights after a long day at work I'm standing over the glowing stove trying to get dinner ready and the kids are fighting and the laundry is piled up and my mate ambles over, pinches my long-fallen fanny, and whispers oh so romantically . . . "Get ready! I'll be hitting it tonight," thinking he's Brad Pitt in his sweatpants and muscle shirt.

"Go to the doctor!" I shout when his hand goes straight to his dimmyjinger.

"I don't need a doctor. I need a blow job."

Of course you do. All of you do. Every man I know thinks that would cure the world's problems and bring peace among all nations. And most women I know would say the same for hooking a man up to a Prozac IV.

"You're lucky you get one on a regular basis," I say. "Grace Ann from the book club only gives Bob one at Christmas. She says it's a sacred special thing."

"Well, my sacred special thing is going to rot off if you keep ignoring it."

Boy. Show me a woman that conversation won't throw into a hot, arching, pelvic-thrusting machine.

Not exactly sultry words to hear after we've worked our

butts off all day long and dealt with the evil public and the seething politics of office life, putting in a full day of corporate hell after walking the floors with the vomit-spewing baby till 5:00 a.m.

"If you want love," I tell him, "it starts in the kitchen." What I mean is that it would be nice if he'd pick up a pot or pan, throw a chicken in the oven, some rice on the stove. But he has a completely different vision in his head.

That's when he'll whisper something that would shock the shoe polish off my Baptist-bred mama. They aren't exactly words that warm my blood either.

"I feel like hitting the old booger-roo tonight," he might say as I shiver with the chill of frigidity and slippery chicken cutlets in my hands. He's called my arena the booger ever since the two-fannied woman sold us Putt-Putt.

After supper it's time to clean up, check homework, bathe children, feed the dog, water the hamster, crab, or dog de jour, read bedtime stories, pack lunches, and lay out the clothes for the next day of repeat performances.

By the time I'm done I sure don't want to descend the stairs and see my husband lying on the couch with his friend and those buddies bared for me and our neighbors to see due to his aversion to the words *window treatments*.

What I'd really like, and what the selfish woman in most of us would *really* like, is to sink like a dead whale into a tub of scalding water sprinkled with lavender oil. After an hour's soak we would then slip into a pair of pajamas so big and ugly even our mee-maws wouldn't be caught dead in them.

It takes a special saucy woman to regroup, put on a sheer teddy, and entertain her beloved hornster with the devil's dance at this stage of the day. Give the gal a medal. Especially if her man's words of romance involve "booger" and "buddies" or any such vulgarities.

A friend of mine who never gets any always says to me, "At least he finds you attractive. At least he's chasing you in some form or fashion. Bentley and I haven't had relations in two years."

What can I say? That Bentley is more interested in having relations with *my* husband? That the wife is the *last* to know when the unhorny husband's sex drive shifts into reverse and he's cruising Fanny Lane?

I feel sorry for those women and should be grateful my beloved is taking an interest. I should do as my mother says and give him his twelve minutes so he'll be in a much better mood.

"Well, Mama Know-it-all," I wanted to say, "my husband doesn't take twelve minutes. An hour can pass and he's still got to kick it into second and third before he hits the finish line.

I guess we've got to give these *real* men credit. I mean they don't seem to need incentives like sleep or a flat stomach to fire them into conjugal orbit. Just walk by them. If they detect a heartbeat, that's encouragement enough. They are as ready as the day we met them, never mind it's been 2.5 children, twenty-four additional pounds, boobs like tube socks, and fifteen years since our wedding night. That should give them a brownie point or two, right?

I should let that suffice instead of getting cold as plucked chicken skin when he talks about his balls swelling up and hurting or his prostate doing whatever it is men's prostates do. Maybe it's sort of like a miniature version of an evil uterus.

One night I tried to explain to him that being married as long as we have takes some creative language and variety. That wouldn't it be fun if he could finish in twelve minutes instead of two and a half hours?

"How about a quickie?" I asked, and he stared as if I were hurling a dagger at his region. I had to cough up yet more excuses. "My breasts sag like Putt-Putt's and you call my love arena the 'booger.' In addition, you wear ugly underwear and present yourself like the Grand Slam at Denny's. Understand?"

He took his hands off his region for a moment and transferred them to the remote control, tuning me out with a whir of sound and blur of color as the channels melted into one and another night passed without sex.

As I climbed the stairs, he offered up a blistering comment. "I got more sex than this in high school."

"Don't worry," I told him in my nicest voice. "Once I get my new boobs I'm sure things will change. Your captain will raise a flag and his oarsmen will have cause for celebration."

"I'm not betting on it."

Truthfully, neither am I. Sometimes new boobs lead to self-esteem, which leads to a saucier marriage. Other times, they just lead to bigger bras.

A few days later one of my friends, Tired in Tennessee, told me she and her husband of a hundred years are in therapy due to the infrequency of their Serta moments. They'd seen each other floss just one too many times. The answer, they thought, was a respectable counselor who suggested they watch an "instructional" video together.

"You know," I said to my Tired in Tennessee friend, "when Tidy Stu sees an Oxiclean commercial he can get pretty fired up."

"Did you hear me?" Tennessee asked, shrilling her words. "This therapist suggested we watch a tape of couples coupling, for God's sake."

"I've never heard the likes of such. Well, it ought to be fun! Just pop lots of popcorn and fast-forward the boring parts."

I went on to tell her about the book that arrived on my desk called *The Art of Exotic Dancing for Everyday Women.* The authors claim this is the manual for the *regular* women of the world: mothers, daughters, sisters, friends, preachers' wives, the women with careers and responsibilities—all out there shopping, cooking dinner, chauffeuring the kids, managing households.

"They show these women posing and slinking about the

house using furnishings for their come-hither props," I said. "I never knew a fern stand could be so enticing."

My friend cleared her throat. "I guess I could climb our four-poster."

"That's a good start, but you haven't lived until you've tried the squatting hip roll as he's watching and wondering what hit him. You haven't felt your true inner power until you've slid down the banister in a garter or writhed on the linoleum in cellophane."

"You're sick," she said.

"I'm just telling you what the book says about the benefits of the home dance."

"Have you tried this yourself?"

I paused and held back my laughter. "As a matter of fact, yes. After Tidy told someone I come home from work and ugly up, I stood proudly on top of the toy box and shimmied for a good five minutes in my A-list underwear."

"Did he like it?"

"He asked if I was having a seizure."

"Then what was your point?"

"Point is simple. You do what it takes, darling. That's all any of us can do. And tell him you're game as long as the month ends in R."

The Ultra GrindZapper Treatment

My mother has always liked and respected dentists. That is, until she met one particular TMJ specialist who had other things on his mind besides jaw trouble.

TMJ, for those who have no idea, is a painful condition of the mandibles that in my mother's case caused a clicking and popping noise that drove her nuts and in search of relief.

"It had been clicking for two months," she said, "and I was afraid it would lock up before I could get to the doctor's office. I would be one of those people who can't ever shut their mouths, drooling all the time and looking lost or alarmed."

As soon as my mother arrived the receptionist exclaimed with enthusiasm, "You must be Peggy."

"Yes," my mother said, returning the pleasantry and glancing about at an office in total disarray.

"You just have to be Peggy because we only book one patient at a time. That's our policy. Efficiency with a capital E. No room for greed and overbooking here."

Mama smiled and nodded because people tend to tell her too much and go on and on about stuff. It's the gene a lot of our family has: the tell-me-anything-on-your-mind gene. Who cares if it's gynecological or about the current condition of your colon? Come on and tell us. We've got the gene.

"Have a seat," the receptionist said. "We got new chairs on order, but these are clean enough to eat from because we spray them down good after every visitor leaves. Not all the people who come see a specialist are clean, as you may well imagine. Some," and she whispered this, "are on Medicaid, but we take only three of *those cases* a month."

Mama didn't like that comment because she knew of children in her community who were too poor to see a dentist and suffered such pain they cried themselves to sleep at night. Not one to start arguments, she let the Medicaid comment slide and wiped the imaginary dirt from her pants as she sat on the edge of what appeared to be a standard office chair with a taped-up leg.

"The doc and I have been busy taking care of our cars today, so excuse the mess and excuse me while I eat my lunch," the woman said. She had a short blond bob with dozens of threadlike platinum highlights. Rich lady hair. She was probably the doctor's wife or special sidekick. "I take it you've already brushed and flossed, because we hate it when people come in and have particles in their teeth. If you've not done this, go ahead to that bathroom on your right, the one behind our tropical fish tank, and use the floss on the table. Scope's right next to it." She beamed at Mama, the mayonnaise shining on her chin and her teeth bleached beyond reality.

"I've taken care of that at home," Mama said when in popped a stocky man panting and complaining. He wore ill-fitting pants that bunched up his butt crack and he mumbled something about not having had lunch either and retreated to a back room.

The receptionist, her mouth full and the pungent smell of onions floating throughout the office, handed over a four-page questionnaire asking what my proper mother believed to be a lot of weird and irrelevant questions. "Fill these out, please. And don't worry. You've got total privacy. Like I said, one patient at a time. No greed here."

At first the questions were tame. But then they got bold—much bolder than a woman with a shred of decency would dare reveal.

"How much coffee a day?"

"How much alcohol?"

"How much milk?"

"Do you have missing teeth?"

"Do you have oral sex?"

Oh, Lord, have mercy. Do I have what? My poor sweet mother wanted to run out the door.

"I stopped dead on that one!" she said, laughing so hard she slumped over in her chair. Mama will do that. When she gets to laughing she either slithers out of her chair and onto the floor or she falls over a coffee table, draping herself across the furniture and pounding it with her fists to contain the overflowing mirth.

Oral sex, indeed! The get-me-off-the-hook maneuver. "Why, I've been going to my gynecologist for thirty years and never has that been asked," she told me. "I'm thinking this place is not very professional. So I go to the next question."

"Do you have yeast infections? Genital warts? Pubic lice . . ."

Oh no. This is too much for me," mother said to herself and contemplated her escape. "I thought I was there for my clicking jaw, not my business 'down there.'"

She looked up from the clipboard and saw a telephone. She considered calling my father and telling him she wanted to come home, but as soon as the thought hit her, the receptionist approached and asked how everything was going. "Best hurry along. Like I said, we book one at a time, but our next client is due in ten. You've taken a long time on that questionnaire. Must be some mighty thorough answers."

Mom had a thought. She would pretend to be indigent and without insurance and maybe, just maybe, they'd send her packing. It was obvious this woman didn't like the poor by her earlier comments, and there's no role Mama loves playing more than poverty-stricken at any chance she gets. I used to hate it when November would roll around and she'd always say, "Christmas won't be as big this year. We're flat broke." We were never flat broke but these were lingering fears from her own childhood, so I grew up hearing about being "flat broke" quite often.

"I haven't worked in years," Mama said to the woman, faking a Percocet-induced monotone. She looked down at her attire, happy to have worn what she calls her pitiful clothes due to irregular fading and elastic failings. "And I don't know my Social Security number, nor do I have dental coverage or similar such benefits. Times are hard," she added for effect, not mentioning she'd be heading for the South of France in March and was hoping to be click-free by departure date. "We're flat broke, you see."

The woman eating paid my mother's economic ramblings no mind. "You haven't finished filling out the information, have you?" she asked, mouth full of food reminding Mama of one of those glass washing machines at the Laundromat where you can see everything swirling around.

"No."

"Well then, we will just finish our lunch while you answer *all* the questions. I'm waiting on a call anyway from the mechanic about our cars."

Poor, poor Mother. She just wanted her jaw to quit clicking. She didn't need to hear all this other stuff about mufflers and transmissions or watch these oddballs cramming hoagies down their throats.

She glanced at the molar-shaped clock behind the receptionist. It was 2:00 p.m. She'd been there almost an hour and decided to put down the questions she had no intention of answering. She stood and let her eyes take in the room without a single stick of decent furniture or a magazine within a year of its publication date. She began cleaning up and organizing the outdated periodicals when her mind stopped in its tracks. It spun in directions it shouldn't have gone, specifically to the question related to what Monica Lewinsky made famous on a Democrat my mother abhorred.

"Oh no," she said out loud without realizing it. She grew horrified and wanted to dig a hole and fall in. She has always been quite famous for her sudden public outbursts and doom-begging. "Oh, I wish this room would split wide open and swallow me whole."

Surely they don't think that has something to do with my clicking jaw!

She sat down and scribbled on the questionnaire in the space provided where it asked, *Do you have oral sex?*

TEACHING MY GRANDSON HOW TO BLOW A BUBBLE WAS WHAT CAUSED THE CLICK, she wrote in all capital letters. I FEEL SURE OF THIS. Maybe that would satisfy their prurient prying and they'd lighten up on that other business. She waited another few minutes, her heart racing and her mind brewing more fears.

Finally the receptionist called her name and the doctor entered the waiting room.

"Whew. We just *had* to eat," he said as Mama followed him down the hallway. "I'll bet you can smell my roast beef."

Mama took a seat in the chair and noticed it was as low to the ground as it could possibly go without being buried. The doctor sat on a stool near her head. She was eyeball level with his crotch, which sported bits of lettuce and grease splatters. The door was open and a bicuspid on the wall seemed to be guarding them.

The doctor peered down at my mother.

"So how long has your jaw been clicking?" he asked.

"Well, let's see . . . I guess about—"

He didn't wait for her to finish. "You sure do slump," he said out of the blue.

"Do what?"

"I said, 'You sure do slump.' You need to sit tall. Posture is everything."

My mama wondered how she could possibly be slumping while lying on a dental recliner that was all but underground.

"Show me how you sleep," the man ordered.

"Show you what?"

"Bear with me, this is important. I need to see how you sleep, position-wise."

Mama demonstrated how she puts an arm under the left side of her face and curls into a fetal position.

The doctor slapped his meaty thighs. "Well, I'll bet your muscles say, 'Thank you, dear Jesus' when you get out of bed each morning. They have to be happy to get out of that position."

For a couple of minutes while he scanned Mother's mouth and neck area, all was quiet. "Ma'am," he said, startling her, "we don't do that!"

"What? We don't do what?" Mama's knees were shaking.

The doctor jumped up from his seat and shouted, "Would you look at that! You're jutting your chin. Ma'am, we never ever jut our chins. And what's that noise? Are you gritting those teeth? We never ever grit our teeth. That's a condition called bruxism and you're in luck, dear lady. We have recently purchased a line of products called the GrindZappers that fit around your skull much like a headband. When you sleep, if you start gnashing those teeth the headgear shoots out a current and you'll awaken enough to stop immediately."

Get thee out of here, sweet Jesus, Mama thought, trapped under this freak's bright lights and hovering face.

"We bought the Ultra GrindZappers that you can also set for verbal warnings instead of the electrical. When you grind, a firm but gentle voice will awaken you and let you know what you're doing is inappropriate. They're much more effective than the bite guards of yesteryear. This one's even got an alarm clock built right into the head unit so you can eliminate the one on your nightstand. Pretty clever, eh?"

Mama said she didn't know how to respond because she was busy visualizing a head contraption that would either shock or fuss at her during the middle of the night. She was certain the device would give her brain tumors or aneurisms.

"So, what have we here?" the doctor said, picking up the questionnaire my mother refused to finish filling out because of what she considered vulgar meddling. He tapped it against the armrest.

"Ma'am," he said, "you didn't answer how many glasses of milk you drink a day."

"I didn't answer a lot of those questions, but I have a few for you."

Abruptly, the man squawked at her again. "Quit jutting your chin out. I said it once and I'll say it again. Have you ever noticed little old ladies walking around with their faces sticking way out from their neck and their neck so stiff they can't look back?"

"Yes, I guess." Mama tried to picture an assortment of people hunching toward her, heads protruding a good foot or so from their bodies.

"Well, expect to get that. Expect that to be you in ten years."

I've got plans for this man. He can expect a couple of these if he doesn't hush his mouth. Mama imagined herself throwing a punch or two at the doctor's jaw.

After more of his "exam" and insults, he ordered her to open wide and began banging on her teeth with a tiny hammer. This was followed by more of his oral insights.

"Severe overbite," he shouted. "Boy, can you clamp down! In any other mouth this would be a nightmare. Suits your mouth just fine though. I'll bet you can tear up an ear of corn, can't you? I'll bet that cob looks like it's been through a paper shredder when you get done with it."

My mother when angry can't help jutting her chin and grinding those teeth. Her mouth must have been going to town like a set of false choppers wound up and clacking to beat the band. This was too much for the dentist.

"What's that?" he shouted. "Ma'am, what's that offending

noise? Are you gritting your teeth again? The only solution, I'm afraid, is the GrindZapper or I could pull every tooth from your pretty little head. Your choice."

Mama was so startled she bolted from the chair, bib and chain still attached around her neck. She told him she was jobless and without insurance or intention of buying a $395 zapper with built-in alarm clock or having her teeth pulled. "We're flat broke," she said. "I'll learn to make peace with my click, thank you all the same."

She did her best to get away, but he followed her down the corridor, lumbering unevenly as if one leg were shorter. He had grabbed a bag of chips from a counter and stuffed a few in his mouth as he continued making suggestions.

"You will sleep forty days and forty nights without that arm under your head," he ordered as Mother rushed to leave. "You will drink lots of water and sit tall and not jut that chin."

Mama tore a check for $95 from her billfold and was almost out the door when the dentist had to get one more word in.

"By the way, ma'am. Human beings have two bites. Dentists have names for them. The *rat* bite and the *cow* bite. You have the *rat* bite."

My mother slammed the door to the establishment and had a single thought as she jutted, gritted, and slouched in the afternoon sun, her head leading her body to the car.

"I'd rather live with a clicking jaw than ever step foot in that man's office again. At least I'll be clicking in the South of France."

Miss Glorious Priss Pot

There's nothing quite as horrible and haunting as running into the past when you look as if you've been dug up from the cemetery three years after burial.

There we were, in Myrtle Beach, South Carolina, the proletariat playground, the Redneck Riviera, when I stumbled smack into my history, looking as if the years had been firing in my direction with AK-47s.

Some days you can look like a four-pack-a-day smoker when you've never touched a cig in your life and are engaged in a skin-care program that costs more than a new TV. It was one of those days.

And there she was, Miss Glorious Priss Pot, the third most beautiful girl in my sorority at the University of Georgia—Miss It from Tiny Town, Georgia, which also produced Deborah Norville if that's any indication of the beauties.

Miss Prissified was looking as if the years had forgotten to march her way, just skipped Her Preciousness altogether. I wanted the ugly fairy to swoop down and give her some eye bags or a nice flap or two hanging off the sides of her little bared tummy with the pierced belly button. At our age, for goodness' sake!

Why don't you just carry a sign that screams TUMMY TUCK around your neck, you uppity ho? I wanted to shout but could not because I was having a massive attack of the uglies and looked like a hungover chain smoker with a bad tan and $10 highlights.

I recognized her right away, the honey-skinned sultress who was that ageless mix of luck and a combination of genes and mystique that set her apart from the rest of the southern sorority types in pink and green dresses and espadrilles.

Miss Priss Pot with the exotic skin tone and lyrical accent wore hand-beaded shirts made of silks and rich colors and wove jewels and tiny braids in a mane of the most perfect black hair I'd ever seen, even counting those computer-enhanced women shaking all over the Pantene commercials.

Other than the fact she dry-humped a Kappa Alpha during a fraternity beach trip in broad daylight along the gulf shores of Florida, she was a classy girl with haughty airs. And her hump-a-thon didn't even begin to touch my indiscretion in terms of shocking behavior—the night my sophomore year when I won $20 as runner-up in the Erotic Bull Riding Contest.

And here she was all glorious in the supermarket.

Which was precisely why I should have heeded my own advice—either dress in full "every day could be a reunion of sorts" designer gear—or hide. The Kraft Easy Mac display was right around the corner and wide enough to conceal most of me, save a thigh or ass vestige.

In case you haven't noticed, these run-ins always occur with someone you'd rather not see unless you've just emerged from two weeks at Canyon Ranch or shed eight gallons of flab at the Jiffy Suck Lipo-Rama.

The unfortunate day I ran into Her Extraordinariness after a twenty-year hiatus was a day I had forgone makeup, slimming clothes, and a few sessions with Jolene, Nair, and Crest Strips. Not that I have a mustache, but truth be known, Miss It did have a trace of one in college.

On this day, of all days, I had a bulbous zit on my nose,

which lengthened the thing a full half inch and was all I could see. The zit throbbed and I'm certain my nose visibly pulsed.

To add insult to injury was the most unfortunate fact I'd chosen an A-line blue jean wrap skirt—a fashion flop that widens a rump so that it appears to be a rhino hide at close range. The hair, to top off the whole affair, was a tangle of chlorinated straw in which the Eckerd brand highlights had turned alien green.

My swaggling triceps weren't looking so grand in the Wal-Mart shell I had thrown on, and I suddenly felt as if they were turning into giant pelican pouches.

Miss It was strolling by the cheeses and yogurts, her own arms sticklike, her two lovely children cooing in their smocked Lenox Square Mall selections while my daughter guffawed and hee-hawed in a compromising getup handed down three generations—a most unpleasant variation of the elasticized tube top. She appeared to have been plucked from a Feed the Children infomercial and planted right in the center of the grocery store.

How could it be that this woman from my past was virtually unscathed by time? That her teeth had bleached their way into a blinding flash and that her waistline had shrunken from even those rat-metabolism college-girl days?

Our children played in the aisle together, but she didn't seem to recognize me at all, praise the Lord. She was busy keeping a close watch on her own pristine children in case they touched my daughter, who she probably thought carried impetigo.

I continued hiding, figuring it was for the best. Always hide when one's best foot is not forward and in Prada but completely amputated or exposed in a Big K flip-flop.

I'd made it to the checkout without incident, burrowing in those highbrow magazines like the *Star* and *National Enquirer*, when wouldn't you just know it, she ends up in my line right behind me, purring at her just-hopped-off-the-cover-of-the-Lands'-End-catalog children.

"Don't touch that little girl," Miss Priss whispered, eyeing my angel in her faded getup. "She's . . . she may be contagious with something."

It was most unfortunate my angel joy was also sporting a crop of red swollen mosquito-bitten arms and legs. She looked like the poster child for Neglect, like the daughter of a Vicodin addict or the child of a woman with a half dozen abusive boyfriends and who can't get up on a Saturday before 3:00 p.m.

I wanted to scream out that we smother the child in love, sunscreen, and OFF! But if I opened my mouth, recognition would occur.

As soon as I grabbed my baby's hand and pulled her toward the checkout line, it happened. Eye contact. Miss It was staring a hole into me, focusing on the nose zit and throbbing nostril. She tilted that adorably empty head to the side like one of those lapdogs that wears bows and lives in a penthouse.

"Millie?" I said, hoping it really wasn't her, that maybe this was a much younger sister or first cousin.

"Yes," she said, raising her tweezed brows. "Millicent is what I prefer."

Shit. I was stuck. "Remember me? Susan Reinhardt . . . well, it was Gambrell back then. From Georgia? We were Tri-Delts together?" *You got trashed and dry-humped that alcoholic KA on the beach and everyone stood around to watch,* I wanted to add but graciously held back. "It was 1980 something or other. I had a sister, Sandy?"

Her eyes widened and I swear I heard a squeak. I could read the banner sliding across her mind. *What in the world happened to her? Boy, did she slip a few rungs! She has flat-out gone to pot. Must have been all those keg parties. Why, I'll bet she lives in a single-wide without a cathedral ceiling or a sunken tub.*

Millie, trying to make up for the fact that she was in tacky old Myrtle Beach of all places, went on about her husband and his prep school and the family coat of arms and how she was here only because her in-laws owned a "vacation villa."

"What brings you *here* to this sort of beach?"

Well, I felt like saying, *we're here for the Jerry Springer reunion convention. Maybe you ran across our episode, 'Catching Your Husband Cheating with Sheep, Bleating Goats, and other Attractive and Available Farm Animals.'*

Instead, I addressed my tube-topped toddler, who was pulling Skoal from a shelf: "That's not candy, sweetheart."

Priss Pot continued to show off her superior pedigree. "We're going to be in Hilton Head for our *real* vacation," she said, trying to hide her shame at being in Myrtle. "On the private end of the island. It's exquisite and exclusive. Where the Clintons always go."

Well, I'm sure Bill would love one of your famous dry-humping sessions, I started to say but am smart enough to realize impressionable little ears were amongst us. Though my tot already knew what a booger and pussy were thanks to the two-fannied woman from Hickory.

Before I could throw my purse over my purchases, Priss Pot's eyes zoomed in on my grocery cart's contents, which I had all but forgotten due to the shock of seeing the woman. Her cart was packed with high-dollar delights and wines priced in the double digits for bottles that would serve no more than two.

In my buggy sat a package of Price-Buster brand mozzarella, a jar of Vienna sausages (the one meat my daughter would eat), a six-pack of O'Douls because college had turned me into a bit of a drunkard, and four bulging bags from the damned Dollar Tree where we'd shopped first.

I wanted the floor to divide and swallow me up whole. Out of the corner of my eye I noticed my Skoal-obsessed cherub picking her nose and announcing to me and Miss Glory, "I've got a booger. I've got a booger and nowhere to put it." She held her finger toward me, and Miss Finely Bred lunged protectively for her smocked and scrubbed Junior Priss Pot children.

She jumped back as if startled. Her eyes darted from my

booger baby to my shopping cart filled with the Dollar Tree bags.

By then, I'd had enough. Especially after she muffled a scream.

"Oh, to hell with all this pretense," I said, taking my daughter's finger and wiping it across my A-line wraparound. "I don't guess your girls' noses ever run, huh? I don't guess a mosquito has ever found their virgin skin?"

Miss It stared and held her children tight while I continued this PMS-and snoot-induced mini-fit. "In case you're wondering what's in our bags, wonder no more. As a former sorority sister we're close enough to share such things." I leaned in and she pushed her cart to block me. "I ran out of Poligrip. The stuff goes fast here in Myrtle. Can't have enough, you know, especially since we're boiling corn tonight in the motel room, Budget Bob's Motor Court. We were thrilled to see it had a fridge and hot plate for the price we were paying." I swept out my arms like Vanna White and pointed toward the other bags.

"Inside those we got some two dozen of the Heifer Queen Maxi Pads they had on sale two boxes for a dollar. What we don't use, I'll save for craft night. We're going to make flip-flops so we don't burn our feet on the hot sand."

Miss Priss seemed to be choking on her tongue, but I didn't let it stop me. "Thing is, I saw the idea in a craft book. You take one heavy-day pad and loop it with the medium-flow pad. Be sure to leave one long for the foot. Fits most sizes. The great thing is you can take your Tacky Glue and adorn the tops with little seashells and whatnots. We did the same thing at Christmas, only used Santa heads, and the kids' teachers loved them and wrote us the nicest thank-you notes."

She said nothing, pretending she'd never met me, digging in her purse for her double-platinum triple-gold VIP Elite American Express card.

The checkout lady had finished ringing me up. I turned back for one last look at the third prettiest Tri-Delt at UGA in 1980 something or other.

"Bye," I said, as hicky as I possibly could. "It was good you got to see me." Her tiny nose tried to curl, while mine throbbed and grew puffier by the minute. "Maybe we can get together, talk about the good old days."

She sucked in a breath and I could see her rib cage. "I really don't think it would be a good—"

"Maybe next time I see you," I interrupted, "you'll be wearing a bra! I might be having an ugly day and my daughter and I might, on this one unfortunate day of the year, look like a mama hag and baby haglet, but we are good-looking 364 days of the year. And we know when to wear undergarments."

Miss Priss may have been thin and rich and unwrinkled, but she had a set of pendulous bosoms that made Putt-Putt's look right firm.

"Target makes a water bra," I said in my sweetest voice.

Before she could utter a word, the bells dingalinged and we were out the door, breathing that hot-as-pizza-oven air and rummaging for the goodies in our Dollar Tree bags.

When One Elvis Is Not Enough

The only time Mama openly shows her sexuality or even acknowledges she has urges is when the word Elvis is mentioned. She purely cannot contain herself or her God-given and usually suppressed drive.

Her first date with my daddy was to an Elvis movie—not his choosing—and I find it hard to believe she could keep her hands off him after the show, having learned what I know now.

It's a double miracle she managed to remain a virgin 'til marriage when Elvis was all over the radio and her heart, heating her blood like a fever that wouldn't break.

When Elvis died it was my younger sister who delivered the tragic news and had to console our hysterical mother. It was a muggy August day in 1977. I was fifteen and my sister was thirteen. We were old enough to have heard countless Elvis stories from our mother and witness her getting all worked up whenever his songs came on the radio or his movies on TV.

My sister found Mama outside pulling weeds in the central Georgia air that feels like breathing steam from a swamp. She ran from the carport door and down the front yard to the flower garden.

"Mama, Elvis is dead!" she screamed. "Elvis is dead!"

My mother lifted her head, processed the information, and rightly collapsed into the rich soil, crushing with her five feet eight inches the Gerber daisies, lilies, impatiens, and dahlias. My sister said the sound her body made when it hit earth and the noises bubbling up from her throat have forever marked her.

Our mother burst into hysterics and wailed and moaned, scaring my sister half to death. It was as if she were being scalded alive. She rolled back and forth crying and groaning, her tear-streaked face coated in mulch and dirt, along with defeated petals. She was still carrying on when my daddy drove up the driveway, coming home after a long and tiring day at work.

He stuck his head out of the open window of his new Cutlass Supreme. "What the hell? What the hell is going on?"

Mama cried that much louder and kept on flopping around in the garden, beside herself with grief. "Elvis Presley died," my sister said in a pitiful voice, the voice of a girl afraid her mother had gone mad.

By this time my sister had hit the ground, too, figuring if this sadness was worth her mother's entire allotment of tears and turmoil, it was also well worth hers. Together they commenced in their grief fest, the chorus of their noises echoing throughout Piney Woods Drive and surrounding streets. It was 6:00 p.m. and daddies were coming home from work, moms and kids on porches and in backyards, enjoying the evening until suppertime. Everyone heard the commotion in our front yard.

Daddy was livid and stormed from his Cutlass. "Y'all get in the house right now! I bet no one will ever shed that many tears on me in a lifetime. Now get your asses on in the house! The neighbors will think I've beaten you both. You can take this crying to your bedrooms."

They rose slowly from the garden, dirt piggybacking the tears down their faces. Mama had to lean on her youngest daughter for support and trudged along as if mortally wounded, unaware until later that plenty of Piney Woods eyes had been on them.

"Oh, meeeee," my Daddy said. "I can't believe I came home and found this going on in my own front yard of all places. What's the deal here? Are y'all going to the funeral or something?"

Both cried even harder. "They could pay you good money for those wailing services."

Once they got into the foyer and out of neighbors' earshot, Sandy told Dad, "You owe the cuss jug seventy-five cents for saying three bad words."

He grumbled and headed toward the closet that he'd turned into a wet bar and poured a stiff bourbon.

Mama has never gotten over Elvis. And with all the impersonators around, she doesn't have to. While she never saw the original in person, she's discovered an imitator so close to the real thing, he brings her to her knees and she all but collapses the way she did in the flower bed that hot August afternoon. When this man comes to town, Mama heats Daddy a meal and bids him adieu.

"Have fun with the church ladies," Daddy said shortly before her inaugural concert with half a dozen women from the little Baptist church they'd recently joined. He sipped his bourbon, figuring he'd probably get lucky later that night if he could only stay awake. He shared a few words of warning before she walked out the door in her snug corduroys and that giddy, schoolgirl excitement.

"Don't come rootin' around for me when you get in," he said, not meaning a word of it. "I'll be asleep."

She waved him off and jumped into the car with ladies she knew only from church. She says it's one thing to see them in Sunday school all prim and pearled, but she'd never given much thought to what they did outside of church. Now she knows.

They invited her to see Elvis at Spartanburg Auditorium—

only it was this impersonator who Mama swears is the only Elvis copycat worth spending $26.50 to see.

"Eddie Mills," she said. "No . . . Miles . . . Eddie Miles." She was all tongue-tied and worked up the next day when I phoned to find out how her concert went.

Initially, she'd been hesitant about going for a couple of reasons. "I got this huge fever blister and the pinkeye," she said, "and I didn't know how to act with the Baptist church ladies." She knew it would be hard to contain herself when a delectable version of the King glistened and gyrated, chest heaving from those open rhinestone jackets.

Mama reported spotting three thousand gray-headed women and a few men in poet's blouses at the Eddie Miles "Elvis" show.

"I just couldn't sit still in my seat. He was neat and clean and so cute. He was in shape and not like how the real Elvis got there toward the end, all sweaty and pot-gutted."

She continued her excited ramblings. "There were all these women yelling, 'Sing the next song backwards,' because his fanny looked so cute in those blue bell-bottoms."

I imagined these were the same women who on Sunday mornings shouted, "Give your sinning souls to the Lord," but I said nothing. All God's creatures deserve their fun and were custom-built to crave the Act. Much as one tried to pray away desire, it always found its way back, like a tiny flower through ten tons of sidewalk.

As soon as Eddie Miles returned to Spartanburg the following year, Mama and the same crew with a couple of additions decided to see him again. Only this time they paid top dollar for seats six rows back and center.

And this time they invited me and wouldn't take no for an answer. I later learned why my mother insisted I go with them. Naively, I assumed it was out of sheer love for her oldest.

"Be prepared," she warned. "Anything can and *will* happen."

Mama and her troop of Baptists truly adore Elvis and can't

seem to let him rest in peace. With Eddie Miles doing the resurrecting, Mama glows with euphoria when talking about him. "I hate to say it and I hope the dearly departed Elvis can't hear me, but this one's somewhat cuter than the first." She said it as if we were talking about a breed of dog that after a few cycles tends to produce finer litters.

"You told me that last time about him, remember?"

She paid this no mind. "I'm the teenager tonight. You are to be the mother."

The six of us exited the relieved Buick and entered the auditorium along with all the other women who would soon have more hot flashes than during the peak of menopause.

"Let's hurry now," Mama said. "We need to get a good seat."

"Peg," Margaret, the head Baptist, said. "We have our seats. We're on the sixth row. Remember, sugar? That's as good as it gets."

"We are a full two hours early," I said, feeling a migraine pulsing and wondering if I'd make it through the entire event. I love my mama and her friends; otherwise, I never would have gone to see an Elvis impersonator. Then again, witnessing all that hibernating estrogen resurface as soon as Elvis the Pelvis rocked the stage was worth every dime and more. Forget hormone replacement therapy. Just put these women in a room with Eddie Miles and watch the estrogen levels rocket! Long exited urges make a comeback and the ghosts of what *was* forget they're dead and begin carrying on hysterically.

As the auditorium lights dimmed, the Baptist next to me was Barbara, the firecracker of the bunch who flirts and makes even the ugly men feel alive by batting her huge blue eyes and breaking into frequent smiles. She may work it a little, but she's a pure-hearted soul who never hides her feelings. She sings in the choir and pulls double shifts in two nursing homes. She was first to let out a whoop that resonated throughout the auditorium.

"Come on, baby," she shouted, hearing the first strains of

the guitar. She flung her head this way and that. "Whew! Come on, now!" The man in front of her turned to stare. The music had been a false alarm, just generic tunes played from a big set of speakers while everyone found their seats. Barbara wasn't happy. "I didn't pay my money to hear no tapes," she bellowed and the man in front of her scowled again.

She elbowed me hard. Mama had mentioned Barbara and her elbow, saying I would be feeling it most of the night. "My heart's a-flyin'," Barbara hollered as this duplicated Elvis at last bounded onstage. "Wait 'til you see him turn around."

Almost as soon as the words were out, Eddie whipped his fanny toward the crowd and this did Barbara in completely. She flung out her elbows and whooped like a wild turkey.

"Lord have mercy, I'm going to be on my knees at altar call in the morning." She fanned herself with a program and squalled like a colicky infant. I wished I'd brought a horse tranquilizer to put in her Coke or in mine.

Mama, meanwhile, reached toward heaven with her two fists punching the air like that mean 105-year-old who tried to kick my ass and was hollering and yelling and acting sixteen. It was a frightening sight, marking me for life the way my sister was marked out in the flower bed that August day when Elvis died. Mama shoved a camera in my lap.

"Run up there to the stage and get his picture," she ordered. "Hit the zoom and focus. Go on now. Hurry." I hunched in embarrassment but did as told, snapping a few pictures and feeling stupid.

Eddie started up about "Don't disappoint me," and Barbara shouted, "I won't disappoint you, baby." The scowling man in front turned and made a face that raised the flesh on my arms.

About every five minutes, when Barbara could take no more, she yelled, "If you need CPR, baby, I'm certified . . . 'At's right. I'm certified with a capital C, baby. Oh, mercy me, you sho' are purty. Ain't he purty?" she asked, elbowing me.

"Uh-huh."

About fifteen minutes before the show ended, Eddie hit the first notes of "Love Me Tender," and what sounded like a herd of elephants thundered from their seats.

"Get up," Mama demanded. Gone was her kind and playful nature, and in its place was a fierce woman on a mission. "*Get up now!*"

"Why do you want me—"

"Get your butt down there and rush that stage." I understood at that moment why she wanted me to go and had paid for my ticket. It was all making sense.

"Run down there and get me a scarf. Please. He only has about a dozen and I didn't get one last time." She was about to cry and I imagined her back in the flower bed grieving, and so I rose from the chair and waddled toward Eddie. It wasn't easy trying to navigate what appeared to be a stampede of spooked cattle. Abruptly, from the corner of my eye, I spotted Mama already ahead of me and center stage, those arms reaching high and her pitiful voice warbling like the gravely bereaving. "Eddie! Eddie! Look here, Eddie."

He took pity on her and draped a scarf around her neck, causing such a commotion of screaming and swooning we had to grab each of Mama's arms and escort her to her seat.

Barbara was still going on as loud as her lungs would allow about CPR and her gift at giving it, and the man in front had finally given up and moved to the farthest end of another row.

After the applause for "Love Me Tender" died down, Eddie broke into "You Ain't Nothing but a Hound Dog," and a hundred-year-old woman with no teeth flung the tubing from her nose, hurled her oxygen machine, and rushed the stage squeezing a teddy bear in her arms.

Once the show was over, we left the auditorium in a Buick packed with six Baptists on a big Elvis high.

"I thought I'd died five years ago," Barbara said, "but now I'm cured."

The next morning at church Mama faced the same ladies

who the previous night were shouting and salivating over a fake Elvis.

"I didn't get much sleep last night," Barbara admitted, fanning herself with the church program featuring the morning's sermon, "Don't Let Lust Bar You from the Kingdom."

Mama smiled knowingly.

Field Trips from the Edge

Officially, I'm still not a camper. The fear of camping rests in my pores, blood cells, the mitochondria and strands of DNA.

We don't camp in my family. Maybe sleepovers in a tree house or on top of a trampoline as a youngster, but adult and camping are two words that don't coexist in my mind.

My idea of fun is an ocean, white sand, and a hotel—nothing fancy, just not tents, tarps, air mattresses, and pee-peeing in the wilderness. I like a roof over my head and an assortment of electrical outlets.

"You're so high maintenance," a coworker with gristles for toes said. He wears Patchouli, the earth daddy scent, and is always playing his six-string and pretending he spends his evenings sculpting and painting when I know he's really on the Internet trying to meet slutty artists. "Camping is a Zen experience of communing with the cosmos and listening to the melodic rushing of the streams."

"Hotels are a normal experience of communing with soap and warm water, flushable potties, and listening to the melodic pounding of the ocean."

"You just don't get it," he said, half closing his eyes as if he'd been summoned by a member of the spirit world.

I would love to buy his fungusy self a pedicure. He doesn't get it. Why is it that those who hate camping are looked upon as flawed humans? Can't some of us *love* the outdoors but still want to come indoors at bedtime?

"You're wrong," I told him. "I'm not high maintenance. I never get my nails done. I dye my own roots and I drive used cars off eBay with missing parts. You're the one who gets your colon irrigated with Folgers."

"Everyone would benefit from a sparkling lower digestive tract. I also have my chakras balanced and my spine adjusted for optimal energy flow."

I want to knock people like him out cold, but Mama says that would be a sin so I don't. I've harnessed enough bad karma from those naughty dance floor days.

Even with the promise of nature's healing offerings, I still shudder at the thought of camping; however, I knew one day soon—real, real soon—I'd have to do it.

For I am the mother of a Cub Scout. And mothers of Cub Scouts cannot escape such joys as the Pinewood Derby and camping in twenty-degree weather.

I dodged the bullet when he was a Tiger Cub, a Wolf, and a Bear Cub. Now that he was a Webelo, I couldn't get out of it. He came home from school one day with a story he'd written called "The Only Boy Scout Who's Never Camped." Whoa, sistahs. I felt my cheeks flame with shame.

Recently, a chance at redemption arrived when Pack 34, Den 8, led by the indefatigable Scotty Kingston, a man who obviously gets laid regularly because he volunteers for everything in sight, was headed to Camp Big Foot for Operation Snowshoe—a traditionally frigid trip designed to make men of boys. Designed to make guilt pie of mothers who refuse to go. I turned in desperation to Tidy Stu.

"Well, looks like you and the boy are going camping," I said.

He stared at me as if I'd said we were having ground hog au gratin for supper. "It'll be fun, all that male bonding and shooting targets, maybe a bit of knot tying. Y'all can eat beans and hot dogs and drink instant coffee in those cute tin cups."

His eyes squinted and he scrunched up his long nose. "You don't think I'm going out there in the middle of February, do you?"

"You know I don't camp," I said. "There are people who camp and people who don't camp. Just like there are people who smoke and those who don't. You can't really have in-betweens."

"I'll camp when the thermometer hits sixty," this son of an Eagle Scout said. "The Weather Channel is predicting the flood of the century. Did you hear me, woman? Flood of the *century*. Go look at the weather map."

On Saturday morning, rain roaring and creeks rising, I packed up our gear and provisions and carted my Webelo to camp. I had sweated, feared, and obsessed over this for two weeks and here we were, in the wilderness, guns and cannons blasting and boys everywhere chanting and carrying flags and giant snowshoes, joyfully sloshing mud as they flapped and trudged along.

My dear friend Ma Ferguson and I sat in the lodge and ate all the provisions while the terrain washed away and the devoted Scout leaders in yellow rain ponchos had a grand old time splattering about in the monsoon.

That annoying Village People song about being a macho man kept playing in my head.

"That can't be fun," I said, opening a bag of Lay's potato chips. "Surely that's not what men really like to do."

Ma Ferguson mumbled and swayed in her rocker, closing her eyes to the sound of rain beating on the lodge roof and the distant squeals of boys shooting things and Scout leaders cheering them on. "I'm going to the car to get more food," she said. "I brought three packs of Oreos. Regular, Double Stuffed, and Reduced Fat. You know my motto: might as well eat if there's nothing else to do."

She returned and we started in on the Double Stuffed, gobbling them up, drawing the attention of an enormous Unclaimed Blessing (also known as a Freak) in a red vest covered in Scout badges perfectly sewn and placed, row upon row. He displayed badges for hunting and fishing, carving, whittling, cooking, target shooting—you name it. There must have been a hundred badges on his jumbo vest. He sort of glided over to us breathing heavily from the effort.

"My gosh, he looks like Jabba the Hutt," Ma Ferguson whispered.

"Hey," I said to the poor monstrosity. "You thinking of calling this off? Look out there. Everyone's drowning."

A thunderous boom erupted from his pontoon-size lungs. "Nooooooo! They are having the time of their lives." He said these things in slow motion. I couldn't stop staring at his badges, thinking there must be one for everything, including pedophilia and campsite molestations.

"How do you get your badges sewn on so nicely?" Ma Ferguson asked, and I wanted to slap her for making sweet conversation with Jabba the Scout Hutt.

As if a slow-pulled hunk of taffy, he looked down at his vest and said, "I. Take. All. My. Badge-work. To. The. Dry. Cleaners."

What a winner, I was thinking. What an amazing dude. Ma kept talking to him, which meant one thing only. That she'd had ugly thoughts about him and was trying to relieve her guilt. I'll bet anything she wished the campsite had a prayer room with candles and Mary and Jesus wallpaper. She must miss the smell of Tide along with her vanilla candles. She laid it on thick with Jabba, this spread of niceness in order to de-sin her truest and meanest thoughts.

Since I'm in between denominations, waffling back and forth, I could think what I wanted and not have to say sweet nothings to the vested hulk. All I wanted was for him to cancel camp and send us home. Home sweet home. Dry land. Dry beds. Warm showers.

"Don't be making conversation with him again," I said to Ma as he finally glided away ever so slowly.

"He's precious," Ma lied. "He's the sweetest thing."

"Please. Just say what you really think and take your sins to your laundry room later. At least your religion has a purgatory. Y'all got a holding tank for the semisinners. With my kind, your choices are limited to bliss or burn. Nothing in between. And don't go making out like he was anything but a freak."

She hushed and ate a cookie, but I think she was working a rope of rosary beads in her pocket. We sat there most of the day, eating and watching Jabba.

About 5:00 p.m., rain relenting for seven full minutes, Jabba announced over the public address system that we were to "make camp" and set up our tents. Of course at that point lightning flashed, thunder rolled, and the sky emptied its yearly allotment, all of us like drenched rats with soaked sleeping bags. I turned to my left and saw the creek dashing from its banks. I couldn't see far due to the thick sheets of rain. This was misery with a capital M and Scotty and his buddy, Fredd with two Ds, were laughing and acting like it was a day at the beach. I saw another den leader and his friend passing a flask. A flask! Maybe that would earn them the "I can hold my liquor" badge.

As one of our members began whimpering, rain pouring from his scalp and into his ears, I pictured a night of misery, tents floating down the river with the Slim Jims and Pop-Tarts, icy wind lashing wet skin. The men stood under a drenched tarp and tried to light a fire for the supper. But the only thing getting lit was them.

Ma Ferguson and I made a decision.

"There's camping, and then there's stupidity," we agreed, yanking up the tents so fast stakes flew and nylon whistled. The tipsy Poncho People looked at us like we were Priss Pots instead of the Flood Dodgers we really were. "I'm sorry," I said. "This is highly dangerous. When men prefer bravado and machismo over good common sense a woman must intervene."

Within minutes we'd loaded up half our group and rushed the dirt road moments before the creek overflowed, leaving all campers stranded. By 8:00 p.m. we were home in our warm dry beds, watching the Weather Channel and its warnings concerning the biggest storm of the decade, the red tape rolling across the bottom of the screen telling everyone death was likely if they didn't cart their dumb asses home.

I just hoped the Scouts who braved it out were doing well and would at least earn an "I survived snowshoe" T-shirt with matching high-water britches. Bless their badge-happy hearts.

"I'm never going on another camping trip," I told Ma, and she nodded and fanned herself. We would end up eating our words a few months later when the mother of all field trips stared us in the face, daring us to be crappy moms and bag out. The trip had been planned as an end-of-year fourth grade excursion, beginning at the western tip of the long state of North Carolina and continuing all the way to the other side. From west to east. We were to board a bus for four straight days, countless hours of confinement with a rowdy and roaring bunch of kids and one screaming, yelling, and cursing teacher.

"I'm afraid of Mrs. McFarland," Ma said. "She says the F word more than she says 'good morning.'"

"At least she can keep them in line. The bus is supposed to be one of those huge luxury things." All this convinced Ma Ferguson to go along with me. About one-third of the mothers signed up and were assigned three children each.

Ma and I, in the days prior to the trip, remembered well Jabba the Scout Hutt and his vest of many badges and thus broke out in hives, humps, and fear-induced welts.

"I got the mange and a bald spot near my part," I told her.

"I'm all broken out, too," Ma whined. "My chest erupted and I got these hives on my arms. You know those same two lumps that pop up when I get disturbed? I was in the prayer room for three hours yesterday but managed to finish the laundry and get started on the ironing."

What my best friend and I were facing was a trip even former city councilman Troy McFarland, husband of the cursing teacher, couldn't face.

Four days and nights trapped in a bus with fifty-two fourth graders—a trip from Asheville all the way to the Outer Banks and back. We must have been either hypnotized or just plain temporarily insane as we signed the forms to go as parent chaperones.

On this day, Monday, April 28, twelve hours until departure at 5:00 a.m., Ma Ferguson and I began panicking. We love our babies, but Lord have mercy, our nerves. Our poor inflamed and exposed nerves!

Troy, whose wife, Bertha McFarland, organized the event and does wonders with this type of thing, said emphatically, "I don't do class trips. I decided that a long time ago. It's one of the things I don't do. You're in for a long ride."

I called Bertha, an academic mover and shaker known for her ability to pull off a trip and a sizzling strip of profanity, a woman who could call someone an obscene name in one breath and then pick up the phone, take another breath, and charm heads of state and celebrities into coming to the school. Rumor was she had lined Bill Clinton up as the elementary school graduation speaker for the following year. If anyone could do it, Bertha could.

"Are our fears justified?" I asked her.

"Oh no," she said, her voice gravelly from all the yelling over the years at unruly children. "I fully expect this group of young . . . uh . . . ladies and gentlemen to behave beautifully. But you know there was a time a few years back, at an elementary school other than ours, when the entire event fell apart. Remember now, this was at another school and not mine.

"It was the trip from Hades," she said, using her best manners, the ones she teaches in fourth grade etiquette classes. But the more she recalled of the trip the madder she got and let her manners fall by the wayside. It all started with the mild words, the training pants of cussing. As the story progressed she simmered and steamed, her tongue forked, and her mouth grew foul.

"I had to tear a new asshole out of several of them little sons a' bitches," she said, scorching my Baptist-bred ears. "They loaded my bus at four in the morning and by the middle of the day I was needing a saltshaker and a bottle of tequila. I stood up and delivered a few of my choice words and they shut the hell up. I had to pin one of them sniveling snot rags to the side of the bus. I told him if he didn't shut his mouth I would roll down the window and throw his ass to the curb. Everybody got nice and quiet after that and we sang our Christmas program even though it was May. We sang all the Christian songs the damned government won't let us sing under normal conditions. I figured the little loudmouths needed some religion and sure enough, their heathen asses got quiet after that.

"We had a lovely time. Everyone behaved beautifully and used their best manners. Our group, I can assure you, isn't gonna act ugly. Not with me on that bus."

My office phone rang shortly before quitting time on the day before departure. It was Ma Ferguson again. "I'm so happy," she chirped. "I've decided to take my car and drive. I don't have headphones, and I'm scared of the noise on the bus. I'm also really scared of Bertha McFarland. She called me a 'bitch ass' one day and a week later had the nerve to tell Dane he wasn't holding his fork properly or 'masticating' his food enough for digestion. She just wanted to say 'masticating' because it sounds dirty."

Despie, one of my coworkers, a childless but vivacious "aunty" who cherishes every moment with her nieces and nephews, put the upcoming field trip into perspective.

"It's just little fourth graders," she said. "Nothing but sweet little cherubs. How bad could it be?"

Well, I'll tell you how bad it was. The bus driver, a wizened man with a cigarette-shrunken face, announced over the intercom: "For those who need to do business besides that of a bladder nature, we'll be stopping frequently at rest areas."

"What's a bladder nature?" the little boy in front of me who reeked of sulfur asked.

"Tinkling," I said.

"Macy just vomited and had a wet fart a while ago," the boy said.

Macy will be hosed down like hogs at auction time, I felt like saying.

The Scout leader's wife and I had the seats in the back near the bathroom. Every time a child came by to potty we were obliged to quiz them.

"What are you planning to do in there?"

"Number one," they'd say.

"You positive?"

"Yes, ma'am."

"Proceed ahead. I'm timing you. Remember that there will be no number twos ejected on this bus."

The next four days were a blur of activity and tours and rushing about in the name of education and experiences. When it was all over, we returned to the bus for a twelve-hour trip home.

When our chartered septic tank finally wheezed into the school parking lot and the door opened, I collapsed onto the pavement. One of my eyes snapped shut from lack of sleep while the other worked fine, rotating around like our Stinky Stripper's the night of Leslie's bachelorette party.

"How was it?" I heard one of the nonchaperoning parents ask. Of course this person looked fresh and suntanned, exfoliated to within an inch of her toned musculature.

I rolled my lizard eye at her. "Fine. It was the finest trip in all of school history." I wanted to add, *In skipping out on this festival of farts, you will regret forever that you didn't give up your tennis game and foil highlights to join your child in this great adventure.*

Ma Ferguson, who smelled like vomit because she helped tend those with stomach flu at the rest stop, elbowed me and set her suitcase down with a loud thwack. "It wasn't that great," she said to the poor woman I'd been ugly to. "We just saw a few lighthouses and the state capitol. We got to go to the ocean for ten and a half minutes one day."

"I'll tell you what you missed," I said, trying to sit up on the school's sidewalk so others could greet their parents and go home. "You missed the almighty hand dryer. The thing had a V-8 engine and blew more air than a category-five hurricane. My toilet paper holder nearly flew off the wall and the woman next to me lost a shoe in all that wind. I could have sworn I saw a pair of eyeglasses and two sets of partials hitting the exit door."

"She's just tired," Ma said, explaining my delirium to the aghast woman, bless her sweet aerobicized heart.

"The seventh time I popped in to check out the dryer, I put my face up to it and the skin literally peeled back from my skull. I got to see what I would look like partially decomposed. See what you missed?"

The woman made a disgusted sound way down in her throat and walked off with her half-asleep child.

I remained on the pavement, waiting for my husband to come and rescue us, my son sitting beside me on top of his suitcase.

"Are you OK, Mom?"

"Mmmmmmrrrrpppphhhh."

The Worthalots

This is the Christmas letter I'd really like to mail when anyone sends me a form letter talking about their genius children and fabulous careers, sprawling homes, and spectacular vacations. Such letters make me want to upchuck. And so do letters and e-mails where people write LOL after every dumb joke or semiwitty remark.

So I write these spoofs every year, thinking I'll actually mail them. So far, I haven't. But one of these days . . .

Dear Ever-Growing Massive Circle of Friends and Loved Ones:

Wow, what a year this has been for us!!!

I'm just not sure where all this talk about the failing economy is coming from because we've enjoyed a boom like you wouldn't believe☺. My savvy Theodore invested stock in all these pharmaceutical companies, the ones that make stuff to get you happy and "firm," and we're as rich as the Clampetts but classier than the Kennedys. Teddy's third double cousin by direct descent is a Kennedy, as you know, but we've not fully traced the path that no doubt will lead to THE KENNEDYS. We're confident the connection is there.

My Ted is soooooo smart, people. He also bought into the Botox deal early on when it was still being tested on Sharpeis and before the soccer moms decided they simply *had* to have it. Not only is the entire family wrinkle-free, we're swimming in the profits, although unable to smile at this point.

We couldn't even work up a grimace when our poor dog got hit by lightning, or when Nana announced she was having her buttocks augmented at age ninety-two now that she's found love on the Internet—in the "Wild Widows" chat room of all places. Seems she's told the poor man that she's forty-five and a former Penthouse Pet. We advised her that *Penthouse* was the nasty book where they sprawl out their naughty bits for the whole world to see, but she doesn't understand and is insisting the nude human body is pure art. We tried to tell her that art appreciation typically doesn't extend to subjects well into their nineties, but she says there are plenty of ways to stop and reverse the clock. Good old Nana. She's a true example of our family motto: "Nip it, Tuck it! Fix it or Fuck it!" LOL. LOL. LOL.

You know, it's just so darn easy to see when looking at her, *and us*, why everyone thinks we're the perfect American family: four cars, several homes, baby Einsteins for progeny, and those constant trips abroad. I'm so lucky my Theodore is successful and hasn't screwed up our marriage by using all that money to lure in little boys and young strippers like so many of your husbands have. I pray that will end for you, poor dears. I realize some of you gals are going through not only wretched financial times, but have lost in the love field as well. It's hard being our age, when our men typically begin cruising the high school parking lots for second wives or dilly-dallies. I feel for you. Really, I do. LOT. (Lots Of Tears!)

I have to say you have no one to blame but yourselves for not investing in Botox and the Atkins plan to stave off time like our Nana and myself. My own mother always told her daughters, "Never, ever let yourself go." If such occurred, it's no one's fault but your own that the men run off or turn gay. I hate to sound like a homophobe, but if I were married to some of you I'd probably shift the Beemer in reverse too, if you know what I mean. LOL! LOL! LOL!

Just remember, it's not too late. The clock is always willing to tick backwards for a certain price, my precious drooping and bloating friends!

Bless your hearts, you poor, less fortunate people. If you don't mind, I have to tell you about the joy of Viagra, and not because we have stock in it, but because it can put a tiger in the tank! A crocodile in the Duckheads!!! 'Course, Theodore has plenty of water in his hydrant, so to speak. Whoa! That man is a tidal wave.

It has helped that I haven't uglied up and have remained a size negative 2 for him all these years, thanks to my devotion to bulimia and liposuction. I don't care if you people *did* think I'd aged in my last family photo. (Don't think I didn't hear through the grapevine that y'all said I looked like a withered corpse in need of a Big Mac and a Crisco IV.) I heard about it, but since I'm more of a Christian than some of you will ever be, I will find it in my heart to forgive you for your obvious jealousy. I'll admit, my skin shriveled and sloughed off in chunks and patches when I quit eating, and part of my skull was exposed for three months, but life's a trade-off. And I chose to be slightly wrinkled and cadaverish in exchange for a size negative 2. You chose to eat. My Theodore can always turn me over if he doesn't like the view. Better than turning me away. Put the freakin' fork down, people. Call a surgeon!

Well, I didn't mean to get off on one of my tangents. I'm just so hungry since all I had were four very Atkins-oriented sirloin tips the size of Le Sueur peas, and I'm trying hard to resist throwing that up. Progress, not perfection, people. All that said, we at the Worthalots' estate are still hoping with all our hearts you people will manage a semi-merry Christmas. We're sure having our best one EVER!

On the festive front, we've decided against a Christmas tree this year for our main living quarters. Instead, I've hired a dozen midget mimes on which we're hanging our Waterford ornaments along with fourteen-karat gold mini cell phones that ring "The Twelve Days of Christmas." Adorable! The mimes were so grateful for the work, too! Seems that if *The Wizard of Oz* isn't in production anywhere it's hard to come by good acting jobs. Oh, and they can sing! Prettiest baritones you ever heard. Like whales bellowing secret messages.

The kids are in heaven. I'll admit, they really wanted a tree, and not just festooned mimes, so we went ahead and hauled the biggest fir from the federally protected forest (don't tell!) and loaded it atop our Ford Titanic, which gets an amazing one-half mile to the gallon. We've also installed an espresso bar in the dining area of the Titanic and an aerobics studio near the rear end, to help tone my own hindquarters that Teddy is always comparing to a whippet's lower half. LOL. I have my own minifridge completely stocked with Tab (bottled Tab to die for!!!!) and my teeny, tiny meat kabobs—no CARBS!

Let's see. What else? Oh yeah . . . all our travels. No Christmas letter would be complete without a travelogue from the family to make all other families want to throw themselves onto the nearest train tracks or loop a noose over the tallest interstate bridge. We've been traveling so much it's hard to keep up, but since the weather's so mild here, we won't be going to Bora Bora until February or March. I still have five pounds to lose before I'm down to eighty-eight, my "Go Phi Delta" princess fighting weight. LOL. LOL. LOL.

My only complaint is the mild weather, and thus the reduced chances of having a white Christmas. But Theodore, being ever so thoughtful, wanted his children to have a white Christmas, so guess what???? We're FedExing some snow the morning of. Can you believe it? It's supposed to stay white for up to six hours and only costs $11,500—even less than Nana's new ass.

Oh, life is good. I guess we've come to that part in these letters where protocol says we're supposed to go over our medical procedures, talking about new ta-ta's, goiter removals, colonoscopies, and appendectomies . . . so here we go . . .

We've certainly had more than our share of outpatient surgery. Whew! I had a third pair of doorknobs (LOL) installed; far superior to my other two surgeries and so natural looking I'm considering a Web site and a billboard. Picture me—soon to be eighty-eight pounds with a set of double Ds. Cute City, peeps. When I healed from that, I underwent a breast lift, because my motto is simple: if they aren't on the shoulders, they aren't high enough! And Teddy says it gives him something to hold on to when he's had too much single malt scotch. I worried if they were jacked up there so high I might appear freakish, kind of Quasimodo-ish, but my Theodore assured me they are cheerleader perfect. Isn't he great? He swears he's going to stop attending pep rallies at the high school now that he's got what he needs right at home. He sticks around much more since our sweet Angelica, child by my first husband but one Teddy loves as much as or more than our own, turned fourteen.

Speaking of Ted and surgeries . . . now, don't tell, but he had that "enlargement" procedure they keep advertising on the Internet. He finally understood the Lord was trying to tell him something due to the heavy volume of ads we were getting on our computer. Every time one popped up, an ad, that is (LOL), it got more personal. Things like, "Teddy, you're not giving your spouse what she needs most! Inches, buddy. Girth, my friend. Raging orgasms for the lady of the house." Or the one that really hurt him: "Teddy, my boy, all the other men know where their wives' G-spots are. With a skin-tag like yours, you'd be lucky to find her Heavenly Hallway at all!" The nerve of those people! He finally just up and called the company and ordered the services. All I can say is Ted Rocks and Rules!!!

He was so excited about his new and improved "Teddy Tower," formerly known as the "Teddy Tot," that he got brave and told his dentist he was tired (and I'm whispering this) of his dentures. I realize everyone thought his teeth were real, but the truth reared its ugly toothless head during our trip to Belize while yachting our hearts out. Ted had a problem with his snorkeling equipment and his dentures fell to the bottom of the sea. Poor man had a choice: swim up for air, or die trying to fish out a pair of $800 teeth. God love him. I know you all understand that when a man has it going on *down there*, he wants it going on up top, too. Well, the poor darling didn't have the gums to keep his smile up, and none of y'all knew us when he was a crack dealer and all of his precious corn kernel teeth fell out. One by one, bless his heart. Drugs are awful. Remember that. The only good drugs are Botox, Viagra, Prozac, and Phen-Fen. LOL.

The beauty of this whole story is that a wonderful surgeon has implanted the most gorgeous uppers and lowers you've ever seen. Bicuspids to die for. You can see his smile from two blocks away. Each tooth must be an inch and a half long. And then—get this—all the "Plump up your lips, my buddy Ted" ads started flying across the e-mail. Our spam zapper couldn't even get rid of them. He's planning to blow up his lips with collagen in order to cover his whopper choppers. He overheard someone whinnying like a mule one day and hasn't been the same since.

As for our incredible children, they're doing great. Both are getting the new "Homework Pal" from Santa—the cute little robot that will block the door to their rooms and shoot mild to medium electrical currents if they don't finish up class assignments or clean their rooms. Wonderful investment. LOL. LOL! They are still gifted and smarter than all other children, so we are no doubt proud. Angelica and Teddy spend so much time together, it's the sweetest thing you've ever seen. They even go away on stepfather-daughter trips. The other day Angelica said she would have a huge surprise for us in about six months and we just can't wait. Wonder what that could be???

In closing, I'd like to say we've gone ahead and done a bit of charity work. You know . . . giving back to the community,

I believe is what they call it. I have personally hand-stenciled some "will work for low-carb food" signs in the prettiest lettering you ever did see. I've also decoupaged precious coffee tins for their fortified wine collecting. The message I'm trying to send is that it's worth it to pay a little more for the better wines. My hope is the signs and such will bring in more money to buy something with a cork in it. LOL.

I'm also volunteering at Teddy Jr.'s school, reading the Rush Limbaugh newsletter to all the children the principal suspects of having parents who vote for Democrats. The very thought of that makes me shudder even though Ted is a raging liberal, God love the man! I sure do!

Mercy me! The Christmas spirit has struck with a mighty bang at the Worthalots' home and hearth. Merry Christmas, everyone! Hope this letter has lifted your spirits as high as Nana's surgically enhanced ass. LOL! Kiss Kiss. Until next year . . . Remember our family motto: "Nip it, Tuck it! Fix it or Fuck it!" Also remember the lipo wand is the only wand a woman really needs. LOL.

Yours Truly,
The Worthalots

I Wanna Sang!

My granny never drank or smoked until after she birthed Uncle Steve and hit menopause right around the same time.

When she was forty-three the doctors told her she had a tumor. Instead, three months later, she pushed out my uncle. My dad was off in the service and his sister was studying in nursing school.

Meanwhile, Granny suffered a nasty bout of hot flashes and hormonal swings, bless her heart, and this wonderful Church of God lady took up the bottle and Winston Lights.

Thank goodness the drinking didn't last long, but the cig thing would carry on for decades, only she would hide it and say things like, "You know I don't smoke," all the while gray clouds of tobacco smoke puffed from her apron. She'd cup my face with her moist hands that always smelled like Jergens in the white bottle, and later, a trace of tobacco.

That apron was her secret hiding place. All southern girls who smoke and were raised right hide the fact they partake. I'll never forget being in college and all of us sorority girls sneaking into the bathroom, inhaling Virginia Slims Menthol Lights and then stuffing our faces with Velamints.

Granny would wet paper towels and stick them in her

apron. When someone came to the door, she'd toss her cigarette into the ruffled pockets and hope it landed within the soggy Bounty. Only sometimes her apron caught fire.

She and I had a special bond; we'd hold hands and walk from her house on Main Street in Ware Shoals, South Carolina, to the Piggly Wiggly, the only grocery store in the entire town.

"Tell me a secret," she'd whisper, though no one else was around.

"I've got a new boyfriend and Daddy wouldn't like him at all," I'd say and she'd squeeze my hand and smile, wink as if to say no one would know but us.

I was her favorite, but only because I was most like her. I inherited her flaws and her gifts, and she had plenty of both, but was a strong woman who managed to feed her kids even when her husband drank his paycheck and wouldn't come home for days. She was tough and always landed on her feet, making money by keeping others' babies and frying chicken dinners for the shift workers at the mill.

The years didn't just slow my granny down, they dimmed her, changed her, robbed her of these many gifts.

The smoking and small fires continued to the point something had to be done. She was in her late seventies, losing a grasp on reality, and falling down a lot in her home. She'd sit in her Naugahyde recliner, watch her soaps, and smoke. She'd fall asleep and burn holes in the vinyl.

My parents were scared she'd burn the house down between her smoking and running the kerosene heaters so close to the curtains in the wintertime. When she broke her hip the doctors said she couldn't go back home, and thus began the guilty but necessary trip to the nursing home.

She had enough of her faculties to know she wanted to stay home and smoke until time to go fry chicken in heaven and diaper the baby angels.

"I'm sorry, Mama," my daddy and his sister told her. "The doctor advised this was for the best for right now." It broke their hearts they couldn't take Granny home with them, but both had families and couldn't babysit given the nature of her fiery feats and the progression of her dementia.

On the way to the rest home, Granny sat in the car between them, her hair perfectly curled and permed, Avon's Sweet Honesty on her neck, and the valley of her ample bosom dusted with powder from a pink satin puff.

She pouted and stared at the road ahead, not saying much as Daddy and Aunt June drove her to a rest home in South Carolina to begin this new and difficult chapter toward the end of her life.

On the way they stopped at a convenience store for gas and snacks. Daddy needed a Diet Pepsi and Aunt June was probably, at this point, ready for a glass of wine. She got out of the car and leaned into the window where her mother sat rigid and unblinking.

"Mama," my aunt said, "if you want some cigarettes, you tell me right now because they have designated places where you can smoke."

Granny blinked once. "I don't smoke," she said. "You know I don't smoke."

My aunt walked away from the car, was a few steps from entering the store when Granny and her hundred and eighty pounds jumped into Daddy's lap, rolled down the window, and hollered out to her daughter, "June, get me two cartons of Winston Lights."

Once at the rest home, Granny delighted in that she could smoke all she wanted and no one seemed to care. But soon the nurses noticed her danger with all things lit and took away her matches.

One day during a visit, several residents wheeled forth to tattle on Granny.

"She's gonna burn us up in here," they said. "She's always trying to buy matches and lighters off us. Y'all gonna have to do something or ain't none of us gonna live to see our funerals. Ain't gone be no point in wearing our purties if we's burned up like beef jerky."

The staff decided to keep a closer eye on Granny, personally escorting her to the smoking areas. When they weren't looking, Granny would dig through the ashtrays for butts, hiding them anywhere she could on her body.

"We found twelve butts in her bra today," Aunt June said, her voice tired but trimmed with laughter. "And that was while she was wearing it." Several of the butts still had fire, which was my grandmother's ultimate goal—to have fire in her room so she didn't have to walk all the way to the smoking area six corridors away.

"So sad putting lit cigarettes in your bra," Mama sighed. "Can you imagine?"

"Well, no one can say her ta-ta's weren't smokin'," I said and Mama claimed that was trash talk.

She changed the subject. "Granny was brilliant. She concocted an idea that next time they took her to the smoking area, she'd take her purse with her. She was determined to get some fire in her room one way or another so she could chain-smoke in there."

My granny smoked for a while as if everything were normal, but when all eyes had turned away, she tucked a lit cigarette butt in her purse, snapped it shut, and began the slow journey back to her room. She didn't allow for the length of time it would take and suddenly her purse billowed with smoke. The nurses, shrieking and squealing, knocked the purse from Granny's grip and stomped out the fire with their big white shoes.

Poor Granny. Once when Mama came to visit, she noticed her hair looked pitiful. That's the thing about my mama. Being a former beautician and graduate of a cosmetology refresher course at forty, she knew a thing or two about hair.

"It looked awful," Mama said. "It was straight and un-fixed. Her hair used to be her pride and joy. I asked the lady working the beauty shop if they could give her a permanent, but they claimed it was too hard to get her in the chair and I said, 'You put her in the chair and that will lift her spirits.' They took her right away. She looked beautiful."

Over the years Granny adjusted to nursing home living while her mind continued slipping gears, forgetting it was in reverse or park and that it would never kick into drive again.

Even so, my granny was not one to sit still for very long. No matter how uplifting the entertainment or how good the smokes, she was good for half-hour stretches at best before she got the itch to get moving.

Daddy and Aunt June would visit her on weekends, and on most occasions, these outings were quite eventful. One Sunday my daddy accompanied her to church services held in the cafeteria and attended by an assortment of variously clad residents. Some were swaddled in pajamas and dementia. Others rolled into the room in wheelchairs and dignity, many wearing their Sunday best.

At a small podium a woman reverend smiled apprehensively, as if she knew anything could—and probably would—happen. And just as sure as she began with prayer, all sorts of chaos soon broke loose.

"One little woman," my daddy said, "was cursing, saying things you wouldn't believe, taking the Lord's name in vain every other breath. She called the preacher a hussy and hippy. After a while of it, an orderly came and took her away."

"Blessed is he who has regard for the weak," the composed lady reverend thundered, "for the Lord delivers him in times of trouble."

Over in a corner a woman leaned forward in her wheelchair, dentures loose and jutting. She wrinkled up her face and yelled in German toward the podium each time the preacher spoke a word. "Nein! Nicht!"

Undaunted, the reverend continued. "The Lord will sustain him on his sickbed and restore him from his bed of illness."

The woman's German grew louder. "Nein! Dass ich Nicht Lache! I'm still in my bed of illness, fool!"

From somewhere in the wings, a nurse's assistant appeared and escorted from the services the disruptive and disagreeing. But just as soon as the second noisemaker was led down the hallways, another resident took off yelling.

"Guess who had to jump in there next?" my daddy asked.

"Granny?"

"She told the preacher she was ready to 'sang.'"

My grandmother, who rarely missed a church service while still living on the outside, took up where the others left off.

"I wanna sang!" she hollered and my daddy stared ahead and smiled, turning white everywhere but the tips of his ears, which burned red. "When we gonna sang?"

Daddy patted Granny's powdery arm and said, "Mama, we'll sing in a minute."

That did not satisfy her. She swatted him the way she used to when he was a little boy tugging on her apron and wanting another piece of fried chicken, long before the years her apron had become an ashtray.

"I'm ready to sang! When we gonna sang?"

The ever-patient reverend closed her Bible and allowed my grandmother to sing, her voice warbling loudly, as if Jesus was sitting on her right, Billy Graham on her left, and the gates of heaven within walking distance.

It wasn't too many years after that day that my grandmother died. I still miss her and think of her often, can see her face when I look at my own or my daughter's, my aunt's or father's. It's as if she's always with us, immortalized in our half smiles, widened eyes, or in the way we make fusses over babies, even when they aren't our own.

I wrote to the angels shortly after her death, wanting them to know who was coming and what to expect. I only wished I had slipped the letter into her coffin next to the red rose my sister placed by her beautiful face.

Dear Angels:

I guess by now you've met her. Smelled the rich Crisco crust of her fried chicken, the flowers and almonds imparted by her Avon Sweet Honesty and Jergens lotion.

I figure the pearly gates opened with a clank and in swirled Jessie Mae all renewed and shed of her worn-out mind and wasting body as she climbed the stairway to heaven.

I just know the halo crowd had a wonderful time leading her to her Maker and the long-lost kin and friends who'd earlier made the grade and advanced upward. I can see her face, picturing it the way it was before disease dimmed those pewter eyes, alive and anticipatory and asking, "Who's that over yonder?" and, "You reckon they have three meals a day up here?"

I guess you know about the way she was before ascension, when she was my solid, Lane-Bryant-shopping granny who wore a size 18 or 20 and favored taupe work shoes that were far more functional than beautiful. I wonder, have you felt her lap? Did you know it could hold several of her grandbabies at one time? That she never refused us, letting us climb her like an oak, one arm around her neck, our free hand pawing the table heavy with her Bibles, dog-eared and underlined and sliced in sections with slips of scrap paper.

I figure you're aware of her house on Main Street with the big wraparound porch, aluminum sliders, and wooden rockers. The house always seemed mysterious to me: the hardwood floors outdated in an era of wall-to-wall carpet, the glow of fire in a furnace frightening to a child with central heat and air, the black telephone heavy as an anvil.

The bedrooms were like secret hiding places, mattresses way up high and as cold as if taken from the refrigerator and piled with handmade quilts and old blankets.

You realize how hard Granny worked to get that house.

I'm sure that scored her a few heavenly points. For the first years of my daddy's life they'd moved seven or eight times, chased out by rent collectors because Granny's husband guzzled his paycheck. But Granny was smart and learned how to intervene and get to the bank before he could get to the bar. She learned, too, to fend for herself, taking care of three children and making sure that even if they went to school with holes in their shoes, they never went to bed with holes in their tummies.

She fed them well. Fact is, she fed everybody. In my memory Granny will always be a big woman who liked to fry sausage patties every morning, walk to the Piggly Wiggly for iced lemon cookies, and wave at everyone, whether she knew them or not. She liked her church more than anything and would sing loudest of all, skin of her neck powdered and trembling as her voice rose with the chords of the organ.

Tell her, dear angels, if you get a chance, that I can close my eyes and feel her hand, damp in mine as we strolled from town, her walking crooked from hip trouble and lugging paper bags filled with coffee, Jimmy Dean, and those iced lemon cookies. She'd lean over when we were halfway home and say what she always said: "Tell me a secret. You know I'll keep it."

We did this for years, until her mind forgot her children, forgot herself, and looped back in time until once again she was an infant. Silent. Crying. Spoon-fed. Eyes following people around a room the way a baby's follow a rattle or toy. If she knew anything, any of us, there were no signs.

Year by year the weight of the world fell off her shoulders and her big-framed body. By the time we saw her in her maple coffin, smiling regally from a pink satin pillow, she was a size 6.

I'm sure you angels have a sense of humor, so I'll tell you what I said to my aunt June through tears.

"Not many women can say they went to heaven a size 6." My aunt laughed and hardly anyone could take his or her eyes off my grandmother, who was positively radiant, like a queen, only prettier. Every wrinkle she'd earned had somehow vanished and she honest-to-God appeared thirty years younger as she lay forever silenced in this life, probably en route to another.

"If I look that good when I die," I told Mama, "please, have them prop me up on the square downtown for a full two-day viewing."

I'm sure, dear angels, that my granny is busy in heaven, offering her lap to all the children, frying chicken in self-rising flour, and telling harmless secrets to those who'll listen. I'm sure you'll hear her singing to the babies, smell the powder on her neck and bosom, the Avon on her wings.

She'll be the one waving left and right as she walks the roads of eternity.

The lady with the gray clouds rising out of her apron pocket. Or the one with beautiful hair and purse aflame.

Smiling from the Pool Table

My mama is obsessed with death. She just can't wait to die and thinks of little else unless it's going to church, getting ready for church, cooking casseroles for church, or helping others in her church. During the three days a week she's not at church, she reads her Bible and keeps her husband happy with the wifely duty—all in preparation for that one ultimate goal. Meeting the good Lord. It would not surprise me in the least if this sweet woman prayed for the souls on her favorite show, *Big Brother*.

I'll never forget when she called all excited because she'd bought her mausoleum slots. At one point in their humble lives my parents thought being buried in the hard dirt was good enough for them, but when the slick-talking mausoleum salesman called one evening and Daddy had consumed his bourbon allotment, he decided to consider buying a couple of fancy slips in the grand burial bureau.

"Your mama kept saying she didn't want to end up in a sinkhole," Daddy explained. "She saw all those coffins bobbing down the Flint River during that big flood a few years back in Albany, Georgia. She didn't want to have to be buried twice or take a chance on someone seeing her pop out of her casket not looking her best. You know your mama."

Because my father had just retired and wanted Mama to travel all over the world, she decided to get every affair in order for the big Fune. This included choosing the perfect outfit to match the casket and blend with the flowers she anticipated receiving for living such a good and pure life.

The prospect of travel, especially by air, left my mother swamped with fears. She thought of her two daughters. She thought of plane crashes and terrorists, and visions of her funeral would break through these images like a migraine. She didn't trust my sister or me to plan her funeral and was terrified we'd dress her like a spinster and forget her lipstick.

"You girls wouldn't know how to do a funeral," she said.

"I believe we could figure something out, Mama," I said. "There's only so much wiggle room you can allow for a funeral."

"Oh no. A funeral is like a wedding. You've got to plan and organize or the big day will never be memorable. I want to remember my funeral forever. I'm not getting on a plane, thinking of my daughters burying me in something ugly and my hair not fixed right. I want to go out with a bang."

"Ohhhh meee," my father sighed. "Peg, have you ever thought that if the plane goes down, there is no need for a funeral?"

She didn't care to visualize the event, but one doesn't argue with my mama when she's taken a notion to something. It's best to let her have her way and life will continue running smoothly.

"Sam, don't you go ruining my funeral!" she said. "The coffin can be empty. They can just lay my outfit in the casket with an eight-by-ten picture of me coming out of the neck of my dress. Same with you in that nice blue suit with the American flag in the lapel. Only thing I'm worried about is we don't have a decent picture of you. The one I have is what the girls took last Fourth of July when you had that ratty old beard and they hung that 'Will Work for Food' sign over your neck. We'll have to get you a new picture and that's all there is to it."

My father, not the most patient person alive but one who sure tries because he's madly in love with my mother, let her rattle on.

"We can spread these outfits on the pool table before we leave to get on a plane. We can have our Kodaks coming out of our collars and the will next to the cue ball. This way, when we go traveling everything will be taken care of."

He took a long deep gulp from his bourbon and water and shifted the gears of his green leather chair, releasing it to a full recline.

"Just think," Mama said, "how our girls will feel when they come into our house after the plane crashes and see us on the pool table."

My father tried to picture this. He had a vision: his suit laid out where he racked the balls, his head nothing but glossy paper peering from his necktie. He wasn't thrilled. "You mean to tell me that we are putting ourselves on the pool table before we travel every time?"

"I can travel in peace knowing I'm on the pool table with you."

She turned to our father and continued with her instructions. "We need to get the plots first. I want a good location and you know good and well how I feel about sinkholes."

My father had only days earlier received his clock and commendations for more than thirty years of exemplary employment. Not forty-eight hours had gone by when the mausoleum salesman came calling. "I can't believe that I have just retired in good health," Daddy said, "and my first week at home I'm planning my funeral. I'll go tomorrow and hear what this graveside charlatan has to offer. You can come with me, then we can hit the skies."

Mama wasn't about to go. She's a busy woman. It was

bridge day and she has played cards faithfully since I was old enough to remember.

"You will have to go without me. I have to go to my Bloody Mary Bridge Club tomorrow. I just wish they could make a Bloody Mary as good as yours. Theirs are always too thick. Now you just go and get us a nice final resting place. I'm going shopping before bridge for my final outfit, the last set of clothing I'll ever need."

The way she said it you'd have thought she was shopping for a cruise to the Bahamas. I'd never seen her so excited. She called me the day she discovered the outfit, the day she found true love in the mall hanging on a mannequin, a blouse fit to meet Jesus in.

"I went to Belk's and there it stood before my very eyes," she said, rapture in her voice. "I was paralyzed at the sight. That store mannequin looked just like an angel. A beautiful, heavenly white satin blouse and a long white skirt swirled at her feet.

"I stood in awe, visualizing wings and a halo and hugging the good Lord in that blouse." She decided to ditch the former outfit she'd been planning for the big day and upgrade the ensemble to fit with the current trends.

"Now wouldn't that blouse be the perfect outfit in a white satin-lined coffin?"

"Please, Mama. I really don't feel comfortable talking about this." I knew it was futile and that she'd rather discuss her demise than anything on earth. "Why do you dwell on this?"

"I don't know," she said. "I guess because my mother died at thirty and her mother at thirty-one. Makes no sense though since I'm already sixty-four. I just decided when I turned thirty to get ready. I didn't get serious though until your daddy retired and wanted to travel all over the world. He told me, he says, 'Peg. It's not fair that I've seen Germany, France, Italy, Belgium, Denmark, and you haven't. I want to see them again with you. I want to see your sweet eyes taking in everything. And I know I will enjoy it more this time with my sweet bride.'

"He is so good to me. He knows my eyes are baggy but he calls them 'sweet eyes.' Anyway, hon, one of my rules is to never buy unless it's marked down so I go over to the wooden angel to check the price. Seventy-nine dollars. And that is just for the blouse. Heavens, I'm thinking to myself—no pun intended—I can't find a markdown."

Mama said she walked away all pouting and sad. She cruised the mall shopping for clothes she could wear to the French Riviera, Spain, and all the other places of the world she'd yet to see. She said nothing compared to the blouse in the window at Belk's.

"All the other mannequins were ordinary. I kept thinking of the angel in white satin. I could see her as I ate a hot dog in the food court. I felt her presence as though she left the store and was sitting there with me. If I told people what was in my thoughts at times I know they'd have me committed, but I truly believe this angel was walking beside me. We were together for two hours before it dawned on me that I'd heard all my life rules were made to be broken and that includes the don't-buy-unless-on-sale rule."

She figured she already had a skirt at home and she'd save by not buying the one on the mannequin. She also had a party to attend and could wear the satin blouse while she still had a heartbeat, pray she didn't spill something on it, then pack it away until time to lay it on the pool table with her Kodak head.

When Mama searched the rack for her size and couldn't find it, her heart dropped. A salesclerk appeared. "There's no size ten," Mama said.

"Oh yes, there is." The woman beamed. "It's on the mannequin."

Mama watched as the lady stripped the mannequin, placed the garment across her forearm, and followed her to the dressing room. She unlocked the doors and my mother stood in silence with her blouse. She slipped it over her bare skin and sighed. "When I turned around, I saw a cloud of satin and my face was glowing. I felt spiritual and knew this blouse was meant for me. The Lord is good, hon."

Mama cradled her blouse and walked it to the counter, Visa card in hand.

"You must be going to a party," the salesclerk said, ringing up the item, her fingers punching keys.

Mama smiled with confident serenity. "Yes, I am. A party that never ends." The clerk's eyebrows shot up but she said nothing.

With her attire in order, my mother was ready for anything. She joined her biddies during Bloody Mary Bridge Club and couldn't get her mind off her funeral, even as the cards sailed through the air and the conversations kicked into high gear.

As soon as she got home, my dad met her at the door. "How was bridge?"

"Fine. I shopped before we played and you'll love what I bought. You want me to try it—"

"Peg, we need to run on over to the cemetery," he interrupted. "How would you like to be buried in heat and air since you said you didn't want to be buried in a sinkhole?"

"What are you talking about?"

"Peg, you know how you are always cold. Well, when you die you will always have heat."

Mama pondered that for a moment. "Are you saying I'm going to hell?"

"No," he said. "I'm talking about our final resting place. It's not a sinkhole. It's a choice location. A mausoleum."

Mama was explaining all this to me on the phone one night, sounding as thrilled as if she'd bought a beach house. "I have to tell you the truth, Susan. It was beautiful, Oh, they're in the prettiest building with carpeting, central heat and air, and bathroom facilities. Your dad and I won't need a thing. Oh, and guess what? We put the whole thing on Visa and earned Frequent Flyer miles. What about that?"

"I guess it's good, but I really don't think you'll be needing—"

"Mercy, I have to tell you the truth," she interrupted, "it did have a downside to it."

"And what was that?"

"I smelled the formaldehyde. But I'll let that one slide. At least there's a restroom and I'll never be cold."

On the way home from the cemetery my parents turned toward each other and died laughing.

"We each knew what the other was thinking," Mama said. "Heat, air, bathrooms, a chapel, and carpeting. A far cry from six feet in the ground."

When they got out of the car, Mama ran inside the house to try on the blouse she'd bought for burial. As she stared at the garment nestled inside the shopping bag, she had second thoughts.

"I decided to wait. We were going to a weekend party with other engineers and their wives and I wanted to see your daddy's reaction when I wore it for the first time. I knew I wouldn't get a reaction the second time."

When the night of the party finally arrived and Mama put on the blouse for Daddy, he had the fit she anticipated.

"He said I looked prettier than I'd ever looked in my life. When I got to the party, I got lots of compliments. One girl named Beth went on and on. I knew her sister had just died of breast cancer and her mother had recently been diagnosed with lung cancer. She was real sad and this was her first outing after her sister's death. She was so sweet and couldn't stop talking about my blouse. We sat with them and she just kept talking about how her mother would just have a fit over my blouse. We ate and chitty-chatted. I didn't think a thing about it."

That night Mama took off the blouse and returned it to the satin hanger, tucking it gently into the protective bag. She slid into bed with my daddy and was soon asleep. But hours later as the moon climbed and night wore on, she awakened wide-eyed with her heart wildly beating.

"Something lifted me straight out of that bed," she said,

"and I got up to check on my blouse. I'm not sure why but I got it out of the bag and set it out on the table, then went back to bed."

She had a final thought before sleep overcame her. *This blouse isn't meant for me.*

The next morning the wives met for breakfast while the men held meetings. Mama searched all over for Beth but couldn't find her. A few minutes later she came through the doors and Mama handed her the bag. "Here's something for your mother."

Beth opened it, saw the blouse, and started crying. "I can't believe you would do this. Are you sure?"

"Yes," my mother said, a loving hand on Beth's arm. "This was meant for your mother."

More than a year passed until the two met again. Beth informed Mama that her mother had died and was buried in that white satin blouse.

My own mother had a sense of peace and closure. "The whole time I felt like that angel in the mall was walking beside me, she *was*. But not for *me* to be buried in her clothes, but for me to see that Beth's mama got the blouse."

After I told my mom she was the sweetest woman alive, a burning question got the best of me. "What are you planning to lay out when y'all go to Italy since your blouse is already six feet under?"

"I've got a bunch of cute clothes," she said. "Your daddy and I are going to the portrait studio next week, so if we die in a plane crash, don't be sad. You'll see us smiling from the pool table."

Eye Cues

The truth is, I tried to kill the Diaper Genie. I never realized how intellectually challenged I was until I gave birth and all the baby gear began arriving, parts unassembled.

The car seat was bad enough. I drove with my fresh catch buckled in with prayer and loose straps to the police department, honked the horn, and two cops came rushing to the car, badges catching the blinding October sun.

"See my baby?" I cried. "He's still got the birth cheese on him in spots and I don't even know how to buckle him in safely. They don't explain it on the box. I got the Spanish instructions but no one put the English instructions in. Or maybe my husband threw it away during one of his cleaning fits."

They knew they had a hysterical and hormone-swinging new mother in their midst. "Why's the little fellow hanging upside down?" one of them asked as I turned to see my infant's head flopped over and his tiny body suspended by the very straps designed to protect him from harm.

I boo-hooed from the sight of him and from staying up two nights straight, my faced pressed into the crib slats making sure he didn't quit breathing. Within minutes they had fixed my new baby, tucking him snugly into safety.

"They have a parenting class at the Y," one said and I wanted the entire parking lot to open up and swallow me whole.

"Thank you so much. My mother's going to teach me all she knows." They must have figured I had spent my life in special ed, but the truth is, most of those students could put things together far better than I could.

If it required more than three steps to the process, forget it. The stroller was a nightmare, the playpen an abomination, but the mother of all bad gadgets was that fiendishly wicked atrocity called the Diaper Genie.

I thought that after two days trying to figure it out and failing, I could handle anything my husband brought into the home, including household appliances. He frequently wore them out, abusing them to death with his obsessive washings and overloadings, smashing the giant pet sofas into the washer and setting the dryer on the hottest cycle—Scorch and Torch.

The old dishwasher had a terminal illness from swallowing too many household objects and from overuse, and the new one arrived, all but giving my husband complete euphoria. I thought we might need to medicate him.

The Sears men wheeled it in and hooked it up. The rest was easy, right? Load and press Pot-Scrubbing Super-Duper wash?

I never would have guessed the simple-looking box would turn into an issue of grown-up shape sorting. But loading the dishwasher did indeed become a big deal in our house, a precise science requiring a Ph.D. in physics or engineering.

I was feeling rather wifely one evening and decided to load the new Whirlpool, packing it with plates and saucers, cups, glasses, utensils, pots, pans, and infant toys. At least, I figured, this was better than letting them ooze and grow life forms in the sink.

Big mistake! It seems man and dishwasher have a relationship based on some hidden truth about the inner meaning of appliances. My own mate, Tidy Stu, has his theories and strategies regarding cleaning and domestic chores.

Tidy Stu, a man who organizes a drawer by dumping the entire contents into the garbage, thinks there's one way—and one way only—to load a dishwasher. That there are no shades of gray.

One evening as I sat on the floor holding a wooden spoon and playing "Kill the Diaper Genie" with the children, I heard thunderous noises, crashing and banging, hair-raising sounds that meant one thing and one thing only. He was at it again. Rearranging the dishwasher to suit his neuroses.

He mumbled under his breath, puffing out snorts of disdain, then marched toward me, cheeks red and shining, a spaghetti noodle splattered on his T-shirt.

"When are you going to learn to properly load the dishwasher?" he said, hands up in the air, granules of Cascade on his forearms. "Looks like a chimp loaded it."

I emitted monkey noises, scratched my fanny, and he got even madder. "You don't go around putting a bowl here, a plate there, and hope for the best," he said. "There's a space for everything."

I brought the issue up at the office one day.

"Sure, all men can load the hell out of a dishwasher," said Tuck Early, circulation director. "I haven't met a woman yet who could do this thing right."

"Didn't you take Dishwashing 101?" asked Brent, a graphic designer and hum-and-strum singer on the side. "Everyone knows there's a certain way to load one."

I asked a man who writes thought-provoking editorials and has managed to stay married a long time if there was even a kernel of truth to this.

"My wife and I were discussing it just last night," he said. "I didn't read the instruction manual, which, being a man, goes against my credo. If it fits, God intended it to be put in the dishwasher."

He and I load dishwashers similarly. If we find an un-claimed spoke or space, we fill it. Pure and simple. If only the Diaper Genie had been so easy and good-natured.

Tidy Stu, the Wizard of Symmetry, stormed back into the kitchen making more noise than a bulldozer operator as he re-arranged my handiwork and put everything into his scientific order.

While it may be true that certain male types are better at dishwasher know-how than certain female types, put those same men in front of a washing machine and all their smarts swim down the drain with the Arm & Hammer.

Take Tidy, for example. He either packs our meager ma-chine so full that some items never even get wet, or a single garment will float on a sea of foam. There's no in-between, no normal-load mentality. Give him a laundry basket and any-thing goes.

Cold Water Only. Say what?

Dry Cleaning Recommended. Not for the poor.

Lay Flat to Dry. What, and junk up the house?

Warning: Do Not Overload. No way I'm having four loads left after this.

And he wonders why all his underwear is Pepto pink, why we keep giving the Maytag men enough money to hit Cancún every winter. He wonders why we've had six washing ma-chines in fifteen years of marriage and nearly as many dish-washers.

"At least I scrub the food out of the plates before I put the dishes in," I said. "Your ex-girlfriend didn't. She says a dish-washer is meant to grind food like a disposal. What do you think about that? Sounds chimpish to me."

"I think women shouldn't be allowed near dishwashers."

It didn't take him long to decide our newest model was in-efficient and he called Sears for an upgrade. One evening the poor old broken-backed deliveryman reappeared, wheeling in a brand-new trilevel unit that requires one to wallow on the floor to load the bottom. No way I would even attempt to get near that contraption. No way.

"I'm on strike," I announced. "Either get rid of that dishwasher or I'm getting a room at the Baymont."

"The Baymont?"

"It's a new hotel that's both affordable and has an indoor pool and hot tub plus free breakfast 'til eleven and a *USA TODAY* for every guest."

"Great. Leave a number."

"I'm serious. No more loading the dishwasher." He shrugged and waltzed into the kitchen to admire the new appliance, probably taking out his new digital camera to shoot it from every angle and e-mail the photos to friends as if it were a Playmate of the Month. He did the same thing with our smooth-top oven, and I would catch him late at night gently running his hands over the flat burners.

To be quite honest, I'd rather have a sink filled with hot lemony suds and a window where I can watch life as the wind moves it through the leaves and the children's hair. I love to plunge my hands in that warm soapy water and solve problems as I scrub macaroni and cheese or broccoli casserole from the bowls that nourished my beloveds.

"We had to have this," Tidy said. "You know good and well the other one was skipping the rinse cycle and leaving grit on the dishes."

"I didn't know they made three-tiered dishwashers. It's like a high-rise hotel. I'm scared to death of it."

"It's the best you can buy."

"But the door . . . why . . . it's a mere inch from the ground. The only creature that could possibly load the thing without rupturing a vertebra is a centipede. My back's bad enough from picking crumbs and dog dribbles from the floor. I'll be happy to scrape plates and stack them on the sink, but there is no way I'll bend that low to slip in a cookie sheet. It's not worth it. This baby is all yours."

His face puffed with anger. "This is the number-one dishwasher in America," he shouted, looking eerily like the Juice Man, a televised fright with eyebrows thicker than most mustaches, a creature who hawks his juice machines and scares my babies to death. "It's number-one rated! Check out the features."

"I'm not setting foot near it."

"You have no taste."

"I'm not ready for a hip replacement or back brace."

"Maybe it takes a special type of brain to do this right."

"Listen up, hon," I said. "You've already ruined a half dozen washing machines by stuffing them with clothes, dog beds, and king-size comforters. Super Wash doesn't mean you can throw in five baskets of laundry, then sit on the lid to get it to shut."

"It was a faulty washer."

"All of them will malfunction if you abuse them."

"I'm not talking about a washer. I'm trying to show you how to use the new dishwasher."

"You didn't let me pick it out, so why should I have to read a forty-two-page manual on the thing?"

"It's the best on the market."

"Take me off the market. Consider yourself its sole parent. I'm giving you full custody. I don't even want visitation. As I've said, I'll be at the Baymont."

He stood there staring, then grinned and waved bye in his infuriating stubbornness. "If you love dishwashers this much, I can quit my job at the paper and you can wear a pair of cushioned shoes with Dr. Scholls pads and sell the sons a' bitches at Best Buy. You can pose by these number-one rated units until the bliss is overwhelming and your feet swell up like Pillsbury Grands."

"Do you have PMS?"

I picked up the Diaper Genie and pretended to throw it at the new dishwasher. "I'm sorry," I said, trying to be nicer, "but

I cannot justify back surgery just to get the burned cheese off my Pyrex."

"You flick it up with your foot," he said, about the unit's ground-hugging door. He deftly kicked his sock-footed lower leg and managed to position the door upright.

"My black boots will have that door ruined in a week," I said.

"This is the only one around that has three racks," he continued, growing euphoric. "You can put all your frying pans and casserole dishes on the bottom so you can get them clean. No way I'm getting rid of this, 'cause it's by far the best one."

At that point in life, pretty close to the midway mark, I began doubting my intellectual abilities. The baby gadgetry was the first test, then the dishwasher, and finally, the math word problems my son was bringing home that I couldn't solve. I had a suspicious feeling my I.Q. was lacking in the portion of the test where one does calculations and figuring, the section that secretly predicts one's later success or failure with appliances.

Some of us possess more personality than logic, more charm than scholastic gymnastics.

Take for instance my little girl. The first parent-teacher conference I had with her was in kindergarten where her no-nonsense instructor said, "Your child knows only two of her shapes and six of the smaller letters."

"She's only in kindergarten," I said ever so sweetly. "Hey, it's the first two weeks of school. And she knows all her *big* letters."

"She only knew *two* shapes," the teacher continued, about to rattle off my wee one's lack of knowledge when it came to triangles and rectangles.

That's right, I thought and wanted to tell the woman the two shapes my daughter *really* knows. *She knows Standard, which is a woman with a back fanny. And Nonstandard, which includes women with fannies in the front as well.*

I held my tongue as Mama would have advised and the teacher pointed to a book pasted with numbers. "Your child knew three numbers," she said, raising both of her eyebrows as if to say, *What have you been doing all summer while the other moms attended Read with Pride every Wednesday at the public library and bought the Jump Start and Leap Frog series? You musta been sitting around watching* Lifetime *and popping pain meds.*

"It's different with the second child," I explained to the teacher. "We wanted her to enjoy her years at home as much as possible and didn't push her."

"Well, it would seem to me you could have at least read her a book, maybe gotten her interested in a bit of *Sesame Street*. We have children from the worst backgrounds you can imagine who know their shapes and letters from watching *Elmo* every morning."

Well, la-di-da. "We thought kindergarten preparation was just learning to share and say 'thank you,' and 'please, ma'am.' That's how it was in my day."

"Well, your day is long gone," she said and cracked her first smile. I gazed at the paper in front of me where dozens of numbers swirled at random. Some were even three digits.

"Why are these on here, like 58, 644, and 179?"

"Oh, well now . . . those . . . those are for our smarter children. Those who at least saw half a dozen episodes of *Sesame Street* or went to Read with Pride day at the library."

Well, I'm just so glad my daughter is normal that I don't care how many shapes or little letters she knows. There's no need for little letters anyway. I knew my baby girl was brilliant and just tricking those teachers. My angel was born an old woman. She exited the womb an ancient hundred-year-old lady with more wisdom than most of us will have in a lifetime. She came out asking for homemade yeast rolls and a set of knitting needles. She loved Lawrence Welk and Bob Hope. She watched Red Skelton with her grandpa. Those were her idols. Not the damned Teletubby flamers.

"She can load a dishwasher, my baby girl," I said, but the teacher didn't seem impressed. "She puts the forks in one side and the stemware in the other—"

"Here's a packet of supplemental learning materials. Don't let it collect dust."

Not long after that conference, my sister in Rich City, Georgia, called to let me know her seven-year-old son was a genius who "blew his California Achievement Test right off the charts."

"Wow," I said. "Could he help with my kid's word problems?"

"Oh, heavens yes. He scored at the tenth grade level in math. I just wonder where he gets it. We were cute but not the brightest bulbs GE ever made. I've been tempted to take one of those I.Q. tests on the Internet because I bet he gets it from me, not his daddy."

The next evening she sent an e-mail with an I.Q. test attached. I knew right off she wouldn't have mailed it had she not scored in the "Blazing Genius" range. The fifteen-minute test featured thirty-two true-or-false and multiple-choice questions. Over the years I had asked my mother about my I.Q. scores in childhood, and she always said, "Y'all have never been tested to my knowledge."

I knew she was hiding something and didn't want to sabotage our potential by letting us in on a secret: that we were two neurons short of qualifying for the primate program.

I stared at the test. Then I took it. My heart skittered and palpitated. My hands perspired. About fifteen minutes later, I had completed the questions. The news was grim. Beyond grim. In bold type was my two-digit score—75. So this is what Mama had been hiding. So this explains the remedial math, the Diaper Genie failure, and why Mama never had to cover up naughtiness with such words as "brilliant," "bored," or "off the charts and completely unchallenged, my oldest daughter."

I called her to report the deficiencies. Later, my sister and I compared scores. She informed me she's a bona fide genius and I informed her I'm "struggling but happy." Trainable and educable. Chimplike. Unable to perform certain domestic tasks such as working Sears appliances or assembling bitchy Diaper Genies.

That night I took another look at the test. The 75, I discovered, was only one part of the score and the total number was at the top of the page in faint pastel type. Not that I felt any smarter with three digits rather than two.

Shortly after that testing episode, I was Googling around on the Net, and another I.Q. test popped up, daring me to take it and see what the world had in store for my particular brand of genius. I thought, what the heck, and completed the questions. I never would have taken that second test had I not been trying to prove to Tidy Stu that intelligence has nothing to do with loading a dishwasher properly. I was just flat sick of him asking me every night which chimp loaded the Whirlpool.

"I guess it was the same chimp you'll have to beg for a hand job," I'd say out of sheer meanness.

As I finished this particular test and hit the Enter key, the screen flashed with an ad claiming the I.Q. company had matched my intelligence with that of available men in the area. Oh, Lord.

I scrolled down to see what types of manhood awaited should Tidy Stu decide to leave me for the OxiClean Scrubmate of the Month. As soon as I saw the fellers . . . yes, these were fellers . . . I nearly collapsed in a pile of pity.

Woe to the woman who scores a number on an I.Q. test to bring in the likes of Backward boB, from Hootin' Gootin', North Carolina, a man who says "the best things in life are found in prison," and was photographed in a Skoal cap and white tank, sweat stains soaking the chest for added sex appeal.

I checked my I.Q. score again. "Word Warrior," the test

had said, suggesting pairings with six men from this region I'd dare say didn't even know where to find a dictionary. How much can a girl do with a man seeking a "Purtay Thang" to decorate his "two-seater moped"?

He was followed by a feller in a cowboy hat accessorized with a photo collage of every animal one might find flattened on American roadways. His ad says he's into "taxidermy, baseball, and wants someone to snuggle with after a long day of persevering critters. I even own a Whirlpool dishwasher with three levels," he wrote and I quickly exited his site.

Feeling doomed and dumb, I called my bright but normal son into the room and asked him to help me take a third I.Q. test. I knew he'd get the math part right, thus increasing the score enough that I'd be matched with respectable human beings. A girl cannot go to bed thinking she should have married a roadkill specialist or a man with a two-seater moped. It's just not well tolerated. It could trigger a nervous breakdown.

My child and I zipped through the questions and then clicked Submit Score, hitting the semigenius jackpot. I anxiously waited for these Top Notch brainy men to flash up on the screen, knowing they'd be scientists and specialists, philosophers and inventors.

Wrong!

There was "Five Toes in the Sand" looking to "hang ten with the woman of my dreams." And there was "Why are we here? Want to know more?" a man in full golf swing and pondering face, proving only that he has plenty of pretension and enough cash to pay a greens fee.

Backward boB may be a better catch than I had earlier thought. I'll bet he can't load a Whirlpool or GE or anything other than a Smith & Wesson.

From here on out, I'm done with I.Q. tests. It really doesn't matter since they don't etch your score on your tombstone. It reminds me of dieting. What's the real point unless you get paid millions to wear a Victoria's Secret thong and parade your lanky skeleton on world stages?

I mean, really. The bottom line is simple: Ted Bundy was a genius. And Forrest Gump a peach.

At least I'm smart enough to have taken the Diaper Genie, decoupaged the barrel-like gizmo, and placed it on the hearth as an antique butter churn. Now that's called using your brain. Let's see a chimp do that.

Gooooood Miiiiiiilk!

I don't live in the Bible Belt.

I live in the Bible Bra.

Never had I encountered so much meddling as when people discovered I was still nursing a child who sported eight teeth, a head full of hair, and the ability to string sentences.

"Goooooood miiiiiiiilk!" she'd sing in her southern voice as she pawed the blouse and tried to fish out the goods.

When I'd nurse her on a crackly vinyl couch in some smelly bathroom in the mall, people would stop and stare. By their appalled reactions one might assume I was putting a teenager to breast, not a twenty-month-old toddler.

One day I was in a department store restroom, discreetly nursing to the percussion of farting and other "ladylike" bathroom blasts. The old sofa by the stalls served as an alternative to whipping the nack-nackers out in front of all the old men who stroll the mall to pass time and ogle nubile teens as their prostates and Pacemakers fire into arrhythmias.

I had a friend who enjoyed riling up these poor men, and she'd unfurl both her dead-fish breasts and place two of her triplets to nipples as shredded as long, ragged cigarette ash.

I knew enough from Mama's histrionic teachings that nursing in front of the opposite sex would get you kidnapped and raped and possibly even dismembered and you'd be left for dead with nothing on but a torn shirt and not found for three to six weeks, at best. "So don't do it." That was her advice and I took it, most of it.

Ladies tromped in and out as I nursed in the bathroom; they'd glance at my daughter and me, and then quickly turn away. One woman walked over, hovered, and stared with disdain.

"How old is that child?" she said sharply, placing her parcels on the counter.

"She's in middle school," I lied, kissing the top of my daughter's head. The woman made some muffled comment just as the water came rushing from the faucet.

"You earthy types will do anything to feel good, won't you?"

Mercy be to God. "Earthy? Can you not see these two coats of mascara? My lip liner accentuating the gloss? I'm nursing my child so she won't be dumb or sickly. I'm giving up the future of my own breasts, knowing when it's all said and done, suckled and emptied, they will look like two little puffs of abandoned skin, empty of firmness and vitality. This, so that my darling baby can have the best start in life with extra I.Q. points and fewer boogery episodes. I had the epidural and need to make up for some lost brain cells according to a man named . . . Oh, never mind."

The offended party click-clacked in her black pumps and yanked her friend from the stall and they both stood over me as my baby sucked and smacked and paused in gratitude to say, "Goooooood miiiiiiiilk!"

"I just think it's pretty sick to keep them on the breast past six weeks old," she said to her friend who was trying to zip her skirt. "It looks weird. These young mothers today nurse 'til the kids go to junior high, and I read where their panties get all wet when they do. I watch *Oprah*, young lady." She turned to her friend, who had a blank stare on her face and was still fiddling with her zipper. "We had a neighbor lady growing up next to us and she kept her son on that long-as-a-forearm tit of hers for eight years. Eight years! I don't need to tell you he was never picked for the softball team and ended up becoming a champion quilter, now, do I?"

"Ma'am, it's not like I'm getting a thrill from this. I mean, you may have perverted leanings but not me. Would you please excuse us? Why don't you just mosey on back to house-wares and pick yourself out a nice new skillet? Maybe wander toward lingerie and buy a granny gown or some underpants you could also use as a gas grill cover."

"Bitch!" her friend said, pointing in my face. "I'm sick of you modern mothers whipping out your titties for the whole world to see. Just last week at the Rolling Hills pool some thirty of those Le Leche League hookers came prancing down to the pool with their kids sucking up a storm on their breasts. One woman had on nothing but her bikini bottoms and a preschooler on one breast and a kid who looked ten or twelve on the other. He'd eat a piece of his K.F.C., then lift up his mama's titty and have a swig. It was sick. S. I. C. K!"

"I'm in a bathroom, ma'am. Not in the middle of the mall or pool." I was close to adding, *I'm in a stinking doodytar-ium where the odors from rumps like yours are not adding to the ambience of my daughter's dining pleasure,* but my mother would have disowned me had she heard such rude-ness.

Finally, the women left, the air heavy with sighed disdain. Prudes.

Oddly, it's not just strangers who offer unsolicited commen-tary concerning the goings-on of others' glands. It's friends and relatives, including—and especially—my mother, who chirped the entire second year of my daughter's feedings, "When are you gonna wean that child? We are proper southern women and it's not what we believe in, Susan. One year . . . well, I could live with that, though even that seemed excessive and border-line vulgar."

"Vulgar?" I said. "What is so vulgar about feeding a baby from the very organ nature intended it to be fed by?"

"Nature?" she shouted. "Nature? Is that the lord of your choice these days? What happened to God? Why didn't you say as 'God intended'? You are living up in that hippy town in the mountains where anything goes, and look here . . . it's af-fected you. Nobody nurses a child with teeth. Nobody. Not even Yankees."

My parents and in-laws were horrified when they saw Baby Girl tugging at my blouse, reaching into a battered brassiere as if digging for popcorn at the bottom of a bag.

When my toddler purrs, "Miiiiiilk," in that little North Carolina accent of hers, you can almost feel the wind from the head-shaking these relatives deem their duty to submit.

How could they be offended by such an adorable act, such a natural, loving expression of motherhood? How could they not know that this is good for her, good for me, good for soci-ety? Good for the thighs.

"Not only is it sick and perverted to nurse past, say, three to six months of age, but you'll ruin your breasts," the nursing naysayers said.

"Fine."

"They'll hang like rocks in socks."

"Like Uncle Ted's balls," an aunt offered. "He looks like a tired old ox from behind. Every time he bends over I have to see those flapping tentacles."

"Testicles."

"Shaped more like tentacles at his age."

For their information, I tell them, I have a plastic surgery fund started. "I've been saving five years to have them lifted and plumped up when the time comes. For now, my damage is their gain."

"How ridiculous. Plastic surgery. That's for hussies and the mindless."

"That's what strippers do. Get plastic boobs," another aunt said. "No point in having them unless you're doing whore's work. The devil's work."

"Well, when I get them, I'll probably do a bit of stripping. I hear Croaker's Rest Home is into pet therapy and experimental programs. They could probably use a middle-aged stripper. I could call myself Nurse Goodbody. They would be delighted when enema time came around."

My kin walked off to pour wine and forget I was perched within the family tree.

One summer when the baby was fifteen months old, she stayed with my parents overnight and Mama did her best to pry the child from Playtex. She offered my precious child Coke, Kool-Aid, Mr. Pibb, chocolate milk, and other *nutritious* beverages. It wouldn't have surprised me if they had poured a Coors Light into her bottle. Anything to get the child's mouth away from an exposed nipple.

Later in the day as the three of them were out by the pool—baby in Dad's lap, Mother in the next seat—my parents discovered just how attached to the breast this child was.

My daddy had removed his shirt and was slouching just enough so that his chest drew interest. He has one of those male builds that when hunched over in just the right way, resembles a sturdy lesbian woman with a fairly good set of 46-B knockers. My baby saw that cleavage and dove in for the kill. In her eyes lactation seemed possible. Here was a fleshy breast with a nipple. She leaned in for a closer look, threw her head back, and split the air with a curdling scream.

"She saw those old black hairs and red moles a-sproutin' and couldn't stop crying," my mother said, laughing until tears filled her eyes. She fell off her chair, as she does when

mirth overcomes her, and slithered to the pool terrace, howl-
ing and saying she was going to wet her pants.

I told my mother and her troop of nosy hens that the
American Academy of Pediatricians, not to mention La Leche
Leaguers all over the world, agree that breast is best for as
long as a mother and child feel comfortable with the arrange-
ment.

"They're nothing but Communists," my daddy shouted.
But he says that about everybody, even Democrats and Episco-
palians.

It took a while, but finally I buckled to pressure and tried
telling my child, "All gone," or "No more gooooood miiiiilk,
sweetheart." She'd look at me with sad brown eyes, and that
was all it took to give up and give in.

Not long after her second birthday and following a few
sleepless nights of her tugging and pecking as if I were roadkill, I decided to try weaning, first employing the traditional
and doctor-recommended methods such as tapering off or
shortening the feedings.

When this didn't work, I listened to the voices of unreason.

"Put a little vinegar on them," my mother-in-law said, so I
did and it worked.

For about five minutes.

"Dab the nips with Tabasco," someone else said and I considered calling the police on them for child abuse.

The next day, remembering how my baby cowered upon
seeing the Abominable Snowman in the *Rudolph* movie, I had
a great idea and took a pack of washable Magic Markers and
drew the creature on my chest—one abomination on each
side, jagged teeth included, hoping she'd be deterred.

It worked.

For about five minutes.

After that she started laughing and pointing, saying,
"Thnowman," as she bobbed her head toward the source.
"Thnowman wants goooood miiiiiiiilk." I washed quickly be-

fore someone called Social Services. Seemed the mural method wasn't going to work either.

The following morning as I sat in the rocker trying to relax, she toddled up with a fist full of markers and a bright pink Popsicle-smeared smile. She yanked my blouse to the side, pushed a red Magic Marker into my hand, and said, "Thnowman. Draw thnowman, please."

Now I've got two problems.

Not only a child who wants a meal at the mammary, but one who also requests art and atmosphere to complete the dining experience.

Leasing Life's Blessings

One of life's hardest moments arrives on a sidewalk. It approaches faster than a parent can prepare, this day when a child who was just yesterday a baby, steps away from our arms and into those of her first teacher.

I didn't want to let go.

Late August is a time of giving up, the sun tiring and summer a season parents must bid farewell too early. It is also a time of turning points, of opening hands as if in offering: here is my little boy, my only daughter.

Please, our hearts say and we suppress the voice that begs, *Treat him well, love her as if she were your own.*

This morning I turned in the keys of summer and with them my little boy's days. This child who would awaken at the sound of his own laughter would spend the first day of his life in a new setting, one that didn't include a daddy who dined with him daily at the cafeteria, shredding and hand-feeding him tender strips of chicken, bites of trout picked for bones. A man who every day bought our boy chocolate chip cookies, but only if he ate all of his broccoli.

They spent the afternoons roaming the mall, throwing pennies in fountains while I held down the day job that paid our doctor and dental visits, the job we relied on for insurance and stability.

My son wouldn't have these things today. Nor would he have the loving grandparents who thought his every move a milestone, his every smile worthy of film and flashbulbs.

Today, my little boy, my only child at that point in our lives, entered preschool.

I felt as if life were speeding by so fast I couldn't catch the handles to stop or slow it down. I mourned. For the inability to lasso the hands of the clock. For the baby who was growing up and out of a mother's arms. I mourned for a lost era, those days we would never again call our own. Days when I could smell sunshine and chlorine in his tousled hair, Hi-C on his breath. The days I could hold his hand and know his world: mud and chocolate, syrup and watercolors, even a tiny callus from playing on the monkey bars and climbing rope swings.

I also worried. Would he cry? Would he make friends? Would the teacher wipe his nose and tears or ignore and ho-hum him as just another pupil occupying a chair, another child with bangs and Spiderman shoes and a laminated bumblebee name tag?

I wasn't sure about this new life, this latest milestone. Some stones, I reasoned, weren't ready for turning. Let the moss grow, the ferns, the dirt anchor them to the earth.

Couldn't we keep him home one more year? Why did we fall to the pressures of jump-starting our babies into little thinkers and doers so soon?

I realized, as I held the Lion King underwear for him to step into, the life he'd step out of. He put on his favorite red pants and I made sure he chewed his Flintstone vitamin. Dino, always Dino.

During the weeks leading up to this day, I felt confident. I had driven my boy past the church day care center many times, showing him the tire swings and tricycles, the jungle gym and plastic slides. "You're going to have so much fun," I said, taking my voice up a couple of octaves. "This is going to be a wonderful adventure.

"And see there?" I continued babbling, pointing to the big yellow arches behind the center. "If you get lonely, just look out the window and you can see McDonald's where Nana and Poppy take you for ice cream."

I felt as if we had prepared, my son and I. We shopped together, picking out clothes and shoes, me in that phony voice that had found my throat the past few weeks. I'd pitch ideas to him like unsure fastballs.

"Ohhhh," I said. "This will be so nice to wear to play school." Our family had changed the name from preschool to play school, hoping it would ease the transition.

I felt sure I'd be ready on that August morning, but all was erased as that day dawned gray and rainy, as if the sky mourned with me.

Like a fragile drawing on an Etch-A-Sketch, my confidence vanished, replaced by webs of fear and uncertainty. I packed my camera, embarrassed upon entering the classroom to be the only mother with a camcorder and a thirty-five-millimeter slung over one shoulder, my child over the other, clinging like an octopus and whimpering against my heart.

The teachers were both kind and encouraging, but my boy didn't shake loose, even with their bribes of finger paints and cookies. He clamped tighter, pressing his tear-streaked face in my collarbone, and all my preparations unraveled like a weak seam.

"Just three more minutes," he whined. "Just three more minutes, please, Mommy, please."

And so I stayed, long enough to see the smiles on the preschool teachers' faces replaced with a hint of exasperation. *Here we go,* they must have thought. *Another cling-on. This one's going to be difficult.*

The questions came. "Does he nap?"

"No. He won't at home." More looks exchanged between the two teachers.

"Did you bring a blanket and pillow?" one of the ladies asked, using a voice so sweet I imagined children following her eagerly, like a dozen tiny shadows. I noticed a hamster spinning on its wheel in an aquarium near the window. The place seemed cheerful enough.

"Mrs. Reinhardt? Did you bring a blanket and pillow?"

My face grew hot and I could have fainted on the spot. How could I not have thought to bring my baby boy a blanket, a pillow with the scent of home, a soft cuddly animal to grip in my absence?

The women sensed my embarrassment and saved me. "It's OK," one said. "The first day is usually like this." I felt my son's hands clawing my neck, the nails he hates for us to clip digging into my skin. "It gets much easier in another day or two. You'll see."

They talked my child down from my arms as one would a cat from the high branch of a tree. For a moment he stood at my feet, eyes big and looking into mine with a single question both of us understood. *Why?*

For that moment I realized anything could happen. I could scoop him up and run out the door. I could take him to the Piccadilly Cafeteria for broccoli and chicken, to the Disney store where he could sink his round sticky cheeks into a mountain of Mickeys, Pinocchios, and Winnie the Poohs. We could ride up and down escalators and throw money in the fountain.

As I stood lost in thought, a sense of motion underfoot jarred me back into this world of letting go, a world of leasing my loved one to a system that's supposed to work. A system designed to teach and love, to show the way of the world— one watercolor, one puppet show, one letter of the alphabet at a time.

The motion belonged to my son who'd stepped forward and away from me and all that was familiar. He slipped out of sight under a Little Tykes playhouse. When his sweet face emerged, his lips formed a smile. He ran for a rubber dinosaur and climbed the tiny slide to the playhouse.

I took a picture and walked quietly out of the room and onto the sidewalk. I stood there for a long moment in the early morning sun before walking to my car where I laid my head on the steering wheel and cried for an hour.

With my daughter, born nearly six years later, it was different. When I sent her to preschool we stood on that same sidewalk, watching her take those first steps of independence. While she clutched a teddy bear, I grabbed the last wisps of an era that had embezzled time. It's unfair how quickly it sneaks up on you, stealing the babies and replacing them with little people who carry backpacks and Power Puff Girl lunch boxes. She let go with no effort, the confidence of a child born second.

A couple of years later when yet again August arrived, letters from the school appeared in our mailbox, all but ending summer. The letters introduced us to my girl's kindergarten teacher who gave a pep talk about what a great year she had planned, along with a sheet of paper listing the school supplies she'd need.

I promised myself that with this last baby—forever emptying my womb and filling my heart—I wouldn't sob. The tears that fell with her brother wouldn't fall on my face as she marched into kindergarten with her Kim Possible backpack and her clunky baby diva shoes, her long hair flying in a mess of waves and tangles.

She will stomp ahead of me, I said to myself, knowing this child the way one does her youngest when a mother realizes there won't be any more to come.

She is a mother who hangs on longer, stretching this last baby's childhood beyond its borders. She may even break a few rules by sleeping next to her child on some nights, inhaling her baby's dreams as the cool breath leaves her lips. She studies the fringe of dark eyelashes fluttering in a slice of moon, and she longs to freeze time. Just one more year.

That's all I wanted. One more year to wake up late, feeling her warm hand on my face and seeing her smiles even before I opened my eyes.

I knew my baby girl. I knew she would roll her eyes if I cried or tried to hold her back. She would put her hands on her hips and say, "Moooooooom. You're embarrassing me."

She has a plan. She's going clip-clopping into kindergarten that first day in her high-heel denim sandals, and I will see her walking ahead, the backpack overtaking her, attitude in every step. She may turn if I'm lucky and wave good-bye at the door. And maybe, if she's in the mood, she'll hold out her arms as she did as an infant and allow me to stoop for a fleeting embrace.

A mother loves her children the same. It is an unwritten law, a must that the scales of devotion and calibrations of the heart are always balanced. But each child is different. The first is more of a test drive, a practice go-round when emotions are intense, and even the first bath becomes an event worthy of five textbooks on the subject.

We coddle the first, steer him more firmly, unleash all our desires onto this one small child who we learn quickly has ideas of his own.

We won't let the first eat candy from the floor, have cookies or sodas, or wander into other rooms unsupervised. We follow him like a puppy. We read him books and focus on this child as if the world has come to a complete stop except in our own homes.

We watch him grow, guiding as he climbs the vines of childhood.

My daughter was the child I never thought I'd have, the baby who came along after losing one in between. She arrived healthy and olive-skinned and crowned in a thick mat of jet-black hair that slowly turned the color of sand. She ate candy before dinner and stayed up too late. She forgot to drink her milk and no one stood over her forcing the issue. She didn't learn to read before age four as did the first child.

She was the baby we enjoyed, the one we bathed without books, the one who learned her alphabet at her own pace. She didn't have to be the smartest or fastest.

She was simply our little girl. Our second child.

And on this August morning I had to give her up. I watched as she walked into another woman's room and turned her big brown eyes on me, giving them one last roll before the quick flick of her wrist and a wave like an afterthought.

I walked down that sidewalk that steals my children. I opened the door to my car and sat at the wheel, staring at the beige-bricked kindergarten wing and feeling the sting of a tear, the knot in my throat, the threat of emotion's release. I promised I wouldn't cry.

It was a promise I couldn't keep.

The Unglamorous Girl of "Camp Am Not"

Some people were born to lead glamorous lives and others were not. Toss me in with the "Camp Am Not" crew. I once tried to be glamorous, painting a lovely mole on my upper lip during the Madonna "Like a Virgin" rage of the '80s. I went to a dance club, had a few drinks, forgot about my mole, and stood out in the rain talking to the man I'd eventually marry.

He informed me my mole was running. That's how glamorous I am.

Toss my friend Vivian Hamilton at the tippy top of the "Camp Am Too" tower. Vivian is not an ordinary woman. She was born with an entirely different name she wasn't fond of, and after seeing *Gone With the Wind* she changed her name to Vivian with an A, slightly different from that of her favorite actress, Vivien with an E Leigh.

My friend Vivian is the niece of Thurston Truitt III, my ex semi-fiancé who recently wed at sixty-two. She is delightful, delicate, and childlike.

I met her over Thanksgiving dinner at Thurston Truitt's Tara-like mansion. Vivian at thirteen was a big-eyed and pale girl who ate nothing but broccoli and talked like a combination of Scarlett O'Hara and Holly Golightly.

"I just adore broccoli," she said in that cultured coo. "It's my very favorite food. Don't you simply adore broccoli?"

I wasn't sure about that, but I did adore this girl pretending to be Holly from *Breakfast at Tiffany's*. Some days she's Scarlett, other days Holly, and a lot of days she's Marilyn Monroe.

Vivian is quite wealthy by birth, has never held a job other than volunteer work, and enjoys Hollywood like no one I've ever met. She follows the stars the way some people follow their horoscopes. She travels the world in order to catch glimpses of and shake hands with her idols.

She even crashed the Golden Globes posing as a security guard and made her way into a star-packed Miramax party where she spoke softly in her well-buttered and bred southern drawl and ordered Shirley Temples.

She's a pretty girl, thin as a model in her black dresses for evening and khaki pants and polo shirts for afternoons. She wears flats and carries Dooney & Bourke or Coach bags. She is also my children's fairy godmother because women like Vivian are never just plain old godmothers. She is the closest thing to a fairy I've ever known, light as air and flying all over the place, dispensing happy dust with her sweet gifts and voice from heaven. Every time the UPS truck comes or the FedEx men ring my bell, it's often a package containing Viv's prizes, always glamorous and fairylike gifts such as Eloise books for my daughter and Harry Potter merchandise for my son. On my birthday she sent a burst of pink flowers and even managed a dozen long-stem roses on Mother's Day that somehow stayed alive in the various mail trucks between her home on the Georgia coast and mine in the North Carolina mountains.

I knew by the time she was sixteen the girl was never going to be a part of the real world, that she would leap along the edges of reality and show me ways of thinking and existing only a certain few can get away with.

I was twenty-six the year she turned sixteen. One day I

came home from work and immediately noticed the black Cadillac with a Georgia license plate in the driveway. I walked through the front door and found her in my bathtub, as relaxed as a starlet.

"Vivian! What a surprise." A glistening foot draped the edge of the tub and her toenails shone a subtle pink. The house smelled like hot steam and drowsy flowers.

"Oh, Susan, I hope you're not mad, but when you told me about your new apartment and the two claw-foot bathtubs, I just had to drive up and take a *bawth*. Daddy bought me a Cadillac and what's the point of having a car if you've got no place to go? This is wonderful, Susan. Absolutely marvelously fabulous." She had driven six hours to take a bawth in my tub. Who couldn't love a girl like that? Is that glamour or what?

She was always thinking of others and that includes the poorest of poor, to whom she'll bring gifts of food and cards to Blockbuster because the American poor always manage to have VCRs and DVDs.

Vivian is a female caught in the gears that never completely shifted from girlhood to womanhood. And even though the romance with Thurston had its storms and joys and didn't last, my friendship with Vivian has survived two decades and is stronger than ever. She loved me because I could teach her big and luscious words like *parched* and *serendipitous,* and her all-time favorite, *proletariat.* She, in turn, taught me what it was like to be ultrarich and devoid of responsibility other than making herself and everyone around her happy with that infectious gift she has of retaining her childhood in all its splendid forms.

She dazzled me with her experiences of world travel and meeting celebrities. She likes to check into the Beverly Wilshire in the exact room where Julia Roberts filmed *Pretty Woman* and order shrimp cocktails and get real friendly with the service workers and housekeeping help.

She knows they are the ones who can lead her to the stars.

She's met most celebrities and mingles as if she were born to brush against them. She shops on Rodeo Drive and has Jose Eber's people style her sun-kissed hair.

Vivian considered jetting to Tahiti to get one look at Marlon Brando; an excursion worth every expense. When she flew there and didn't see him, she jumped on the next plane out—didn't even stick around to snorkel or sightsee. No Marlon, no vacation. If I'd paid that much for a plane ticket, which I'd never be able to do in the first place, I would have at least dunked my toes in that breathtaking water. Not Vivian. She's a girl on a mission and most of her missions are about seeing movie stars and helping the downtrodden. It's almost as if life doesn't exit for the in-betweens. It's either the stars or the starving.

"I can't relate to anyone else," she says in her celestial voice that's a perfect hybrid of every gorgeous star from the '40s, '50s, and '60s.

When Marlon Brando died she called crying and I consoled her best I could considering I don't have my own office and sit next to a quiet man who wears fancy ties and neatly pressed dress shirts and says few if any words. "I'm so sorry you've lost dear Marlon," I said and he raised his eyes and tried not to seem surprised. Poor man, this office mate who's had to hear talk about all kinds of odd things including midget prostitutes and diapered detectives. "I know . . . I understand . . . Really, let me know what I can do. Yes . . . I'll never forget how much you loved Marlon . . . Right, I'm here for you, sugar."

She was still thinking of the Marlon from the glory days and I was thinking more along the lines of the hefty fellow who played the Godfather. She told me he was in *A Streetcar Named Desire* with Vivien Leigh, and she'd heard how gently he treated the fragile star. She followed his career straight to the grave, and that included three stops in Tahiti and countless phone calls to his publicist. She tried for years to get through to him, telling anyone who answered his phone she was a great sympathizer with the plight of the Native Americans, knowing that was Marlon's big cause.

"I just love the Indians," she purred into the phone, a connection stretching from the Georgia coast to the French Polynesia. "Tell Mr. Brando I'm wanting to make a *sizeable* donation."

The publicist/housekeeper kept telling Vivian that Marlon wasn't there. But the next time my friend called, offering loads of money for the "poor dear mistreated Indians," she heard a familiar voice bellowing from the background.

"Hang up on that woman!" a man boomed. "Tell her not to call here again!" It was Marlon. Poor Viv. And to think she loved him 'til the day he toppled.

Marlon wasn't her only obsession. Hollywood, especially Old Hollywood and the stars she'd watch late at night with her beloved grandfather, Big Daddy, were the ones who made her happiest.

The woman purely loves six legends in this world: Marilyn, Marlon, Vivien, Audrey, Elvis, and Larry Hagman. "Marilyn is the weaker side of me and Scarlett is the stronger side," she said.

She credits *Dallas* with sparing her a fate of pure alcoholism due to Sue Ellen Ewing's terrible bouts with the bottle, and when she met Larry Hagman she assured him the show had kept her from becoming a complete sot.

"Meeting Mr. Hagman was the pinnacle," she said breathlessly at two in the morning while we chatted as if it were 9:00 a.m. and over coffee. She likes to stay up until four same as Holly Golightly.

"I loved J.R. He was such a nice man. I've met all the people I've ever wanted to meet except for Marlon and Burt Reynolds."

Vivian has been flying to Hollywood since 1998. She's shared words with Jon Voight, Claudia Schiffer, Tori Spelling, Jaclyn Smith, Jacqueline Bisset, Jane Seymour, and anyone you could think of. She's seen the stars at their best and a few who were drunk off their well-toned tushes.

She says they were all nice enough with the exception of Sally Kellerman, who showed a complete lack of grace when my friend approached and asked softly, "Aren't you Sally Kellerman?

"I was green," she says of her maiden voyage to Beverly Hills. "I was like Ellie May Clampett. She looked at me and said real ugly, 'Excuse me?' She was as snotty as she could be with her high French twist. She should have been happy. Nobody else my age would have known her."

I thought about the four or five celebrities I'd met and how the only one that had gone fairly smoothly was the encounter with a regular on *The Guiding Light*.

"Don't feel bad," I said to Viv. "Remember when I told you about Andie MacDowell moving to my hometown?" I was at a charity event, the one where I ride my unicycle for Hospice, when I met the beautiful star for the first time. I really blew that one.

The encounter was a classic example of my unglamorous life as a key-holding member of "Camp Am Not." I had shaken the manicured hand of the *Four Weddings and a Funeral* movie star and face of L'Oreal and said the worst thing possible. You see, Andie and I are from towns in South Carolina only twenty minutes apart. She grew up in Gaffney and we lived in Spartanburg. Gaffney is the peach capital of the Carolinas and has a famous water tower that's supposed to be a replica of the fruit but looks exactly like a giant ass. Everyone talks about that water tower. It has a crack and everything and a bit of a knot that bulges like a hemorrhoid.

"I want to ask you something, if you don't mind," I said as I let go of Ms. MacDowell's hand. She smiled and gave her full attention, which made me nervous because I'd been a big fan since *sex, lies and videotape*.

"Uh . . . what do you think of the giant peach in Gaffney?" Oh, mercy, it popped right out of my mouth and was the only thing I could think of—being an Unglamorous Girl and member of "Camp Am Not." I sounded like Beavis or Butthead.

She inhaled sharply and held her breath for a long time. I knew I'd said the worst thing possible. But she surprised me. Once over her initial spell of either shock or disgust, she put on a front and smiled. "I really like it," she said graciously.

An awkward pause ensued. The rest was up to me. "It looks just like a monstrous fanny, doesn't it?" She raised her eyebrows—a feat not easily accomplished by some of Hollywood's more Botoxed beauties—and I ran off embarrassed and haven't talked to her since, even though I occasionally see her about town and have friends who go to her church.

Vivian never would have said such a thing to a major celebrity. She always gives them what they want—a big old pat of butter to their egos. Vivian would have said, "Ms. MacDowell, I just loved you in *Green Card*, and *Groundhog Day*. You are such a role model to women over twenty-five and those of us from the South."

This is because Viv knows the exact art of schmoozing celebs and getting on their good side. Her travels have taken her to the most glamorous spots and hotels. She stays at only the best—those places where bumping into a star is as easy as turning one's head.

"I go to all their stops," she said. "Beverly Hills is very small." She checks into the Beverly Hills Hotel, the Beverly Wilshire, and visits the Four Seasons, the Peninsula, and the Sky Bar in West Hollywood where drinks are about $20 each—even her Shirley Temples.

Her most productive trip to Beverly Hills was the year 2000 when she crashed the Golden Globes posing as "Mindy" the Security Guard. The real Mindy never showed for work and my friend had made connections and ended up wearing her badge and credentials.

"I just feel comfortable around celebrities," Viv said, explaining she understands them because for the most part they are just like her and prefer not to live in the real world. Just plant Vivian in the Rainbow Room at Rockefeller Center, the Plaza, or Waldorf-Astoria. Stick a Shirley Temple in her hand and she'll own that room. The night is hers and any celebrity who finds her line of vision is fair game.

While posing as Mindy the Security Guard, Vivian saw all the biggest stars up close, though she tried not to gawk. The big coup for her was sneaking into the Miramax party afterward.

"I waited until the security guards weren't looking and walked right in," she said. "I just act like I'm one of them." Viv homed in on an old TV star who hadn't seen prime time in half a century and was sitting alone at a table, drinking something potent and staring into space.

"I had to sit with somebody," Viv said. "She kept asking me, 'Darling, what do you do in the industry?' and I'd try to change the subject, but it would always come back to that. She kept on asking so finally I said in a whisper, 'Ma'am, I do not work. I'm a blue blood and love to travel and visit places. I was the debutante who declined.'"

Vivian said the old woman was satisfied with that and changed the subject to Kate Spade purses and how her granddaughter who was only eight wouldn't carry anything *but* a Kate Spade to school.

All of us love Vivian and enjoy her escapades, like the story of her meeting Steven Tyler prior to an Aerosmith concert. She waited three hours in the lobby at the Ritz Carlton, hovering and drinking hot tea, pretending to read, until he finally appeared in his sunglasses and dashed for the elevators.

She stopped him with her dove coos. "Mr. Tyler, I just have to tell you, you are such a wonderful person and your music is what helped me get through my daddy's coma."

Tyler touched my friend's arm and said in all sincerity, "Now, tell me. How's your daddy doing?"

"He's doing so good," Vivian gushed, "and your daughter Liv is the most beautiful, wonderful actress . . . God bless you!"

After the encounter she mailed him a letter and gave him what she thought the highest compliment. "You're just like Elvis," she wrote.

Which brings her to the time she and her ex-boyfriend traveled to Graceland to see Elvis's home. She was sitting in the bar at the Peabody Hotel when Robert Duvall cast his eyes her way and said in his grisly accent, "I'm watching you."

"I looked up and he was with a group of men and said it again. 'I'm watching you.' I got up and went over to the table and said, 'Oh, hello, Mr. Duvall. It's such an honor to meet you. I loved you in *Tender Mercies*. And it's so neat you were in *The Godfather* with the person I love so much.'"

"Oh, you mean Marlon Brando?"

"Yes, sir."

"We had a good time mooning everybody on the set," he said.

"Robert Duvall was flirting with me, in a way," Viv said. "I probably could have gone out with him but I was in love with the guitar player before I met my drummer."

Other stars Viv has met are Catherine Zeta-Jones, Michael Douglas, and Kelly Osborne. "I told her how much I just loved her family."

She also informed director Oliver Stone of a thing or two at the Miramax party. "I said, 'Mr. Stone, you are the world's best director. I love how you seem to have the devil in your eyes.'"

Vivian, who has no fear or credit limit, saunters up to celebs the way the hungry hit concession stands.

"Wynonna Judd prayed with me," she said. "She's the sweetest person I ever met. She was sitting with a girlfriend and I was drinking my Shirley Temple and playing with my straw. She said, 'You have really interesting eyes,' and I told her it was an honor to meet her and that I dated a drummer, too. She said, 'Oh, Lord, let me pray for you, sister friend,' and we sat there and prayed."

The other night Vivian called to wish me a happy and glorious birthday because she loves using words like *glorious* and *divine* and can do so without sounding pretentious.

She wondered what fabulously marvelous birthday surprises my husband had in store.

"I just know y'all went to an exquisite restaurant," she said in her Marilyn voice. "Tell me y'all went to the Grove Park Inn with that heavenly view?"

"We dined at the Econo Lodge," I said, Unglamorous Woman that I am.

"Is that like the lodges in *Dallas* where the wealthy go skiing or sip cocoa? Oh, I love a beautiful lodge that's rustic and romantic."

"It's a motel where you can get a room for under thirty-nine dollars," I said and was met with silence as she tried to process this ugly thought into something delightful because that's how her precious mind works. She can turn dirt into diamonds, that girl. "There was a nice Thai restaurant hooked to it, sort of like an afterthought."

More proof I'm an Unglamorous Girl. I never imagined my romantic birthday dinner would end up at one of those places attached to another joint, but it had.

"I'll bet it was beautiful," Vivian said.

Imagine a gas station all lit up, and then to its left or right, a Subway or a Taco Bell has been slapped and cemented right next to the pumps. Even our local Denny's isn't tethered to a Texaco. It goes to show as I said earlier that some people were destined to live glamorous lives. And others were not.

Vivian is a glamour-puss, and so is my sister, who has magnetism dripping from every tanned pore. She once had this really rich husband who flew her all over the world until he hit a midlife crisis, stapled his scalp with an Elvis-like wiglet, and bolted with Miss Wisconsin.

Long before all that went down she discovered she was pregnant while in her grand hotel in Hawaii, in between scuba diving and hula dance excursions, the waves rising like shrines behind her. I discovered I was pregnant in a Kmart bathroom that smelled like a prison latrine, another reminder of my nonglamorous ways. She pees on her stick in Maui. I pee on mine in Kmart.

Even after my sister's marriage to Wig Man soured and he and Miss Wisconsin went on with their trying-hard-to-be-glamorous lives, she bounced right back and didn't even get fat or require liposuction or Lexapro. She found her an Internet husband at christianmenwithgoodteeth.com who's thoughtful and kind and fits right in with our family. Like the rest of my kin, his personal Bible has a wingspan of three feet and he's fond of opening it to the middle and sitting amongst the covered-dish platters while he absorbs the Word and Mama's sweet iced tea.

He may not be quite as rich as the first husband, but at least he and my sister don't dine in restaurants sticking out of motels with names like Cheap Sleeps or Hump Days Inn.

Vivian would never do such either.

One of these days when the kids are sort of grown I'm going to pack a suitcase and fly to L.A. with her. We'll check into the Beverly Wilshire and stroll all over Rodeo Drive hitting various hot spots, trying to meet the last couple of stars on her list.

But no matter how many stars Vivian meets or how often she checks into the Beverly Wilshire or the Plaza, she'll never get over Marlon. He was the man who brought her closest to her Big Daddy on those nights he'd take her to the picture show—Vivian a little girl of six or seven staying out past midnight with the grandfather she adored.

Those were the nights she learned about true glamour and make-believe and worlds that can take her away from her own.

My Old-Lady Swimsuit

My sister lives in Rich City, Georgia, where the women have babies and shop and spend most of their free time, which is *all* the time, in some form of exfoliation or firming regime.

If they have the energy after lengthy hot-stone massages and shopping excursions, they undergo plastic surgery.

Oh, but what a caring and loving group of people. Just yesterday Sister Sandy, my younger, skinnier sibling with the fabulous husband she plucked right off the Internet and married a month later, sent me an e-mail—rare as she's so busy, poor thing, riding her golf cart all over the burb and ordering her yard man to paint her grass green because winter lawns bring on bouts of depression.

Sister Sandy had baked from scratch a low-fat, organic, free-range chicken potpie topped with a seven-grain whole-wheat crust crisscrossed in fork tines. A delicate suffering soul from her section of Rich City had just undergone *elective* surgery and the townsfolk rushed to their stoves (and delicatessens) in support.

"This sure is a funny town," my sister said, toning down her hick accent and rounding her vowels. She is sounding more and more like her sweet Yankee Internet husband. "Only in a wealthy place like Rich City would the church people be baking casseroles for the family to eat while the mom recovered from breast augmentation."

"Breast augmentation? You're kidding?"

"No. She's the sweetest woman. Flat as Gumby, poor girl. I'm using her as my litmus test. I wanna see how well she bonds with them."

"Sounds like a couple of stray kittens."

"I think I'll wait a year or so before I go under. Now that I've put on some pounds and am not a waif, I actually have a little cleavage. A water bra does them wonders."

I've searched my town dry and have never found a water bra anywhere. "I have a better trick than that," I told her.

"Really?"

"Oh yeah. You know how I told you about all the sleek and busty women at the neighborhood pool? It's not easy going down there and lying on a chair next to them, but I've found the ideal solution."

"What's that?"

"A roll of super-strong duct tape that could lift a boulder. Hoisted up everything my swimsuit top didn't. I looked eighteen until water hit them."

Sandy gasped. "You're kidding. You didn't go to the pool taped up like that, did you?"

"Sure did. It was all working beautifully until I had to jump in and salvage a toddler. I was climbing up the ladder and a woman called me over and whispered, 'I believe you have a . . . um . . . a tag coming out."

"I said, 'Tag? That's not a tag, hon. That's my two ninety-nine breast lift.'"

My sister wasn't laughing. She must have felt an emotion akin to horror that a blood relative would do such a thing. She changed the subject back to her recuperating friend.

"I not only baked her the free-range chicken pie, I had the

florist send her a two-rose bud vase with pink ribbons and a card that said 'A Warm Welcome to Your New Additions: Congratulation on the Twins.'"

"Gosh, I'd have to lose an organ to get flowers or a casserole. If I had a boob job in my town, the only thing people would give me is hell."

"Well, it's different here in Rich City, I assure you."

"I see that. Where I live it's high fashion to go saggy and braless and have underarm hair you could curl on hot rollers. We're known for our high population of precious granolas and I don't know a single earth mama who runs out and pays five thousand for new milkers. No way. They use that money to visit rain forests and canoe in Costa Rica."

In Granola City if you have breast augmentation, it's best to keep it a secret. Or if you can't, then at least add a few redeeming comments such as, "I'm a yoga aficionado and a soy milk drinker. I'm a lactose-intolerant vegan and not religious but *spiritual*." That's how it is in my town, not hers. She inhabits a keeping-up-with-the-Joneses city on the outskirts of Atlanta.

"As I was saying," Sister Sandy continued, "if my friend's look good—and every one of my tennis team girls now has them—I'm going for the installments myself."

Hmmmm. "Well, good for you. Listen, I was thinking about that water bra you were talking about earlier. Where might a drooping maiden fetch such a garment?"

She thought for a moment. "Well, certainly not in the duct tape section at ACE Hardware."

We laughed. It's wonderful having a sister in Rich City with the perfect Internet husband and a circle of . . . shall we say . . . well-supported friends.

I must say the fact that her tennis team and other recipients are so happy about their saline mounds has got me rethinking my own Putt-Putt nack-nackers and the rapidity with which they are falling.

I almost ordered something off the Internet that promised

to plump them like Boobie Ball Park franks. I'm not alone, either. Plenty of us with upper body challenges listen intensely to all the ads and infomercials assuring that we, too, can look like Elizabeth Hurley in that wonderfully hussified, safety-pinned Versace plunger.

It's really not fair how we must fret over our proportions while all the magazines mollify men by saying, "Oh, you sweet thing, of course size doesn't matter. You know, baby cakes, that it's not the size of the wand but the magic within." Or how about the controversial study that 72 percent of women today prefer smaller penises for the great versatility they offer?

Where, I wonder, are the morale boosters for women? Or is the only boost we're likely to get is one that will fill our Miracle bras?

When I hear the ads for creams and potions, lotions and pills, I revert to the shame of junior high school and see the smug face of Hank the Plank who used to corner all of us flatties after band practice and say: "Hey, I hear pirates were at your house last night."

"What for?" we'd asked until we learned better.

"They were looking for a sunken chest." Hank the Plank guffawed before returning his gangly self to his rusted tuba.

Nowadays anybody with a few thousand dollars can have bosoms. Of course, the fashion models who were once flat as sand dollars are now 36-Cs and Ds. And they didn't get that way on their usual diet of celery sticks, Starbucks, and cigarettes.

Even the regular women who carpool and shop at outlet malls are sporting saline. They are easy to spot, in case you're on the lookout. They are the ones squeezed into tops made of Lycra and Spandex, those mammary-enhancing numbers that are tight as sausage casings and cut to the navel.

These women aren't about to shop at Talbot's and hide away what good money hath purchased. Such is why a dear friend of mine decided against a boob job.

"I'd feel like I had to show everybody my new goods in

order to get my money's worth," she said. "How would I face my Sunday school class if they heard I had a Web page called 'Look What Five Grand Can Buy'?"

I could relate. It would be similar to buying a Jaguar and keeping it in the garage. Or graduating from Harvard but wearing "Happydale Community College" sweatshirts.

The quest for chest is an age-old goal that can first hit a girl about the same time as puberty. In the sixth grade, prior to a gymnastics performance in front of the entire elementary school, I had the great idea of padding my leotard with Charmin wads. Needless to say the auditorium roared when after a front handspring, one of my paper bosoms went flying across the stage and the other hung in frail defeat from an armhole.

It was a moment that called for action; thus my sister and I ordered the Mark Eden bust developer, which was shaped like a pink clam with a tight spring between its halves. The idea was to squeeze the two sides and gradually we'd wake up looking like Raquel Welch.

One day I caught my daddy working out with it, and from then on the Mark Eden didn't seem as attractive a product.

While I haven't heard of Mark Eden in decades, there are a couple of new developers on the market. One is called Sprouting-Buds, a vitamin compound originally created as a hormone balancer for women with bad PMS or menopause.

According to SproutingBuds marketers, an unexpected benefit was soon discovered. Chests began expanding and filling out as if by magic. Small breasts swelled from one to three full sizes and larger breasts suddenly felt firmer and uplifted.

Just listen to the testimonials.

"I have had three children and thought I had lost my breasts to their hungry little mouths. Pecked to death, I was," said Miracle Tinsley of Idaho. "After using your product for three months, my yummies have returned to the way they used to look and are so firm I don't need a bra anymore. We even used one of my nipples to sand down our son's Pinewood Derby car."

Please, woman, spare us.

Another happy user says, "My breasts don't feel like Quaker Oats anymore. After as many babies as I've had, twelve, until we finally got cable hookup, I never thought I would get my breasts looking nice again. SproutingBuds did just what the name implies!"

I realized after Mark Eden these ads are too good to be true. Some days I think I'll just keep my ugly pair until they fall to my waist. I'll then tuck them into my blue jeans and pray I don't sit on them. Other days, especially in the summer when the bronze goddesses grease up their store-bought globes by the pool, I feel like . . . well . . . a sock monkey.

It's bad enough that I have lost my chest to gravity, but when my own mama starts telling me to cover up the rest of me, that I'm too old for even a tankini . . . well, that hurts. She had the gumption to announce it was high time I ordered swimwear from the "Proud Matrons Poolside" catalog, which has some of the homeliest suits known to womankind.

Lord help the poor woman who buys her first old lady bathing suit. Give her a medallion, a trophy of bravery to place on the shelf next to the family photos reminding of her thinner days.

The granny suit is a symbol, a rite of womanly passage. It is the flashing red light signaling that time has marched across one's physique like eager soldiers in boot camp. No woman really wants to enter the mee-maw zone, but hefty portions, birthing babies, and too many Happy Meals have forced the doors wide open for all but a lucky few.

We are reminded of this every year as winter wears onward and the new swimsuits arrive in stores, rack after rack of bikinis, tankinis, and rhinestone-encrusted one-pieces that have legs cut up to the armpits. These were suits I could have worn during the summers of '79 and '80, before I blew up from beer and pizza and college life.

It was during a recent trip to Chattanooga, Tennessee, to see Ruby Falls and Rock City, the subject of swimwear selection came up. My mama and the kids and I had checked into a hotel with a rinky-dink indoor pool, shucked our jeans and sweaters, and broke out the bathing suits.

I heard Mama gasp and mutter, pointing to my selection, a low-key number despite the mesh netting across the bodice. She tried to talk but all she could do was sputter and jut her chin. No one messes with Mama when that chin is in jut formation.

Finally, she composed herself.

"Those would be fine for the beach," she harped, "but not for a family pool environment. Don't forget you've had two babies. Not everyone's bodies bounce back."

"Well, I can only guess who you're talking about, dear Mother," I said, eating a stack of Pringles. She certainly wasn't talking about Sister Sandy in Rich City who had two kids and somehow managed to look like the next *Baywatch* lifeguard.

"You've got your granny's shape," Mama said, and I pictured my big sweet husky granny thundering through the house in taupe Hush Puppies and a flaming apron. "You don't need to be displaying too much skin at your age."

Mama rummaged through her canvas bag and produced an elephantine T-shirt appliquéd in sea turtles, which she demanded I put on over my swimsuit. "You cover yourself up, hon," she said. "It's time for a 'Mommy' bathing suit. The kind with some material and those cute little skirts around them."

After our Chatanooga trip, I came home and within three days the "Centenarians In Style" and "Proud Matrons Poolside" catalogs appeared in the mail. I decided to order the ugliest garment on the pages. It was so loathsome retailers had slashed the price 75 percent. That would show my mother during her annual Fourth of July pool party attended by all the kin and friends. She'd most certainly prefer seeing a roll or two of fat after getting a load of the number I was planning to sport.

I dialed the 1-800 number, hoping the monstrosity had sold out.

"Item number, please," a nasally voice demanded.

I reluctantly gave her the number. Maybe it was my imagination, but I'm almost sure the woman typing in codes and keys was giggling.

"Confirming item number 238GP7," she said, giving up the pretense and allowing herself a full-blown hissy fit of snorting and chortling. "That would be the 'Vise,' our very own circulation-reducing ultra girdle tank with steel-belted radial horn-a-plenty bra, piped seams, heavy-duty stays, and detachable knee-length skirt. Correct?"

I said nothing, placing a finger on the hang-up button.

"Ma'am?"

Silence.

"Ma'am? Are you there? Will there be anything else with this order? Perhaps our matching duster? See it on the page? We call it the 'Gripper.' It's truly the perfect complement to the 'Vise.'"

"No, thank you."

"How about the orthopedic pool slippers? We have them in Taming Tan or Big Girl Black. Taming Tan is our most—"

I'd had enough of her probable size 2 condescension. "I'm not quite a porkstress in need of the 'Gripper,' thank you all the same," I said. But what I really wanted to say was, *I know a place where you can put those slippers, Little Miss Stickbug Thighs.*

Later that day I called Mama and told her about the grandma tank and thanked her for signing me up for the great-granny catalog companies. I planned on sending her the Adam and Eve catalog of sexual toys as a nice surprise. I pictured her face as she unwrapped the booklet's brown modesty cover and turned to the page offering the "Erectus Mega," the "Senso Pocket Penis," and the "Backdoor Buddy"—apparatuses sure to make that trashy woman in beauty school with the hole in her crotches seem virtuous by comparison.

She sighed with relief when I told her about my new swimwear purchase. "I'm so glad, sugar. You know in your heart and thighs it was time."

"I'm certain from the looks of it that if it doesn't fit or strangle me, we can use it as a nightstand or a clothes ringer. The saleslady laughed at me, Mama. She had the gall to suggest I buy a pair of pool slippers that looked like something Herman Munster would wear."

"Hon, we all have to age with grace. Women your age who shop in the junior department are ridiculous-looking. Buying mature clothes means you're a classy, confident person."

"No, it means I've gone to pot. Flat-out and straight to pot."

She hung up because *Big Brother* was on and I suspect she loves that cast more than she loves us.

She left me holding a dead receiver and thinking how hard it is to enter middle age—to zoom from Cute Girl to Attractive Woman to Proud Matron Poolside. A woman who's ma'am'd to death and offered love only from those who need their Depends changed and visas renewed. Anyone who says it's easy should be given a scepter and crown, a sash with Mrs. Denial splattered across her chest, enhanced or otherwise.

I'm beginning to crave an organic free-range chicken pot-pie, a twin-bud vase, and a note welcoming my new additions.

Surgery is sounding better every day, people. Graceful be damned.

Nobody Wants a Bone
But a Dog

As soon as I hit forty a few "days" ago, my metabolism packed a bag and went on vacation. It was as if someone slammed the Off button; thus every morsel with more than three fat grams and any trace of a carbohydrate permanently lodges itself in for the long haul.

Every time I eat Sunday dinner at my mother-in-law's, who's an excellent cook but has a heavy hand with the saltshaker, I don't urinate for two days. And any fluid—even water—is hoarded as if I were a camel getting ready for a desert sabbatical, humps sprouting all over my body.

Talk about disheartening. Of course when I appear in public in a standing (key word is "standing") position, few would heckle and shout, "Heifer!" Once I sit down I look like a baby hippo; however, one cannot spend her entire life walking around and avoiding chairs and sofas.

An evil former coworker who scared us raw most days, ambled by my desk on her way to being exported to another paper and said, "How's it going, heifer?" I sat rigid with my mouth wide open until finding the words to respond.

"Just fine," I said. "Fine as a T-bone. Fine as a fillet. Fine as top sirloin. Fine as—"

"Give it a rest!" she barked and thundered like a football player to the watercooler.

Another time I was in the grocery store with my newly birthed daughter when a vituperative shrew decided she'd rake her claws across my ego. I should have heeded my mother's sage advice about trips to the grocery store. "Always look decent when you go shopping," she said. "You'll run into everybody in town and the worse you look, the more people you'll see. It's a given. Soon as they see you've gone to pot, they'll start up a phone tree and the whole town will know you've let yourself go."

I didn't have the energy on this particular day to don the finery and makeup. The baby was two months old and nursing round the clock. I stood in my fatigue and cleanest outfit at the checkout line when I heard the grating voice of an old friend. My pink frost lipstick was fresh and my hair clean on one side, the side the baby's projectile vomit hadn't smeared.

"Why is it," the familiar voice whined, "that women with big butts have to walk around sticking them out?" Her words were loud enough for everyone in the grocery store to hear. I whipped my head around and faced this acquaintance who'd marched off as soon as she spouted her meanness. She had her back turned and wasn't about to answer for her actions.

Ordinarily, I would have ignored her as Mama taught. But when a woman's had three hours of sleep and has somehow managed to dress her sweet newborn in Gymboree and Baby Gap yet no one is ooing and fawning over her, this won't do.

If someone's going to say I resemble a heifer or my butt's like a steer's, that's fine—as long as they pause first to admire the new baby.

"My hiney may be on the large side," I said, hollering across two lanes of shopping traffic, "but at least it isn't southbound." Her jaw dropped. I felt mean and feared something bad was going to happen because of my hormones and naughty uterus acting up. I could tell my Witch Switch had been tripped.

As I paid for the groceries, the man in line behind me put it best. "Women can be really vicious to each other. You'd never hear a man saying nothing like that."

He had a good point. The truth is, women don't fix up and dress to the hilt for men; they do it to one-up each other. Men don't care if we're ten pounds over ideal weight or if we've got sagging breasts and crow's-feet. They aren't measuring the circumference of our pores or checking for rosacea. They're just looking at the big picture: *Can I get laid?*

It's the women who scrutinize, criticize, and search for every flaw. They're the ones talking about how fat we've gotten or who's let herself go. I've never heard the following conversation from a man: "I ran into Brenda the other day at Sam's Club and she had gained at least twenty pounds. She's aging poorly and her skin looks like she's seen one too many tanning beds. All those cigarettes and not drinking a drop of water haven't done her a favor in the world but add ten years to her face."

When a certain type of woman diets, she's mainly doing so to rise above the other women, to remain high on the rung of the competition ladder. If someone is losing too much weight, it's the women in the office who gossip and accuse Miss Thinness of anorexia and bulimia.

Admittedly, it's hard not to get caught up in the whole business of losing weight and looking great. And along about March or April of each year, I consider going on a diet and doing something about gravitational pull and wiggly skin, anticipating summer's curtain parting and revealing rippled thighs and unsavory upper arms. Even with exercise mine seem to have taken flight from bone. I long to ban tank tops and spaghetti straps, midriffs and pants cut to the pubis from department stores. I fantasize about force-feeding Baby Ruths to the lithe Gwyneth Paltrow types whose arms look like twine. I have what can best be described as super-friendly triceps. They are always waving.

When a person turns forty and is abandoned by metabolism, life is never the same. We're facing a weapon deplete of ammo and left with something far more fragile—our own devices and willpower.

The latest trend is to eat entire farm animals, stuffing one's face with every bit of grease and gristle, anything one desires as long as it doesn't have the dirty four-letter word in it: CARB.

These protein queens are not pleasant after about day three. I can spot a bread-free, carb-starved woman from a mile away. She's mean. She's vicious. She'd do well with one of those red warning signs or flashing lights, maybe even a siren if it's been a good while since she and Mueller's sat down to a decent meal.

There are many signals pointing to the bread-free woman, but be forewarned. She is dangerous to others. Worse than a pit bull that hasn't had a steak or a vampire trying to feed off the likes of Lara Flynn Boyle, who has no fat except in her upper lip. Too many people on this planet are beginning to resemble praying mantises.

Every time I see on TV one of those Texas Walking Stick starlets they are always drinking a big mug of Starbucks and telling reporters: "Me, anorexic? I eat everything in sight." I'd like to see these Twizzlers' line of vision. I'd like to know why their focus and periphery don't include French fries, cookies, chips, rice, pasta, and chocolate—all the happiest foods in the worlds, foods that will raise serotonin levels. I'll bet these hunger babes haven't seen a croissant or fully dressed bagel in a month of Sundays.

Oh, but it's not just the stars who are whittling down to tendon and bone. Everywhere people are eschewing Sunbeam, even the whole wheat breads, and going for beef, bacon, cheese, and mayonnaise. People have quit buying as much toilet paper because no one poops anymore.

Hey, but as long as they forgo the breadbasket the pounds will drop like bricks. But mean? You wanna see mean? You don't even want to sit next to the carb-restricted woman at work unless you don't mind her chewing your head off since she knows it's carb-free and she's hungry and crazy enough to eat about anything.

Not long ago when I chose to write a big feature called "Shunning Carbs and Losing Friends," a vicious woman got on the phone and let me have it.

"May I speak to the bitch who wrote the column on being carb-starved?"

"Uh," I say, thinking the poor caller means well. "This is she."

"My name is Heather Ann Porter and I'm canceling my subscription and calling your editor. How dare you write a story saying people who don't eat bread are worse than rabid hedgehogs? How dare you? I haven't consumed anything but cheese and chicken in two years and everyone loves me. I am an adored woman. *Adored!* My nickname is Miss Adorable."

"I'm sure you are the sweetest thing alive."

"You trying to be funny? Is that your idea of humor, saying those of us who don't eat bread or pasta must somehow be deficient? That we want to look like Texas Walking Sticks? I've seen those bugs. You aren't fooling anybody. Is this the new American prejudice now that all ethnic groups and sexual orientations are off-limits?"

"Well, that's not exactly what I was—"

"Oh, just run your mouth off about those of us who are espousing healthier living. Call us stick bugs if it makes you feel better."

"I'm proud of you for sticking to your guns."

"Did you say guns? Are you threatening me?"

"Ma'am. I'm going to hang up now. Before I do I'd like to suggest you raid the Merita wagon. If you consume an entire Boboli crust within the next half hour, chances are you won't kill somebody and your life will resume to a near normal state."

"You aren't funny. You bread people think you've got the right way to diet, but you are all getting fatter every year.

Fatty, fatty, two-by-four, can't get through the bathroom door. Look at the statistics. There's fat, and then there's *fat* fat. You breadies are in the *fat* fat boat."

"Please, hon, eat something made by Pillsbury."

She slammed down the phone and called my editor, who delivered a gentle warning, bless his heart. Just like he did when I said Hooters should have a brother restaurant called "Schlongs" and all the Rotarians rose up in anger and jammed his phone lines with complaints.

Though I never thought I'd admit to this, I sure miss that platinum-haired fright Susan Powter, who used to shout, "Stop the insanity," and yell at us for eating fat.

"You can eat ten baked potatoes a day," she shrieked back in the '90s when carbs were queen and fat was the devil with a pitchfork of pounds. Powter advocated pastas and breads, anything and everything with little or no fat. Pork, lamb, and beef were the enemy of the heart and hips.

Here's what I say: give me carbs or give me a cot right next to Martha Stewart in the pen. I'd rather sit behind bars knowing someone was planning to slop me like an incarcerated hog with a platter of cornbread and beans, biscuits and redeye gravy than walk around like the poor Heather Ann Porters of the world, their faces and stomachs sunken as an old man's and their demeanor about as personable as a starved gator's.

It is high time we as a nation got off these kicks and just got healthy. Eat bread. The brown kind. Eat rice. The brown kind. Eat pasta, the brown kind. Eat fruits and veggies, preferably not the brown kind. Watch portions, exercise, inhale, and drink water.

So easy to say but oh so much harder than gobbling a few rib eyes, sucking back a bit of Hidden Valley Ranch, and calling it "healthy living."

For those who would still like to drop a few pounds, but don't want to do so at the expense of others or sever a perfectly good head and personality in the process, I've devised this diet from hard-won experience.

The Reinhardt Diet:
The Unconventional Way

1. Forget the horrified looks society will lob your way and go ahead and breast-feed that thirty-pound toddler with twenty-four teeth. This will burn five hundred to six hundred calories per day, more than running six miles on the hard pavement. Lactation is synonymous with liposuction, my friends.
2. Go grocery shopping with a pack of brats—yours, the neighbor's, borrow if you have to. Chasing them down aisles and jostling them from hip to hip, not to mention the cleanups and stress, the soaring blood pressure and pulse rates, all equal higher metabolism and calories burned.
3. Dine at B- and C-grade restaurants. The food will not stay in the system long enough for digestion.
4. Frequent fairs and street festivals and eat from questionable vendors.
5. Visit beautiful Mexico and drink their yummy water. This is all but guaranteed to whittle pounds off your frame, keeping you permanently attached to a commode or Depends.
6. Have a knock-down, drag-out fuss with your husband

or boyfriend. Angst will zap more calories than a Stairmaster.

7. Skip lunch and opt for the Milk Duds instead. First, they take forever to chew. And second, they yank out most teeth necessary for future dining pleasure.

8. Volunteer one or two days a week in a nursing home. Let's see how much you can eat after changing diapers and bedpans for eight hours!

9. Force yourself to eat one meal a day in a Porta-Jon.

10. Finally, heed the advice of the wisest man I've ever met. He gazed at me with his cataract-clouded blue eyes, his face leathered from sun and years, and spoke volumes in a single sentence. "Hon," he said, "don't nobody want a bone but a dog."

Someone's Knockering on the Door

I'll admit thinking only airheads or adult entertainers had fake boobs. Women with couth, class, and substance never did such a thing in my unenlightened mind. Unless a girl made her living writhing on floors and snaking up and down poles or posing in underwear and birthday suits, no inflatables necessary. Not unless she was insecure, vain, or a sick and snooty woman. That's at least how I used to view the fake boob phenomenon until I wanted them myself.

Funny how we can bad-mouth luxury cars, SUVs, designer clothes, large houses in the burbs, until we decide we simply must possess the item ourselves.

Almost overnight I went from saying to my husband, "Ewww. You like her? What kind of man likes fake titties?" to this: "I breast-fed two children and am tired of trying to locate my boobs in the morning somewhere beneath the bed."

If strippers, models, actresses, and other women could have new breasts, then didn't mothers who'd forfeited their bodies in order to properly nourish their babies deserve them too? Deserve them most?

I was fairly content with my low-slung small Cs until my

daughter nursed for more than two years, shocking many of my relatives and others with no notion of child development.

At forty I had my first mammogram and what was left of my breast tissue turned then and there into bassett hound ears, long and downwardly mobile. I didn't know where to put them or what to do about them. I'd imprison them in a bra in the mornings and by afternoon one or both would have escaped.

I wanted the surgery but was scared to death of the risks, including death from anesthesia and the fact some women's bodies reject implants as the foreign objects they are. In addition, it's not that unusual for new knockers to deflate, ripple, contract, cause pain, and end up in need of replacement. The comforting notion was the majority of those receiving implants were happy. These satisfied customers don't make headlines because most of them are ordinary women with children, jobs, husbands, and non-spotlight-type lifestyles.

I knew the decision wasn't one to make without a lot of research. At first I thought I'd just get a lift because it sounded like the classy, intelligent woman's choice, like getting one's hair delicately highlighted instead of bleached blond. A lift. A nice and low-key sort of procedure—the thinking woman's answer to plastic surgery.

I saved and saved, finally deciding the pros outweighed the cons and scheduled a consultation with our local Booby van Gogh, the debonair Dr. Erasmo Redondo who has restored many a woman to her grandeur, especially those who've lost their breasts to cancer. He came highly recommended and several of his clients who were friends of mine flashed the goods and had me convinced.

I was ready to pump a bit of bimbo into my blood and onto my chest and after viewing hundreds of photos, decided I needed both the lift *and* the implants. The doctors I scheduled consultations with agreed that for my body type and decrepit condition, *two* procedures were necessary for complete restoration.

I didn't want to break the family bank or take away from everyday needs, so I syndicated a news feature that appeared in national and international newspapers, paying a nice fee with each publication. Other women I met on a Web site also saved for their own surgeries, one even going as far as selling half the contents of her home on eBay. The woman's husband was dead-set against her getting implants, fearing she would leave him if she sported upgrades. He wouldn't give her a dime, and as a result, she hawked his beloved car parts and her own household appliances to pay for her baby Ds.

After a few weeks of eBay auctions, she'd stashed enough cash and told her husband she was going away for a long weekend with a friend. Shortly after returning home, he paced the floors muttering and wanting to know if they had been robbed because "my son-of-a-bitching collection's gone missing."

"What happened to my brand-new 1956 full-block V9 Packard 'Clipper' engine?" he asked. "It was in its original crate and I can't find it anywhere, *nor* can I seem to locate the restored motor and transmission from my 1955 Oldsmobile Super Rocket 88. I ain't even got my cheaper shit like the trunk mats and bumpers. Two of my convertible tops are missing."

"Well, I don't have a dishwasher," the woman said, batting her lively eyes and pushing forth her new chest. "Look what I got instead. Two perfectly resorted 'convertible tops.'" And with that she laughed wickedly, all but signing divorce papers in her own blood. She said the surgery was her revenge for his spending nearly $200,000 in one year on old cars.

I set a date, December 10, 2003, and nearly chickened out every day. I had such mixed feelings—vain and selfish on one hand, justified and deserving on the other.

For years, since having children and breast-feeding them, my sex drive has plunged, the loss of libido related to estrogen swings and how I felt about my body. The sagging stomach skin and breasts had begun bothering me, even though I realize there are women who say I should be so lucky that the breasts I did have were healthy and noncancerous. Oh, but they were eyesores! I have the secret photo file to prove it.

Spending that much money on myself was also difficult and went against all the teachings from home and church. So I did what most will do when considering a high-ticket nonnecessity. I rationalized and justified and here's what the little voices chimed every time doubts swam forth.

You're not a fancy high-maintenance person. You do your own nails, and yes, biting them since birth counts. You also color your own hair, or did so until it became a two-process complicated job. And look at you, you poor dear hardworking mom whose husband won't even let you have bath mats or dust ruffles. You've had fewer massages than you can count on one hand, two pedicures, and only one manicure—on your wedding day. Everything has pretty much been a do-it-yourself operation, including your last effort with chemical peels. You poor woman, buying that TCA solution off eBay and adminis-tering it yourself, turning for five days into an ancient old lady until the skin finally relinquished and peeled, leaving you with partial skull exposure. If anyone deserves a professional pro-cedure, poor woman, you do.

If a home boob-job kit were available on eBay, I dare say I might try that, too. But there wasn't and so I found a doctor known for his good work, Dr. Erasmo Redondo, "the Booby van Gogh." Not wanting to back out, I went ahead and placed a deposit with the billing department, reserving the operating room for early morning on December 10. Each day leading up to that hour, I picked up the phone to cancel the appointment. And each day I went on the Internet and found support and a cheering squad, the humorous and wonderful "chatters" I came to know and consider friends at www.implantinfo.com.

Another reason I was gung-ho on doing this thing was my friend Vicki La-La Smith, who owns a lodge and tiki bar and who flashed me one day when I told her what I was thinking.

"I did it," she said, raising her shirt to reveal the most perfect pair I'd seen in my life. And here she was nearly fifty years old. "My friend Sue and I did it together. We asked if we could be in the operating room together side by side, but Dr. Redondo said he couldn't arrange that. She went first and I followed right behind her.

"Sue and I had talked about having a boob job ever since we first met. My husband and I had often laughed about me getting boobs and him getting eye surgery so he could see them. Well, hon, I started saving and in no time, I opened up my right hand and held it out to my husband with the money for his eyes."

"What about you?" her beloved asked, knowing how much Vicki wanted boobs.

She did that sexy womanly smile thing at him. "I got the money for me in the left hand."

After the procedure, their husbands drove them home while they slept off the anesthesia and were essentially out of it. But as soon as the sun rose on the next day, the first morning as C- and D-cup queens of restoration, the women cried out in excruciating pain.

"It was worse than childbirth," Vicki said. "Sue called me bright and early to tell me she hated me and the day went downhill from there. At one point, when I was still very full of painkillers, very skinny, and very swollen up top, I walked by a full-length mirror in the nude. As I stood there looking, I thought about how children were starving in Ethiopia and I had intentionally done this to myself."

We women, if we have half a conscience and a decent heart, suffer postsurgical guilt after packing five grand under our pectoral muscles. It's a given for the gentler of souls out there. Vicki vowed to start a resource center for children who had nowhere to go after school. It was her way of assuaging what I call "boob job guilt."

She is also president of her local chamber of commerce and head of the Lake Lure La-La's, a group of champagne-drinking performers who raise money for worthwhile charities.

The new bosoms only seemed to inspire Vicki to want to do more for others, God love her, and I'm sure he does.

The same goodwill toward others struck my sister not long after she went under the implant knife in October 2003.

Sister Sandy in Rich City had always been a large A-cup and was sick of wearing padded bras. I had a premonition she was getting boobs, and called her to tell her I was considering some type of restoration.

"Probably just a delicate and very classy lift," I said, still not ready to admit a desire for implants, too.

"Oh my gosh," she said. "I'm scheduled to go in for my pumpkins on Halloween!"

Well now, wasn't she always one-upping me? First the rich husband, David "Wig Man" I, then the nice and devoted husband, David II, from the Internet, and now . . . now . . . pretty boobs and me still scraping the roadways with mine. If this didn't convince me to step on the gas and get my saggy self to a surgical center, nothing would.

"What did Mama say when you told her?" I asked.

"They have no idea about them. If they did, they'd be pissed we didn't spend the money on something more worthwhile. If they notice, I'll have to tell them I won them on a radio contest."

My sister's story was like so many I'd heard and read about on various sites.

"All my life I had low self-esteem because I felt I skipped puberty," Sandy said. "I was the last girl to get a period and my breasts never did come in. Don't get me wrong, I wasn't a physiological nightmare, but I really got sick of men complimenting me on my butt."

She decided to stay flat until turning forty when she felt mature enough to go through with the surgery as a gift to herself—not eye candy for men in grocery stores and gas stations.

"These would be for me and I wouldn't care what anyone else thought of them."

After Sandy set her date, she drove home and told her husband. She said the news hit him like a fastball from left field but he was supportive from the start, as David II has always been. He was kind even as he saw his dreams of Lasiks eye surgery going down the drain.

"Poor thing," Sandy said. "But you know, I didn't want him to see my old goods clearly until I'd given them an extreme makeover." She had always counted on him leaving his Coke-bottle-thick glasses on the bedside table during mattress nightlife. That 20/400 vision of his had masked the reality of her situation. Yes, indeed, his eye surgery would have to wait, my sister said, being the practical woman she is. And being the organized woman she is, she trained for new bosoms the way one would for a triathlon.

"I am coming down with a cold and pushing Cs and orange juice," she announced forty-eight hours before B-day. "Damn it, I'm ready anyway." She'd bought a used twenty-five-dollar recliner after learning it's best to sleep propped up for a week or more. She also bought four bags of frozen English peas to place on her chest to reduce swelling, Fibercon and pineapple juice to get her pipes loose.

My sister had every base covered in case of ooze, bruise, clogging, or pain. I was beginning to think she was nuts.

Twenty-four hours before her big day, she was busy washing everyone's sheets and scrubbing the house spotless. She had ransacked the grocery store and spent hours in her kitchen, stocking up on goodies and lunches, necessities for David II and her little boys. She also prepared and froze meals for David to heat while she recovered and bonded with her new pumpkins.

On the day of implantation, David II, hands on the steering wheel and eyes big as pecans behind a pair of inch-thick glasses, drove her to the surgical center. As they sat in the waiting room, Sandy came down with a case of jitters and almost backed out. "We can go home, sweetheart," said David II, holding her hand. "You know I love you just the way you are."

His kindness gave her a boost of courage and she waved good-bye as she followed the nurse into surgery. David II waited and read comforting passages from his large-print sixty-pound Bible. On the way home, as he drove carefully to avoid hitting bumps and rough spots, my sister caught him eyeing the new goods.

"It may have been the drugs," she said. "But I think I remember him grinning."

Up and Grade

My New Best Friends

Vicki and Sue, along with my freshly implanted sister and the friends from the boob chat room, are the main reason I dragged myself out of bed on December 10, and walked into the surgical suite, my husband following behind frowning, as if he'd rather enter an anesthesia-free vasectomy den.

I'm not a morning person and this is an hour of the day I don't even consider morning. Real morning is from ten to noon. Crazy-person morning is between five-thirty and sevenish, when all those chirpy types sip coffee, smoke their cigs, meditate, and greet a new day far too prematurely in my opinion.

I was barely awake when the nurse handed me warm blue scrubs to put on. What did they mean, "No underwear, please"? It's not like I was getting vaginal beautification.

I did as told and sat in a chair trembling while nurses administered an IV of calming medications I wished I had available at all times. Might inspire a gal to get up earlier or make more passes at her poor neglected husband.

After a few moments, the adorable Dr. Erasmo Redondo, who the staff nicknamed "Dr. Erase It," entered the room to draw on my chest in black marker, reminding me of the sweet years nursing my daughter and sketching the Abominable Snowman above my nips.

"I brought some more pictures," I said, my words hazy and half formed from the drugs. "Personally, at this point, I don't care what you do. Go ahead and put them on my shoulder blades so I can get more mileage out of them. By the time I get to Croaker's Rest Home, they'll be in just the right spot."

He smiled and those cow eyes did me right in. "We have plans for you, young lady." Oh, how smart the plastic surgeon who calls his "ma'ams" young ladies. We'd pay double to have this Ecuadorian heartthrob slice us up with his youth-sculpting tools. I felt another surge of joy juice warming my veins and thawing my fears.

I am sure that if the surgical staffs at these booby restoration joints didn't loop their patients with happy bags, most of them would bolt as soon as the scrubs and markers came out.

"You have decided, no, to get de works?" Dr. Redondo asked, meaning the lift and the doorknobs.

"I sure have. Why put new elastic in a pair of busted socks if you don't have ample shin to hold it all together? Why rig up a Christmas tree if you aren't going to plug in the lights?" He seemed confused at my drugged metaphors. "Throw in the Mentor 350s and don't be shy about overfilling."

"I fill to manufacturer limit. Is best, I promise," he said, his accent and big cow eyes precious. "You will be happy. All de gulls are happy and beautiful."

He and the staff, half hidden by masks, assured me that I'd be pleased and led me down the hallway to the operating room, my feet in hospital socks with the slip-free gripper dots.

I shivered. The place was frigid and smelled like absolutely nothing, it was so sterile. Knives and prongs, things to gouge and saw and separate human tissue, were everywhere.

They laid me out like a fetal pig in a high school biology class, placing me on a bed shaped just like a cross, and strapped my arms to the table. I felt my pulse quicken and heart beating irregularly.

"I don't think I can do this. I need to be getting home now. Help!"

"You'll be fine," the nurse kept saying, and someone injected more nerve medicine into the IV. "Remember, Dr. Erasmo will erase all your troubles."

"Can he erase my husband, too?"

This is a man who never made an issue out of my upper body, which looked exactly like a *National Geographic* centerfold. He made issues out of everything else, but not what needed the most renovating.

When he learned I wanted breast work, he lost his cool and ranted for two months. Never mind he hit middle age and fell victim to an expensive eBay addiction and our house is now crammed with six trumpets, a piano, flute, saxophone, computer, and get this—*a car*—from eBay.

At least I wasn't trying to order bosoms from eBay, I told him, but he didn't find a bit of humor in this so we entered couple's counseling to discuss the issue of wives wanting to change their appearance and whether or not this was ethically wrong.

"She won't be the same woman I married," Stu said. He's got that male idea that what's mine is his, including the parts of my body he enjoys. It took a while for the therapist to show him he needed to offer support. That the decision, as long as money wasn't an issue, was mine. They were my breasts. Not his.

He relented but not without waves of moodiness and tests of the marriage that on many occasions made me wonder, *Is this worth it?*

"You know I hate big fake boobs," he said a hundred times. "I'm a butt man." He announced this to our therapist, a proper woman who jumped halfway out of her chair at his words. "I'd rather see a woman with a nice ass and small breasts than a pile of silicone on her chest."

"Saline," I corrected. "Mine are to be saline and placed under the muscle for a more natural appearance."

He is in the minority, but I respect him for his preferences and wish society thought as he did. But it doesn't. He was OK with the idea of a lift, as was my mama, but as far as implants were concerned, everybody close to me said, "Don't do it."

Apparently, a lot of men don't care if they're fake or real as long as they remotely resemble what nature intended. My theory is most men like an ample-sized pair, not necessarily huge, but something in the B-C-D range. His theory is that rednecks like 'em big and bigger and that only redneck women get implants.

After a few sessions in therapy and two months of talking with my sister, the women in the booby chat room, Vicki and Sue and others who'd had the procedure, I was as ready as I'd ever be, at least physically. My "before" pictures had me convinced, same as when a woman who avoids seeing herself as fat can't help but face up when the photos come back from the one-hour processing.

Inside, I felt ambivalent, and especially guilty for spending so much money on myself. At least I paid for them with freelance work. At least I didn't take food from my children's mouths or shoes from their feet.

When that justifying wore off, I figured the fact I didn't smoke saved at least $1,500 or more a year. And the fact I gave up beer and wine spared the accounts another couple thousand when one adds in parties and entertainment.

Other girls in the chat room worried about financing their set. And because they'd helped me so much, it was my turn to give back.

Listen up, I typed. *Get a low-interest credit card. One that offers 0 percent financing for up to a year and gives Frequent Flyer miles to boot. Put your knockers on that Visa and earn a couple of plane tickets to go with them. My mama put her crypt and coffin on Visa and ended up in Spain.*

"Are you ready for beautiful breasts?" Dr. Erasmo Redondo asked and I felt a rush of more drugs and a picture of the

Mexican on horseback appeared. He stood by my la mula and said, "Just one breast. Let me see one mature breast, please."

I tried to smile but my mouth filled with a bitter taste and the lights of mind and body shut down.

And then I woke up. The pain struck as Vicki and Sue had promised, worse than having a baby. It felt as if I couldn't breathe, that two potbellied pigs were wedged against my sternum, topped off with a midsized rhino sitting on the mounds.

"Drugs," I whispered hoarsely, my voice raw from the breathing tube during surgery. "Please. Druuuuuuuuuuuuugs."

By the grace of Percocet and a benevolent God who doesn't mind a broken-bodied mother getting her boobs renovated, I stumbled out of the recovery room and into the new world of Fake-Tittied Women. There was no turning back. I was one of *them*. A redneck bimbo in my husband's eyes. A restored and lovely lady in my own eyes.

Stu kept trying to peer at the merchandise, but I wouldn't let him. He didn't want me getting them, so why allow him a peep? I'd sneaked off to a mirror and lifted my shirt high enough to see two mounds of flesh near the top of my collarbones, the nipples stitched and bandaged, surgical tape going in all directions. I was without a doubt a freaky Frankentit and couldn't have been happier. The dead fish on my chest had soared like upstream salmon from belt level all the way up to my shoulders and were perkier than they'd been at age eighteen. Oh, they were swollen and bruised, black and blue, taped and oozing, and absolutely the most beautiful things I'd ever seen. I wept with delight and narcotics.

It would take years, I thought, for these grand appendages to fall. I took to the bed and my sweet children brought me things. My husband did what he could, but mostly sulked. I realize he could have been more supportive, but then again, I'd done something he wasn't happy about and tried hard to understand his pouting. I never pressed the issue unless he tried to get a load of my new units, when I'd pull the sash of my robe more tightly.

About eight days after the operation, I carefully removed the tape from my nipples to see what they looked like and got the shock of my life. They had gone from ugly, bologna-sized satellite dishes to perky little quarters. My breasts were youthful, and while they didn't match my fleshy stomach, I was completely satisfied with the results.

I decided it was time to show my husband.

"Stuart. Come and see; they are wonderful!" I was so proud and happy, knowing he couldn't help but love them as they were the size (in my eyes) of Halle Berry's and Elizabeth Hurley's.

He entered the bedroom and stood with a grim face. I unbuttoned my blouse and the snaps of the jog bra. I opened it and felt the air hit these magnificent new bosoms.

His eyes narrowed and he began frowning, moving in closer. "What have you done to yourself?" he yelped. "Your nipples? They're so small. Where are the brown bumpy things that used to be all over the edges?"

"I've been restored. I look like a teenager."

"I don't like them," he said, like a petulant schoolboy who didn't get his way. "You've ruined yourself. You look like a freak."

He left the room, slammed the door, entered the guest room, and I didn't see him for almost twenty-four hours. He fumed and cried. So I fumed and cried, too.

I dialed up the Boob Room, and those at www.implant-info.com got me through the worst of it, promising the breasts would improve and appear more normal as time went on. They also said some men are jealous and react in many different ways, though, they agreed, the vast majority are as happy as if they've won the mammary lottery.

My husband's reaction, while unusual, would change over time, they said.

By Christmas he still hadn't accepted my new body, but we had to leave town and meet my family in Spartanburg, South

Carolina, including Sister Sandy and her new Halloween Pumpkins. I wondered what my parents were going to think happened to their daughters. Mama knew about mine, but Sandy, the sneak of the family, never told, and with her former flat-as-a-board chest, the folks were in for a shocker.

"I was sure they would disapprove," she said. "I wondered, should I prepare them in advance? Should I wear a big sweatshirt and try to hide them?" In the end, she bought a tight sweater, redder than Rudolph's nose, and pranced into the living room displaying her two turtledoves as if she'd owned them her entire life.

"They were lovely ornaments, too," she said, "even if I do say so myself."

My sister and I greeted each other with knowing hugs and roving eyes. We immediately rushed to the bedroom to compare notes. Boy, she was huge. I was simply redistributed and maybe a cup-size larger, but she'd shot up two entire cups. We were both so excited about our enhancements they were all we could talk about. My mother handled our surgeries better than I had expected, but she didn't like us talking about them so much because it made us sound vapid, selfish, and quite un-Baptist-like.

"Y'all need to change the subject," she said as the three of us lay on the queen-size bed like old times, Mama in the middle.

"Why? It's so new to us."

"I'm lying here feeling like a little old man with a wilted pecker sitting between two young bucks with nice, giant erections," she said, breaking the tension and surprising us with her bawdiness.

"We're sorry. We won't discuss it anymore, we promise."

I had felt so guilty about purchasing my pair that I signed on to sponsor a needy child from Guatemala for a monthly fee that over enough time would equal the cost of my boobs. That seemed to level the score and melt the guilt.

Moral of the story is simple: if you're going for a major

"me gift," which all women deserve now and again, be sure to at least balance it out by performing wonderful deeds for someone else.

Christmas passed without mention of the surgeries to my father, followed by month after month of his not knowing. Last summer on a visit home, I decided to tell my daddy what Mama couldn't bring herself to report.

"Wasn't my business," she said. We knew the real truth: slight shame at the $10,000 loaded guns beneath her daughters' former God-given breasts.

"I need to talk to him," I said.

"You wait 'til I'm out shopping. I don't want to stay and hear this."

She grabbed her purse and my children and headed for Old Navy and Red Lobster.

I was alone in the den with my father, who sat as usual in his green recliner with the remote in his hand and Fox News blasting on TV.

"Daddy, can we talk?"

He pursed his lips and rolled them back in. "Sure, let me get a box of crackers and a Diet Pepsi first. I'll be right back." I caught Mama as she cut her eyes and jingled her car keys. She knew what I was about to say to her husband and didn't want to be around for the Big Reveal.

"At least have the decency to wait 'til I'm in the car and out of the driveway."

Daddy sat down with his Pepsi and Ritz crackers. "You'd better not be pregnant."

"Pregnant? I'm forty-two years old!"

"I don't want to go through another grandchild," he said, his voice tired. "I'm ready for greats."

My sister had given me permission to share her news. "If Mama's too ashamed to tell him, you do it," she'd said.

"Daddy," I began, my voice tripping. "Have you noticed anything different about Sandy?"

He paused to sip and crunch. "She grew some whoppers," he said, trying hard to keep his trademark twisted smile from pulling both corners of his mouth. "I mean some whoppers. She came in here one day and they were still on the rise from the treatment or whatever that little pile a'jelly is they stick in there that Dupont makes."

"What did you think?"

"Ah, hon. Daddies don't mind things like that," he said, shocking me greatly with his acceptance.

"When did you notice?"

"I noticed it the day she walked in here. She's never worn a sweater and looked like that in one. Those things had a forward thrust to them. I said to your mama, 'Peg? Has Sandy had a boob job?' and she said I'd have to ask her, but that's OK. Men get hairpieces and Viagra and women get boob jobs. Whatever they want to do is fine with me."

I decided at this point to spring my own news on him, since he was filled with mirth and scripture, the acceptance and serenity of having just returned from his Bible study group.

"I have another surprise for you," I said, as he put down his Pepsi and tried again not to smile. "I got a new set, too."

He laughed. "You've always had a sack full of stuff up there, hon. Yours just filled out the sack. Your sister's jumped *out* of the sack."

I sat there in the silence of being comfortable around my father. For years we had been at intermittent odds, but the older we both got, the more our love mellowed and didn't have to engage in battle and controversy to ignite.

After a long pause, he flipped the lever of his recliner and sat upright, his feet on the floor. "Well, I wish your ma would do it. She could take some of her Social Security and get hers done."

About that time Mama came home with the kids.

"That was a short trip."

"The line was too long at Red Lobster so we went to

Burger King." She sat on the sofa opposite my father and me, and the kids ran to the playroom.

"I told him," I said. "He took it fine." She rolled her eyes and reached for her Bible. "I also told him you were planning to have the same surgery in three weeks."

"I am not."

My daddy's facial muscles lost the battle and he smiled fully. "I had my hopes up," he said. "It wouldn't take but a few checks, honey."

Mama just laughed, a woman in full acceptance of her body as is. "I would never have breast implants. There's too much else on me that needs fixing."

"Well, hon," Daddy said, "do it all on the installment plan, and I'll chip in. You look good, but if you wanted to beef up, I'd help out where I could."

Mama, who seeks *all* opportunities to turn any topic of conversation back to the good Lord and the Bible, never missed a beat.

"I'm waiting for my heavenly body. God's going to give us a new body. No cancer. No droopy boobs."

And Daddy is never one not to have the last word.

"How about a little advancement on that heavenly re-ward?"

Growing Older with Grace and Merlot

We are at the neighborhood pool, my friend Shelly and I. Her new boyfriend is here, too, lounging in the sun and smiling at her every so often as if he's afraid she'll slip away.

No other men so much as look our way and we don't care, loving the freedom that age and wisdom bring along with the pouches, flaps, sags, and bags.

We have even passed the stage of bemoaning our ample tummies or the leg veins that pop out like sudden maps to the city of Middle Age. We hold up our arms and do the batwing swing and laugh.

"Mine are like hammocks," I say.

"Mine are growing their own internal organ systems," she says.

Our days of being ogled and eyeballed are for the most part gone. We had them, all that male attention like a powerful drug, and we even loved a few of those poor fellows. But now we can pass the crown and let the younger, more nubile women enjoy the spellbinding effects they cast on these men. They will have to find their own way as they weed through a flock of buzzards to get the one decent bird among many.

My friend Shelly and I are so Over It, we've even passed the stage in our thirties when we whipped out the biggest and lamest excuse of all for lack of male attention: "Oh, he must be gay."

We have moved on in a healthy way. We aren't piercing our navels—truthfully, if I pierced mine it would take two days to find it—nor are we wearing half tops and string bikinis. Even with the new breasts, I realize the other limitations of my body.

We are content in the laughter and memories of how things were, not how we can extend our warranties like plenty of older women who go to tragic lengths and end up sad and painted, tugged and pulled. We aren't crying for our long-gone babe days, but introduce us to one woman who doesn't enjoy reflecting back.

We lower the flag at half-staff for the Babe Years long gone and raise a toast to the Awareness Years. Because it's not just OK being between thirty-five and 105—it's freeing and wonderful. I hope it continues until I'm like the 105-year-old spitfire who bunched up her shrunken fists and wanted to kick my ass.

I vow to Shelly as she is still fiddling with her arm hammocks to never become a grouchy old woman like Mrs. Alma Glehorn, who has designated herself "Pool Patrol" and drives everyone nuts with her whistle and warnings. As I chat with Shell on this glorious day in the height of summer and the entrance to middle age, Mrs. Alma Glehorn stampedes around the pool blowing her whistle at all the children.

"Get off the rope!" she yells and plugs her red mouth until she all but blows out a lobe of lung. The kids laugh because she is so over the top, her head bound in a white turban and her lipstick arching like Joan Crawford's. Her squat and gristled body is covered in a ridiculous silk getup picturing a life-size curvaceous and nearly naked image of a swimsuit model on the front—so that it looks from a distance as if that babe were indeed Mrs. Alma Glehorn. From behind, the vixen on her cover-up is wearing a thong, so that it seems from twenty yards away that Mrs. Glehorn is in possession of a nice ass.

She is purely poisoned with a nervous streak I don't want when I dip into my seventies or eighties. The truth is, there are three main categories of old ladies: the mean-as-hell kind, the sweet-as-sugar kind, and the nutty eccentrics, of which I plan to become.

"No alcohol by the pool," Mrs. Glehorn yips at Shelly, pointing her finger.

"The rules say no glass containers." Shelly waves her manicured pinkie in greeting. "My wine is in a plastic tumbler."

"We're over twenty-one," I say, sweet as I possibly can.

"You are disgusting," Mrs. Glehorn says. "You look sixty-five and not a day younger." She turns to Shelly. "No alcohol period." Then she blows her whistle at two boys. "No diving. None of that horseplay." She stomps around the pool perimeter several times, casing the joint, and finally stops in front of two beautiful teenage girls with illegally terrific bodies.

"Are you members here or simply mooching? Produce your pool key or head on back to your boyfriends' camper homes or wherever it is riffraff such as your kind tend to dwell."

Shelly and I crack up laughing. "Shoot me if I get like that," she says.

"She is a woman who has never been a babe, or who can't get over the fact her babe days are history. You and me, on the other hand, are healthy. We've passed the torch with grace."

"I've passed it with Merlot," she says, raising a Tupperware tumbler. "And you passed it with a boob job."

I tell Shelly that my goal in middle and old age is to impart wisdom and laughter. To sprinkle the world with good deeds and random acts of madness mixed in with the kindness. I plan to relish every moment of stiff joints, extra chins, and skin waggling off the bone. Since I've purchased some knockers, I'll at least have it going on when the competition for available men at Croaker's Rest Home dwindles to a forty-to-five ratio. I'll be the babe of bingo, the centenarian with three or four original teeth and a set of moldy saline numbers somewhere near my kneecaps.

Shelly and I sit around the water's edge for a while, recovering from the wrath of Mrs. Alma Glehorn as the sun bores into us and threatens with its burn and potential for more wrinkles. We swap our heyday stories the way men swap sports glory stories.

"I was such a babe men flew me across the eastern seaboard just so I could dine with them at my favorite restaurants," Shelly informs me, sitting ladylike in her chaise longue, smoking Virginia Slims Menthol Lights and drinking her wine, the salve that soothes her. The way she drinks and smokes doesn't look trashy because she's learned over the years to perform these adult vices with the glamour of a star partaking, as if Audrey Hepburn playing Holly Golightly. She is wearing a gorgeous black-and-gold swimsuit, and like me, sports the badges of life protruding here and there from the sparkly fabric.

"I had a butt . . ." She stares off into dreamland and cups her hands as if to form two oranges. She shakes her head in memory and homage to that fine behind that once was hers. "I could have anything I wanted. Don't *even* get me started on the things that happened to me while wearing a black dress."

As she speaks, kids splash and screech in the pool because Mrs. Glehorn has left the premises. Shelly goes on about the good old days when she could put on jeans showcasing a fanny that was no more than a handful. She talks about the wonderful gifts and trips, the outrageous energy her former suitors invested in the pursuit.

"You sleep with them and it's history," she says, exhaling her menthol. "They go to the ends of the world for you if you hold back."

Amen. I tell her about my rich ex, Mr. Thurston Truitt with the Mercury I tap-danced on and destroyed when he'd cheated one too many times. How I traveled with him to Bermuda, Acapulco, New York, California, and plenty of places in the Caribbean. How I'd procured a three-carat diamond engagement ring just by moving to St. John in the U.S. Virgin Islands and yachting about with men on the verge of coma and eternal peace.

"He was six-five and weighed two hundred and ten well-placed pounds," I say, describing Thurston. "A completely gorgeous man who resembled a bigger version of Robert Redford. Huge cheater when drinking."

"I don't believe I'd want that," she says, telling me about vice presidents of major hotel chains flying her here and there, setting her up in luxury suites stocked with champagne and fine foods and leaving their American Express cards on the nightstand so she could shop like Julia Roberts in *Pretty Woman*.

"Only I never even slept with most of them," she says. "If you do that, they aren't going to buy you a thing. Nada. The chase is the strongest of drugs to them."

She sips her wine. "I loved those days but I don't want them back. It's not easy waking up in the same black dress you wore to bed, then trying to sneak back into your hotel room without everyone else in your party knowing what you've been up to. I've taken many a cab and snuck through many a service entrance. Of course I didn't *sleep* sleep with them, if you know what I mean. I just crashed with them."

Lots of us who came of age in the '80s era of decadence could relate. I knew about those side entrances. Try sneaking into a sorority house wearing last night's pink Izod and

Chinos. You just don't do that as a member of a southern sorority where they have a Morals Enforcement Team and pretend they're virgins until engaged or pinned.

Oh, they may have lived the Betty Crocker life on the surface with their manners and hair bows, espadrilles, and squeaky-clean faces. But more than a few would sneak around when no one was looking, doing things they didn't speak of but always coming home on time at night, slipping into their twin beds and frilly little pajamas, snuggling teddy bears and acting all innocent.

Shelly stares at the blue sky with its clouds layered like petticoats. She says her new boyfriend has been a gift from God, though he's not rich or fabulously handsome and probably won't take her places where there's a need for little black dresses. The air smells like coconut sunscreen and the promise of rain, distant thunder rumbling miles away and causing a few parents to glance up from the dark moons of their sunglasses to check the sky.

"I used to date the hotshots and lawyers, the guys who could give me anything," she says, "but now I just want to be happy. I want someone to love me and be there for me. See that man over there? He's the best. I don't care if he's always saying, 'Shelly, I'm just a simple country boy.' That's fine with me. He's perfect and so good to me."

Life would have been so much easier if we had been this wise at twenty-one. But then we wouldn't be able to appreciate all the mistakes and missteps, the wounds of heart to make it to where we were today. Two ladies in their forties, one drinking water, the other a rich Merlot, discussing the trouble of little black dresses and the powerful aphrodisiac of youth and teacup asses, only mine was more or less the entire pot and then some.

"I had one guy named Jeff calling me," Shelly says, "leaving a message saying, 'I'm still thinking of you.' I'm like . . . Jeff . . . Jeff . . . there had been three other Jeffs since him. He had a small one too. I'm telling you. Tee-tee-niney." She crooked her pointer and wiggled it. "I know it's not supposed to matter, size and all, and for the most part really it doesn't."

"Shelly, don't even get me going on my theories in this department. I'm telling you what. Four inches is one thing. No inches is another."

"No inches?" She gently stubs out her cigarette and faces me with her enormous eyes. The girl has Natalie Wood eyes if anyone ever did. "What are you talking about, woman?"

"I was at some medical school party in Augusta, Georgia, and had this poor date who was an old friend from high school and on the verge of graduating and about to become a surgeon. Oh, he was cute. Cute, cute. I was so excited, I'm telling you. That night we went to the formal and got a little drunk and the next thing I know I'm going fishing."

Shelly sips her drink and tips her head to the side. "Fishing?"

"Fishing for the goods, honey. The clothes were coming off and we were sloppy-kissing and going to town, only I kept my dress on, on account of every time I tried to act naughty visions of my mother would pop into my head and that kind of blows everything. I was flapping for his business and—Lord have mercy—I should have known."

Shelly is trying hard to get the rest of the story out, but I am doubled over in hysterics and can't seem to breathe.

"What? You should have known what?"

I drink a few sips of water and fan myself. "You ever danced with a guy or messed around and, you know, never felt, well, anything? Almost like they don't have a wee-wee?"

"A what? Wee-wee? You have lost me, girl."

"We were fooling around and my hand was going up and down, aiming for what I'm assuming was his pelvic region, when out of the blue . . . well, I reached what I thought would be the you know what and there was nothing but a round . . . I guess you could say it was a disc."

"Do what?" She is screaming and slapping at her thighs. "A *what*?"

I am choking up and unable to get the story out for quite some time. "It was a . . . what you might call a . . . umm . . . patty. A hamburgerish sort of thing."

"Oh my Gawd!"

Shelly begins coughing, and for a smoker to start up, it's not easy to stop. She hits her chest with her fist and tries to pour more Merlot down her throat. She is shouting, "Ewwwwweeeee," and, "Grooooooossssss."

"I may have missed the bull's-eye," I say, "but I swear there was nothing. No wee-wee. No flagship. It was sad because I could have loved that man. Maybe he tucked it back or something, but for that pubic patty to have been on top like it was . . ."

"You sure your doctor friend wasn't a woman?"

"He had an Adam's apple and a deep voice. He had beard stubble. I don't know, Shelly. Maybe. God help us all if we're not one gene twist away from being something else—either a man or a little off-centered in some way or another. Maybe I was just too nervous and tipsy and hit the wrong spots, but I swear the next morning when I had to face him it was just awful. He grinned and smiled and acted like we were in love. He said, 'Last night was wonderful,' and all I could do was nod and act sweet and innocent when really I couldn't for the life of me stop thinking about the patty. I had to keep dating him a few more times just to be nice so that if he *did* have a patty, he wouldn't think I dumped him after discovering it. That would have been too mean."

Shelly is shining and red. She tries to talk but nothing comes out but gurgling and coughing.

"I'll tell you something else while we're on the subject," I say. "The more I love them, the more tragic their genitalia, with the exception of my husband, of course."

I considered telling her about Mr. Fungi Man, who my best

friend in college spent an evening with, but she was coughing and carrying on so much I kept that one to myself. My friend called him Mr. Fungi because he had an ultrathin wee-wee like one of those tiny pencils you get playing minigolf, only the little twiglet was capped with an enormous toadstool-size head. She said he was extremely proud of it and yanked his pants down on the elevator before he could even escort her to her dorm room.

Shelly, still in hysterics over the patty, jumps in the pool and surfaces for air, mascara rolling down her face. "Oh my God," she says over and over until she manages to climb to the edge and catch her breath. Her boyfriend rushes to the side of the pool like a concerned mother checking on a toddler. He pats her on the back and offers her more wine before wandering back to his chaise longue.

"My new fellow is just wonderful," Shelly says, beaming. "I guess he's simple and country but loves me so much I really don't care how much he doesn't make. When you get our age, that doesn't matter like it did. You love them for who they are and not what they can buy, if you have any depth to you."

"You're absolutely right," I say, my skin on fire with the sun as I slide into the chilled pool and breathe the fumes of fresh chlorine.

"When I got rid of my uterus a few years ago," she says as I surface, "I was worried about trying to have sex again and what a man would think of the whole deal."

"I still have mine. I call it the Bitch in a Bag."

"Listen, girl. I got rid of mine at age thirty-eight. I went to Dr. Bloomberg and said, 'I can't live like this any longer.' He went right in there and took it out. I'm blissfully uterusless. I've never felt better than to get that blob of fibroids and pain out of me."

She glances toward her new boyfriend and whispers, "He was the first man I slept with without my uterus. We were both kind of scared. I told him, 'Hon, I may not have the cradle but I still have the playpen.' He was still scared."

"Why?" I never thought of sex being different without a uterus.

"He said he was frightened to death to go into that abyss because he might get swallowed up in the black hole and never come out. I wondered about it, too, but nothing happened. He said it was no different than sleeping with regular women."

She reports how much better she feels and behaves as a uterus-free member of the world.

"I've thought for years about pulling the plug on mine," I say. "Mama said if I got rid of it, I'd grow a beard and maybe a small wiener."

She cracks up and slaps the side of the pool with a free hand, wine sloshing out of her cup. No sooner did we make our way to the shallow end than Mrs. Alma Glehorn reappeared poolside, having refreshed her makeup, her Joan Crawford lips plastered on the rim of a Thermos smelling like Old Grand-Dad bourbon. She takes a big sip and faces us.

"I've been informed you women are discussing filth of a certain nature," she says. "I'm pool patrol as you may or may not be aware. You two get out of here immediately and run along to places where your kind fraternizes. My guess would be pool halls and men's camper beds. *Out!*" She blows her whistle and the smell of whiskey overpowers the chlorine.

"We were talking about uteruses," I say. "How they no longer do us a bit of good."

She again puts the whistle to those fire-engine-red lips. She takes a deep breath and I cover my ears to shield them from her blast.

"Cheers!" Shelly says, swimming off with her wine held high, her huge Natalie Wood eyes focused on a simple country boy who had flipped over on his stomach and was grinning as if he'd met the greatest love of his life. "To older and wiser."

She lifts her forty-one-year-old dripping wet body from the

pool and slides into a chair next to the man who will never stock a hotel fridge with champagne or leave his American Express on the nightstand.

I smile at Mrs. Glehorn and shield my eyes from the afternoon sun. "Cheers," I say, "to older and wiser."